OXFORD ENGLISH MONOGRAPHS

General Editors

JOHN CAREY   STEPHEN GILL

DOUGLAS GRAY   ROGER LONSDALE

Samuel Johnson and Eighteenth-century Thought

NICHOLAS HUDSON

CLARENDON PRESS · OXFORD
1988

Oxford University Press, Walton Street, Oxford OX2 6DP

Oxford New York Toronto
Delhi Bombay Calcutta Madras Karachi
Petaling Jaya Singapore Hong Kong Tokyo
Nairobi Dar es Salaam Cape Town
Melbourne Auckland

and associated companies in
Berlin Ibadan

Oxford is a trade mark of Oxford University Press

Published in the United States
by Oxford University Press, New York

British Library Cataloguing in Publication Data
Hudson, Nicholas
Samuel Johnson and eighteenth century
thought. —(Oxford English monographs).
1. Johnson, Samuel, 1709-1784—
Criticism and interpretation
I. Title
828'.609   PR3534
ISBN 0-19-812899-1

Library of Congress Cataloging in Publication Data
Hudson, Nicholas.
Samuel Johnson and eighteenth-century thought/Nicholas Hudson.
p. cm. —(Oxford English monographs)
Bibliography: p.   Includes index.
1. Johnson, Samuel, 1709-1784—Philosophy.   2. Johnson, Samuel,
1709-1784—Religion.   3. Johnson, Samuel, 1709-1784—Ethics.   4. Philosophy, Modern—18th century.
5. Theology, Doctrinal—History—18th century.   6. Ethics, Modern—18th century.
I. Title.   II. Series.
PR3537.P5H84 1988   828'.609—dc19   87-27779CIP
ISBN 0-19-812899-1

Set by Downdell Ltd.
Printed in Great Britain by
Biddles Ltd.
Guildford and King's Lynn

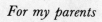
For my parents

ACKNOWLEDGEMENTS

Much of the research for this book was done while I was a graduate student under the supervision of Dr J. D. Fleeman of Pembroke College, Oxford. I wish to express my thanks to Dr Fleeman for his guidance and advice during those years. Large portions of the book were composed at the home of Professors J. R. de J. and H. J. Jackson of the University of Toronto, where I had access to their excellent private library. My thanks for their kindness and hospitality. My grateful acknowledgements as well to Professor C. J. Rawson of Yale University, and Mr D. H. Burden of Trinity College, Oxford, for their help and support over the years. The frontispiece of Moses Pitt's *The Cry of the Oppressed* (Douce P. 633) is reproduced by kind permission of the Bodleian Library, Oxford. My greatest debt is to my wife, whose contribution in time and wisdom has been inestimable.

CONTENTS

NOTE ON THE TEXT

References to *The Yale Edition of the Works of Samuel Johnson*, gen. edd.
A. T. Hazen and J. H. Middendorf (14 vols.; New Haven and
London, 1958–78), have been cited in the text by volume and page
number. In addition, the following short titles have been used in the
text and the notes:

Dictionary	*A Dictionary of the English Language* (1755) (2 vols.; 4th edn. rev.; London, 1773).
Life	James Boswell, *Life of Johnson* (1791), ed. G. B. Hill, rev. L. F. Powell (6 vols., Oxford, 1934–50).
Lives of the Poets	*Lives of the English Poets* (1781), ed. G. B. Hill (3 vols.; Oxford, 1905).
Miscellanies	G. B. Hill (ed.), *Johnsonian Miscellanies* (2 vols.; Oxford, 1897).
Rasselas	*The History of Rasselas: Prince of Abissinia* (1759), ed. J. P. Hardy (London, 1968).
Vision of Theodore	*The Vision of Theodore: The Hermit of Teneriffe* (1748), in Robert Dodsley, *The Preceptor* (2 vols.; London, 1748).

All Scriptural citations are from The King James Bible. References to
the Thirty-nine Articles are from E. J. Bicknell, *A Theological Introduction to the Thirty-nine Articles* (London, New York, and Toronto,
1919).

I have indicated the original date of publication or composition for
my primary texts whenever possible: unfortunately this was not
always possible in the case of sermons taken from the posthumous
collections of divines.

INTRODUCTION

THERE have been numerous books on Johnson's moral and religious thought, but none that has fully examined his relationship with the philosophy and religion of the eighteenth century. But is such a study worthwhile? As I will argue in the following book, Johnson frequently took for granted that his audience understood the context within which his opinions and observations were meaningful. More than many great authors, Johnson intended much of his best-known wisdom for an audience that was immediate and contemporary: he could not have predicted how much of his conversation would be transmitted to us by Boswell; he could have had no confidence that posterity would interest itself in sermons he wrote for a little-known divine; and, though his periodical essays (especially the *Rambler*) were certainly less topical than the *Spectator*, they responded directly to the issues which conventionally preoccupied the moralists and philosophers of his age. By examining the eighteenth-century context of Johnson's thought, therefore, my objective is to help a modern reader to understand Johnson with the sophistication of an informed individual of the eighteenth century, to make a modern readership a better audience.

An important lesson of history is that our beliefs and pre-occupations are not immediately applicable to all times and places. As Quentin Skinner warned in an essay on the history of ideas, a degree of misrepresentation occurs every time we postulate 'fundamental concepts' of 'perennial interest' which bind the ideologies of every age.[1] Undoubtedly timeless and universal concerns exist, but to a large and undetermined extent we are the products of our moment in history. The following book, therefore, makes no claim that Johnson's value lies in the relevance of his life and thought to 'us', or in how closely he 'anticipated' existentialism, or Freud, or other intellectual movements that preoccupy modern writers. I have restricted myself as much as possible to the language and

[1] See Q. Skinner, 'Meaning and Understanding in the History of Ideas', *History and Theory*, 8 (1969), 3–53.

philosophical assumptions of the eighteenth century. My aim has been to familiarize the reader with eighteenth-century ideas, not as they appear in the light of present-day theories and concerns, but as they were conceived and expressed by Johnson and his contemporaries.

This book is far more concerned with Johnson the polemicist and controversist than with Johnson the 'man'. Though it cannot be denied that biographical and psychoanalytical studies have contributed to our understanding of Johnson, they have given rise to the exaggerated perception that his religion was dominated by anxiety and uncertainty. The theory of Johnson's tormented faith is actually based on a small body of evidence, much of it from private journals which offer a very scanty record of Johnson's spiritual condition. Judging from most of Johnson's public pronouncements, he seems to have gleaned considerable confidence from the knowledge that he was carrying on the convictions and arguments of a venerable tradition of Christian orthodoxy. Deeply suspicious of individual claims to originality, he often followed the approved positions with almost verbatim fidelity. While there are many important exceptions to this tendency in his writings, our examination of what is 'essential' or 'unique' in Johnson's personality is often complicated by the discovery that the same metaphor or argument had been used in orthodox writing for half a century.

To say that Johnson's writings are strongly orthodox does not, however, mean that they are entirely consistent and uncomplicated. While it is usually inaccurate to assume that any writer is consistent at all points in his works, it is perhaps particularly dangerous to expect uniformity from an author so ambivalent as Johnson. As Robert Voitle asserted in *Samuel Johnson the Moralist*, 'only a fool would expect to find an elaborate, regular theory' beneath Johnson's ethical statements.[2] But the contradictions in Johnson's thought—and they are numerous—do not necessarily derive from incoherence or, as is sometimes assumed, a reliance on common sense and prejudice. Like so many orthodox writers of his age, Johnson was confronted by challenges and considerations which impinged on his mind from different directions, all containing some element

[2] R. Voitle, *Samuel Johnson the Moralist* (Cambridge, Mass., 1961), 125.

of truth. This book is devoted to the study of these opposing forces and their background in eighteenth-century thought. I am disclosing no single truth about Johnson; I have no over-riding theory. Although, like all interpretations of history or evidence of any kind, my account relies on induction and informed conjecture, my recreation of eighteenth-century thought stresses its division and ambiguity, not the simplicity and coherence which is more characteristic of fiction than historical truth.

Because I view the eighteenth century in terms of contradiction and ambiguity, my major purpose is not to show that Johnson is typical or untypical of some defining characteristic of eighteenth-century thought. My impression is that we can discern an increasing pragmatism in the century's thought, a growing tendency to evaluate moral and religious questions according to their usefulness to society rather than their 'truth'. While much of Johnson's work reflects this trend, it is difficult to generalize: almost as often (as on many doctrinal points) his writings recall positions that were more widely accepted early in the century. Hence, when I refer in the book to Johnson's affinities with contemporary pragmatism, I do not mean that this was a steady rule of either his or mid-century thought; my more vehement claim is that the usual labels and generalizations applied to eighteenth-century thought are inaccurate, and need to be re-evaluated. The eighteenth century has often been described as an age of reason, an age of optimism concerning the beneficence and perfection of the universal system, an age of implicit faith in the essential goodness and nobility of man. These generalizations and others are based on an extremely limited selection of authors such as Locke, Pope, and Fielding. Another selection (such as Berkeley, Mandeville, and Swift) might lead to exactly the opposite generalization. A more basic problem occurs when any set of authors is allowed to weaken our sensitivity to the vast number of conflicting positions that are all, in some sense, 'typical' of that age.

Locke, Berkeley, Swift, Pope, Hume, and others make up our canon of those writers who are really worth studying in the eighteenth century. Yet behind these writers lay a mass of 'minute philosophers', minor divines and obscure pamphleteers. They may be of little importance singly, but together they represent the turbulent flow of conflicting and evolving ideologies. Certainly they were 'influenced' by the great writers, but they also created the conditions which made the great writers possible in the first place. For this reason I have given a prominent place to many minor and 'unimportant' writers. My objective has not been to show that Johnson was a 'Lockeian' or a 'Hobbesian', or to determine which writer most influenced his thought. It can only very seldom be affirmed with any confidence that an author adopted a certain position because he found it in a particular book; the cause-and-effect relationships of intellectual history will always be in doubt. Nevertheless, there is good reason to believe that Johnson's understanding of intellectual problems was closely bound up in, even inseparable from, a broad and complicated background of moral and religious controversy. Though his impact on this debate was not always profound or significant, few writers were so widely knowledgeable, or so able to combine many sides of contemporary thought into an understanding of life distinctive for its humanity and good sense. His learning and complexity make his writings especially useful as the starting-point for a broader investigation of eighteenth-century thought.

A short book such as this does place limitations on what can be covered in any detail. Since it is impossible to discuss every writer and issue of the eighteenth century, I have particularly focused on moral and religious debates between 1730 and 1760, the century's middle decades when Johnson first lived in London and formulated mature judgements on intellectual subjects. These decades culminate with the major period of Johnson's moral writing in the 1750s. No doubt there was some change in Johnson's opinions as he grew older, as I have occasionally remarked; yet such changes are difficult to trace, and seem minor compared to the ambiguities which always existed in his thought. Moreover, because I am examining only those aspects of eighteenth-century thought which are relevant to the study of Johnson, there are some writers who have not been examined with the detail they would deserve in a book devoted exclusively to the age. I have occasionally used the notes to alert the reader to especially interesting works and opinions which are not of direct significance to Johnson.

Each chapter examines a different area of moral and religious controversy. In general, the book moves from the relatively basic issues of faith, reason, and natural religion debated with the infidels and deists, towards ever increasing complexity and ambiguity in the various debates between the Christian writers themselves. My intended audience includes not only specialists of Johnson and intellectual history, but also graduate students and even ambitious undergraduates who require a detailed introduction to Johnson and some major issues in eighteenth-century thought. With this in mind I have added some explanation of terms ('justification by faith', 'the test of ridicule') which may seem rather basic to the specialist. Nevertheless, I hope that the final result contains useful and interesting knowledge for all readers.

1

Preserving the Faith

1. *The 'Sturdy Prejudice' of Eighteenth-century Orthodoxy*

For historians convinced that the eighteenth century's philosophical challenge to Christianity was irrefutable, Johnson has exemplified the persistence of irrationality and prejudice in the age of enlightenment. As Leslie Stephen remarked in his *History of English Thought in the Eighteenth Century*, 'Johnson was little fitted for abstract speculation. He was an embodiment of sturdy prejudice, or, in other words, of staunch beliefs which had survived their logical justification. The depth and massiveness of his character redeem his opinions from contempt.'[1] Recent studies have not been so inclined to dismiss Johnson's faith as 'sturdy prejudice', but it would be difficult to claim that Johnson has increased in stature as a religious thinker. Few have seriously questioned Stephen's opinion that Johnson's Christianity was protected by specious and outmoded reasoning. Of particular interest has been the challenge which Hume's essay 'Of Miracles' (1748) presented to Johnson's beliefs. As many readers will know, this essay did more than discredit belief in religious miracles. In Johnson's time, orthodox believers relied heavily on Christ's miracles as proof that the New Testament was the supernatural revelation of God's will. Modern critics have agreed that Hume advanced a case so powerful that Johnson remained a believer only by failing to understand Hume's arrangements, or by submerging genuine doubts and fears beneath indignant expostulations ('Hume and other sceptical innovators are vain men') and reasonings of self-evident lameness and desperation.[2]

---

[1] L. Stephen, *History of English Thought in the Eighteenth Century* (2 vols.; London, 1962), ii. 175.

[2] See *Life*, i. 444. C. F. Chapin argued in *The Religious Thought of Samuel Johnson* (Ann Arbor, 1968), 88, that Johnson failed to come to grips with Hume's attack. More recently, C. E. Pierce, jun., has contended in *The Religious Life of Samuel Johnson* (London, 1983), 48–54, that Johnson knew that he could not refute Hume, and was disguising genuine fears and anxieties.

While it may seem inconceivable that anybody in Johnson's
time could fail to appreciate the significance of Hume's attack,
we still have much to learn about the nature of the 'sturdy
prejudice' which, as Stephen would have agreed, Johnson
shared with most of those who answered Hume. How do we
explain that not only Johnson, but also most of the orthodox
writers of his generation, responded to Hume's challenge with
little evident alarm or diminishment of confidence? And
similarly, can we accept that Johnson was disguising genuine
doubts when there is hardly a scrap of evidence, even in his
private papers, to indicate that he suspected that Hume or any
other sceptic was right? In this chapter I will re-examine the
question of Johnson's religious 'prejudice'. I believe that it
reflects a profoundly conservative habit of mind typical of the
orthodoxy which Hume and other sceptics assailed. Johnson
was one of the last and most interesting spokesmen for a
tradition in Christian thought which, at least as an important
literary and theological force, was dying—but dying with
absolute confidence.

We should first speculate on how Christians of Johnson's
generation probably viewed Hume's attack at mid-century. It
is significant that the divines who answered Hume, such as
William Adams, George Campbell, and Thomas Rutherforth,
used almost the same defence of the miracles which had been
advanced against previous infidels. For reasons that are to
some extent understandable, they did not believe that Hume
had greatly added to the conventional case against the existence
of miraculous events. Hume himself claimed that he was
extending the arguments used by John Tillotson, the Archbishop of Canterbury under William and Mary, in his attack
on the Catholic doctrine of transubstantiation.[3] Tillotson's
Discourse against Transubstantiation (1684) exemplified a stubborn
faith in experience which would dominate many areas of
orthodox thought during the eighteenth century. It roughly
expounded the same principle which prompted Johnson to
refute Berkeley by kicking a stone.[4] According to Tillotson, no

---

[3] See David Hume, 'Of Miracles', in *An Enquiry Concerning Human Understanding*
(1748), in *Philosophical Works*, ed. J. H. Greene and J. H. Grose (4 vols.; London,
1882, repr. Scientia Verlag Aalen, 1964), iv. 88–9.

[4] See *Life*, i. 471.

amount of reasoning or even Scriptural evidence could overturn the plain evidence of sense that the elements of the Lord's supper did not change into the blood and body of Christ. Nevertheless, he distinguished between the absurdity of believing in transubstantiation, which was accompanied by no discernible change in the physical elements of the sacrament, and the reasonableness of believing in the miracles of Christ, which had been attested by the plain evidence of sense.[5]

As Hume saw, this distinction does not hold, for modern Christians base their belief in miracles not on the evidence of sense, but on the testimony of witnesses. The miracles of Christ in fact contradict our experience of physical reality. Since Tillotson had insisted that no amount of external evidence should persuade us to deny the knowledge of our senses, Anglican writers must reject the Christian miracles on the same grounds that they rejected transubstantiation:

A miracle is a violation of the laws of nature; and as a firm and unalterable experience has established these laws, the proof against a miracle, from the very nature of the fact, is as entire as any argument from experience can possibly be imagined . . . nor can such a proof be destroyed, or the miracle rendered credible, but by an opposite proof, which is superior.[6]

Although Hume's acknowledgement of a debt to a respected Anglican divine served an important rhetorical purpose, the affinities between Tillotson and Hume are superficial and deceptive. Hume agreed with Tillotson that we could never dispense with our common-sense assumptions—what Hume called 'custom'—concerning the laws which regulate the natural world. Unlike Tillotson, however, Hume denied that our customary assumptions are based on valid reasoning. Even belief in that primary law of nature, cause and effect, is really nothing more sophisticated than a plausible *inference* used to explain the habitual conjunction of certain perceptions.[7] Without this inference we are lost, for the most lofty metaphysician could have no knowledge whatsoever without

[5] John Tillotson, *A Discourse against Transubstantiation* (1684), in *Works* (1696) (3 vols.; 4th edn.; London, 1728), iii. 315.

[6] Hume, 'Of Miracles', in *Philosophical Works*, iv. 93.

[7] See Hume's *A Treatise of Human Nature* (1739), pt. III ('Of Knowledge and Probability'), in *Philosophical Works*, i–ii.

assuming the existence of cause and effect. It is only by means of this principle that we can connect our various sense impressions into meaningful conclusions about the world. Since miracles are by definition interruptions of the assumed laws of nature, they belie the only means we possess to reason about the present or the future on the basis of what we have experienced in the past. They violate no laws that, so far as we know, have real existence in the world, but they contradict the irrational assumptions which constitute the basis of human knowledge.

These deeper epistemological concerns are what give 'Of Miracles' its force and originality. Yet these concerns are not fully explained in this essay. Hume's attack on Christianity gains its full impact only when read in conjunction with his speculations on knowledge in *A Treatise of Human Nature* (1739) or elsewhere in *An Enquiry Concerning Human Understanding* (1748), the collection of essays in which 'Of Miracles' first appeared. If 'Of Miracles' is considered on its own, it seems to rely on a common-sense faith in natural laws and a conventional case against Christianity. As we shall see, most apologists had long acknowledged that, with the one exception of the Christian miracles, we should not allow even trustworthy testimony to persuade us to accept claims for events which contradict the perceived 'order of nature'.

In *The Advancement of Learning* (1605), for example, Bacon had urged men to distrust accounts of miraculous happenings.[8] Bacon, however, had in mind the Roman Catholic reports of miracles, and did not extend his discussion to the miracles of Scripture. John Locke also admitted that the strangeness of a report justifiably diminished its credibility among reasonable men. As he observed in the chapter 'Of Probability' in *An Essay Concerning Human Understanding* (1690), 'the common Experience, and ordinary Course of Things, have justly a mighty Influence on the Minds of Men, to make them give or refuse Credit to any thing proposed to their Belief'.[9] But Locke, unlike Bacon, responded to the possibility that this

---

[8] See Francis Bacon, *The Advancement of Learning* (1605), pt. I, in *Works*, ed. J. Spedding, R. Ellis, and D. Heath (14 vols.; Boston, 1861), vi. 125–6.

[9] John Locke, *An Essay Concerning Human Understanding* (1690), ed. P. H. Nidditch (Oxford, 1979), I, xvi, 667.

criterion could be used to justify doubts with the Christian miracles. By Locke's time such a possibility had become increasingly dangerous. Never before had Christian writers relied so heavily on the miracles as evidence of Christ's divinity. Without them the case for the divine authority of Scripture would be seriously weakened. For this reason Locke was careful to make clear that belief in the Scriptural miracles 'is one Case, wherein the strangeness of the Fact lessens not the Assent to a fair Testimony given to it'.[10]

The logic of this assertion is not obvious. How could Locke vindicate this one exception to rules which, in every other case, endorsed scepticism with the testimony for miracles? His explanation was based on the attributes of God as they were perceived at that time. God certainly had the power to change 'the ordinary Course of Things' which he had established. As a benevolent Being he would also wish to interrupt the course of nature if it greatly benefited his creation. For this reason, 'where such supernatural Events are suitable to ends aim'd at by him, who has the Power to change the course of Nature, there, under such Circumstances, they may be the fitter to procure Belief, by how much the more they are beyond, or contrary to ordinary Observation'.[11] The Christian miracles fulfilled this requirement. Since they had so greatly promoted the moral and religious enlightenment of the world, it was reasonable to believe that God, if only in this one instance, had interrupted the course of nature. For most writers in the first part of the eighteenth century, the reasoning used by Locke genuinely appeared sound. That God may, as Philip Doddridge wrote in 1742, 'deviate from the Laws by which he statedly rules the Natural World . . . when thereby the Interest of the Moral World may remarkably be promoted', was asserted not only by innumerable apologists for Christianity, but also by heterodox authors such as Toland and Chubb.[12]

It is important to note that Locke and most apologists were not contending that the Christian miracles were defensible by

[10] Ibid.
[11] Ibid.
[12] Philip Doddridge, *The Perspicuity and Solidity of Those Evidences of Christianity to which the Generality of Its Professors among us may Attain, Illustrated and Vindicated* (London, 1742), 27. Cf. John Toland, *Christianity not Mysterious* (London, 1696), 152; Thomas Chubb, *The True Gospel of Jesus Christ Asserted* (London, 1738), 268.

the ordinary rules for judging testimony. The Christian
miracles, unlike the pagan or modern Catholic miracles, were
the single *exception* to these rules. When apologists wished to
demonstrate the speciousness of contemporary attacks on the
miracles, they suggested that the sceptics had overlooked this
distinction and were attempting to use the ordinary rules for
judging testimony against the Christian miracles. The anti-
Christian speaker in Thomas Sherlock's widely admired
apology, *The Tryal of the Witnesses* (1729), was foolish enough to
argue that belief in the miracles was indefensible because they
contravened the regular course of nature:

In common Affairs, where nothing is asserted but is probable and
possible, and according to the usual Course of Nature, a reasonable
Degree of Evidence ought to determine every Man. For the very
Probability, or Possibility of the thing, is a Support to the Evidence;
and in such Cases we have no Doubt but a Man's Senses qualify him
to be a Witness. But when the thing testified is contrary to the Order
of Nature, and, at first sight at least, impossible, what Evidence can
be sufficient to overturn the constant Evidence of Nature, which she
gives us in the uniform and regular Method of her Operations?[13]

Significantly, the infidels of Sherlock's time were not relying
on the 'Order of Nature' to refute belief in the miracles. The
historian will search in vain for this line of argument in the
contemporary attacks on the Christian miracles by Collins and
Woolston. No infidel seemed to think that this approach would
be effective until Hume. Hume's argument that miracles
violated our 'firm and unalterable experience' of 'the laws of
nature' seemed to reiterate the position of, for example, the
foolish sceptic in Sherlock's *Tryal of the Witnesses*. For this
reason, it is hardly surprising that Hume's essay caused
indignation, but failed to generate much change in the way the
miracles were defended.

This response certainly did not do justice to the full significance of Hume's argument. As we have considered, however,
the real strength of Hume's challenge only becomes evident
when we consider 'Of Miracles' within the context of his other
works. Hume showed elsewhere that we possess no *a priori*
evidence that 'the usual Course of Nature' exists at all, yet
belief in an event which reportedly contradicts the assumed

[13] Thomas Sherlock, *The Tryal of the Witnesses* (London, 1729), 58.

order of nature belies the only means we possess to synthesize perceptions into coherent knowledge. Most important, his other major attack on orthodoxy, 'Of a Particular Providence and of a Future State' (1748), deprived the apologists of their reasoning for the one exception to the rules of testimony. Again utilizing our customary assumptions concerning cause and effect, Hume denied that reason could determine the benevolence of God or even His power to interrupt the usual course of events.

But Johnson considered 'Of Miracles' singly and without reference to Hume's other essays, and it seemed to him that 'Everything which Hume advanced against Christianity had passed through my mind long before he wrote.'[14] He assumed, it seems, that Hume had simply ignored Locke's exception to the rules for judging reports of miracles. When in 1763 Boswell mentioned 'Hume's argument against the belief in miracles', Johnson began with a familiar objection:

let us consider; although God has made Nature to operate by certain fixed laws, yet it is not unreasonable to think that he may suspend those laws, in order to establish a system highly advantageous to mankind. Now the Christian religion is a most beneficial system, as it gives us light and certainty where we were before in darkness and doubt.[15]

Johnson's answer indicates that he had not fully appreciated the significance of Hume's attack (Hume denied the proofs for the existence of 'fixed laws'); yet his misconception was shared by most of his orthodox contemporaries. He produced the standard answer to what he mistakenly, though quite explicably, believed was only the standard objection to the Christian miracles. Hume's apparent reliance on the 'order of nature' must have seemed obstinate and conventional to those well versed—as Johnson was—in the previous literature on this subject.

The arguments which supported Johnson's 'sturdy prejudice' were thus grounded in an extensive background of apologetic writing. Even if we agree that philosophical scepticism had greatly weakened the intellectual foundations of orthodoxy, Johnson was carrying on an eminent tradition of ideas which

[14] *Life*, i. 444.   [15] Ibid. 445.

held unquestioned superiority until at least mid-century. The sheer weight of this authority must have influenced Johnson's reasonings. Indeed, a notable feature of his orthodoxy is the precision with which he followed the established defence of Christianity. He often repeated the usual arguments as if by rote.

For example, the apologists substantiated their case with praise for the courage and honesty of the witnesses to Christ's miracles. This was partly in response to infidels such as Collins and Woolston, who remarked that Christ lived in barbarous times when reports of miracles abounded. These infidels also insisted that people naturally relished superstitions, as the Roman Catholic world amply demonstrated.[16] Christian writers answered that the disciples of Christ were quite a different class of men from gullible pagans and Papists. In a 1731 defence of Christianity, James Foster summarized the conventional vindication of the disciples:

they had no prospect of honour to allure their *ambition*, nor of riches to gratify their *covetousness*, nor of ease and pleasure to suit a taste for *indolence* and *luxury* . . . they were sure of reproaches and sufferings; (not only as the *probable consequences* of their persisting to declare the christian doctrine, but the consequences of which their master had *expressly* forewarned them) all which they unanimously, courageously, and chearfully endur'd, and gave the *highest proof* of an *inflexible honesty*, by dying to vindicate the truth of their testimony.[17]

In 'Of Miracles' Hume was able to cite numerous miracles attested by men whose claims to sincerity were as impressive as those of the disciples.[18] Despite this, Johnson's 1763 rebuttal to Hume returned to precisely the same three marks of sincerity earlier listed by Foster: first, the disciples had no motive to deceive; second, they were forewarned of persecution; third, they finally died in proof of their sincerity: 'the miracles which prove [the Christian religion] are attested by men who had no interest in deceiving us; but who, on the contrary, were told that they should suffer persecution, and did actually lay down

---

[16] See Anthony Collins, *The Scheme of Literal Prophecy Considered* (London, 1727), 71; Thomas Woolston, *A Sixth Discourse on the Miracles of Our Saviour* (London, 1729), 26-7.

[17] James Foster, *The Usefulness, Truth, and Excellency of the Christian Revelation Defended* (London, 1731), 112-13.

[18] See Hume, 'Of Miracles', in *Philosophical Works*, iv. 96-105.

their lives in confirmation of the truth of the facts which they asserted.'[19] The tendency of Johnson's conversation towards this kind of exact repetition attests to the depth of his familiarity with the background of apologetics. But it also indicates a particular habit of mind which is highly typical of eighteenth-century orthodoxy. Throughout apologetic literature, arguments were repeated again and again with the same attention to detail. Like other apologists who duplicated the same logic in hundreds of tracts and pamphlets, Johnson displayed an unwillingness to break even in minor ways from what was standard and approved in the defence of Christianity.

Such a steadfast adherence to the approved responses really prohibits—is even designed to prohibit—the flexibility and open-mindedness which leads to change in established beliefs. The conventional answers seem to check all further enquiry. Boswell, for example, remarked to Johnson that his habitual unwillingness to believe reports of extraordinary events, a sceptical tendency also noted by G. B. Hill, brought him 'near Hume's argument against miracles'.[20] We might have expected that this charge of a private affinity with Hume would prompt an interesting self-justification. But Johnson responded briefly: 'Why, Sir, Hume, taking the proposition simply, is right. But the Christian revelation is not proved by the miracles alone, but as connected with prophecies, and with the doctrines in confirmation of which the miracles were wrought.'[21]

Johnson admitted that Hume was partly 'right': is this not significant? Perhaps, yet most orthodox writers had made the same admission. Although Tillotson had referred to the miracles as 'the main Evidence of Christian Doctrine',[22] an assumption carried into Hume's 'Of Miracles', most apologists had acknowledged that the truth of Christianity could be proved by no single form of evidence, but only by the interconnection between various forms of evidence. John Rogers admitted in 1727 that 'Miracles, without a concurring Testimony from the Prophesies, are not a sufficient Evidence of [Christ's] being *That Prophet*.'[23] In a 1741 reply to Henry

---

[19] *Life*, i. 445.   [20] Ibid. iii. 188.   [21] Ibid.

[22] See Tillotson, *Discourse against Transubstantiation*, in *Works*, iii. 315.

[23] John Rogers, *The Necessity of Divine Revelation, and the Truth of the Christian Revelation Asserted* (London, 1727), 125.

Dodwell, George Benson had written, '*rational* divines do not teach men to rest on one argument, singly and alone, for the foundation of their Faith;—but assert that it is sufficient if two, or three, or all the arguments in conjunction produce, or effect, a rational assent to Christianity'. [24] It was to this conventional position that Johnson made recourse when pressed on the alleged scepticism of his own thought. It was quick, neat, and approved in half a century of apologetic writing. It also avoided the necessity of a deliberation on his personal affinities with Hume which Boswell was trying to encourage.

We have no real grounds, however, to assume that Johnson was unwilling to confront some personal doubt or secret agreement with Hume. His reliance on the conventional formulas indicates a mind that was in this respect unlike Hume's. Hume was professedly a 'free-thinker' who, like others of that group, refused to concede that a belief had any special claim to truth only because it had endured for centuries. Knowledge would progress only if individuals were willing to challenge the long-standing prejudices of orthodoxy. Johnson held quite a different understanding of how knowledge advanced. Like other orthodox writers, he gleaned strength and certainty from the sense of an unwavering consensus within a long tradition. As he once told Boswell, the eminence of this tradition was itself a source of confidence:

As to the Christian religion, Sir, besides the strong evidence which we have for it, there is a balance in its favour from the number of great men who have been convinced of its truth, after a serious consideration of the question. Grotius was an acute man, a lawyer, a man accustomed to examine evidence, and he was convinced. Grotius was not a recluse, but a man of the world, who certainly had no bias on the side of religion. Sir Isaac Newton set out an infidel, and came to be a very firm believer. [25]

A similar sense of belonging to a tradition of great writers was characteristic of much apologetic literature. As Johnson's acquaintance, William Adams, wrote in his 1752 answer to Hume: 'Has the author lived in the time of Sir *Isaac Newton*, Mr. *Leslie*, and Mr. *Addison*? Can he know that these men gloried in the name of Christian . . . and yet think himself at

---

[24] George Benson, *The Reasonablenesse of the Christian Religion* (1741) (2nd edn.; London, 1746), 117.

[25] *Life*, i. 454–5.

liberty to treat all that believe it as men that are incapable of reasoning or thinking?'[26]

Neither Johnson nor most orthodox writers disparaged all departures from tradition. As we shall see, they had their own notion of a genuine and responsible 'originality'. Nor did they wish to relieve the individual of what Johnson called 'a serious consideration' of the proofs for Christianity. But beneath the conventionality and, many have complained, the stubborn illogic of eighteenth-century orthodoxy was a tendency to place far greater trust in the confidence of a tradition than in the brilliance of individuals.

This, Stephen might have remarked, is the very essence of 'sturdy prejudice'. But it is not irrational or groundless prejudice. For Johnson the history of thought was a process of slow accumulation and gradual improvement, not the record of a few reasoners overthrowing traditional beliefs and replacing them with their own. Johnson did not encourage individuals to venture down entirely novel or prohibited pathways of learning; he generally urged men to contribute to what, in *Rambler*, No. 129, he called 'the hereditary aggregate of human knowledge and happiness' (iv. 325). Understood in this way, his 'sturdy prejudice' was related to genuine principles concerning the nature of intellectual progress. It also reflects his conviction in the need for modesty in assessing the importance of our intellectual endeavours. He deeply distrusted the notion that a single individual could suddenly expose major fallacies that had been previously overlooked by all of mankind. And, while this does not necessarily excuse Johnson's heavy reliance on the conventional defence of Christianity rather than his own reasonings, it does help to explain why the confidence of orthodox writers was not greatly shaken by the scepticism of 'vain men' such as Hume.

2. *Faith as a 'Rational Assent'*

Discussion of Johnson's religion has repeatedly turned to the question of whether this 'faith' was weak or strong, often with

[26] William Adams, *An Answer to Mr. Hume's Essay on Miracles* (1752) (3rd edn.; London, 1767), 120. For other examples of this appeal to great thinkers and the tradition of orthodoxy, see Addison's *Spectator*, No. 186, in *The Spectator*, ed. D. F. Bond (6 vols.; Oxford, 1965), ii. 233–4 (all future references to this edition of the *Spectator*); Thomas Randolph, *The Christian's Faith a Rational Assent* (London, 1744), 115.

the conclusion that it was exceedingly weak. Yet it has not
often been considered what exactly is meant by 'faith' when
this word is used by or properly applied to Johnson. There is
general agreement that his faith was based on reason, but we
are under some obligation to be more specific. For there was,
indeed, considerable disagreement among theologians concerning the relationship between reason and faith. Certain
ways of understanding this relationship had been used by
heterodox writers to embarrass the Church, prompting a series
of debates on the precise nature of a 'rational assent' to the
Christian evidences.

According to writers influenced by John Tillotson, Samuel
Clarke, and the 'latitudinarian' divines of the Restoration and
early eighteenth century, the self-evident reasonableness and
goodness of the doctrines revealed by Scripture were, as James
Foster wrote in 1731, 'absolutely necessary in order to its being
a divine revelation'.[27] The 'rational assent' to Christianity
included the individual's acknowledgement that its teachings
were such as were worthy to be revealed by a reasonable and
benevolent God. This criterion for giving or withholding faith
was known as the 'internal evidence', in distinction from the
miracles, prophecies, and other 'external evidence' for the
Divine origin of Scripture. When Johnson told Boswell that
Christianity was proved not only by the miracles, but also by
'the doctrines in confirmation of which the miracles were
wrought',[28] he was alluding to the internal evidence.

But the internal evidence caused some difficulty in the
defence of Christianity. This proof made the teachings of
Christianity subject to the approval of the individual; yet, if the
truth and goodness of doctrines had to be confirmed before
they were attributed to God, then why was it necessary for God
to reveal them in the first place? This was a problem raised by
John Toland's *Christianity not Mysterious* (1696). Toland gave
the usual statement of the internal evidence for Scripture—that
Christianity was supported by 'those *Doctrines* in Confirmation
whereof the *Miracles* are wrought'.[29] But he used this argument
to corroborate his thesis that 'there is nothing in the Gospel

[27] Foster, *The Usefulness, Truth, and Excellency of the Christian Revelation Defended*, p. 172.
[28] *Life*, iii. 188.
[29] Toland, *Christianity not Mysterious*, p. 157.

contrary to Reason, nor above it; and that no Christian
Doctrine can be properly call'd a Mystery'.[30] By thus denying
the existence of any 'mysterious' teachings in Scripture,
Toland rendered Christianity little more than a system of
'common Notions'. Faith was only 'a Perswasion resulting
from the previous Knowledg and Comprehension of the thing
believed',[31] which raised the obvious problem of how it was
possible to be 'persuaded' of what was already fully compre-
hended. Thus, the 'internal evidence' supported a position that
deprived 'faith' of all meaning. 'Faith' was really no different
from factual knowledge of any kind. The absurdity of this
implication raised justifiable suspicions that impious ironies
lurked beneath Toland's show of piety.

Toland's heterodoxies suggest why Johnson and more conservative apologists generally avoided recourse to the internal
evidence. Some replies to Toland advised the apologists to rely
entirely on the external evidence. Peter Browne, for instance,
counselled that,

our way to deal with these men is . . . to insist upon the *Proofs* we
have for the Revelation, and shew that they are such as ought to
convince any reasonable unprejudiced man. . . . For by freely
owning (as becomes us) that we have no notion of all these mysterious
things as they are in themselves, we cut off a multitude of *frivolous* and
impertinent Objections.[32]

Browne's criticism was directed partly at the divines who had
carelessly facilitated Toland's case by laying inordinate stress
on the internal evidences. His recommendation that divines
now avoid relying on the internal evidence was, in varying
degrees, taken up by a large number of orthodox writers.[33]
Johnson also seemed sympathetic to the type of restrictions
favoured by Browne. As he observed of Cowley's poems,
'Reason has its proper task assigned to it: that of judging, not

---

[30] Ibid. 6.

[31] Ibid. 139.

[32] Peter Browne, *A Letter in Answer to a Book, Entituled, Christianity not Mysterious* (London, 1697), 55-6.

[33] Joseph Butler argued that natural religion itself dictated that we should accept the mysteries of Scripture: nature contains many insoluble mysteries concerning, for example, the workings of Divine providence; by 'analogy', it should not surprise us that God has revealed a system of teachings which similarly contains many insoluble mysteries. See *The Analogy of Religion, Natural and Revealed* (London, 1736), II, iv, 188-91.

of things revealed, but of the reality of revelation.'[34] Men, he suggested, had no business testing the validity of Scriptural teachings: we were to confirm by the miracles and prophecies that the teachings came from God, and then accept whatever was revealed without further question.

This argument did require some qualification: neither Browne nor Johnson could totally exclude reason from the task of judging the truth of revealed doctrines. The well-known distinction between doctrines 'contrary to' and 'above' reason was partly intended to guide the determination of what qualified as a revealed 'mystery'. John Tillotson had satisfied most Anglicans that transubstantiation was 'contrary to reason', and therefore inadmissible as a revealed doctrine. And, according to the unitarian writers who sparked a major controversy during the Restoration, Tillotson's reasoning could also be used against belief in the Trinity.[35] This is where the glib distinction between 'contrary' and 'above' reason becomes rather difficult to follow, for orthodox Anglicans insisted that the Trinity was 'contrary' to reason only if it were understood in an erroneous way. As Browne argued:

> They who cry there is a *Contradiction* in this *Mystery*, seem to me neither to know what a *Contradiction* is, nor what is the Christian Faith concerning the Trinity. For we don't believe that the *Divinity* is *One* and *Three* in the same sense; then indeed it would be contradiction. But we affirm quite the contrary, *viz.* that the Godhead is *One* and *Three* in *different respects*. . . . I grant we are not able to *account* for this, and it is this that makes it a *Mystery*.[36]

Johnson's defence of the Trinity in Boswell's *A Tour to the Hebrides* (1785) again demonstrates how scrupulously he followed the standard defence of orthodox doctrines:

> I said, 'Would not the same objection hold against the Trinity as against Transubstantiation?' 'Yes, (said he,) if you take three and one in the same sense. If you do so, to be sure you cannot believe it: but the three persons of the Godhead are Three in one sense, and One in another. We cannot tell how; and that is the mystery!'[37]

[34] *Lives of the Poets*, i. 38.

[35] For a detailed discussion of the Trinitarian controversy, see E. M. Wilbur, *A History of Unitarianism* (2 vols.; Cambridge, Mass., 1952), ii. 185–270; R. S. Franks, *The Doctrine of the Trinity* (London, 1952), 142–51.

[36] Browne, *Letter*, pp. 62–3.   [37] *Life*, v. 188.

This passage illustrates one of the most characteristic features of the orthodox understanding of Divine nature. Even Johnson, a man with a very conservative sense of religious decency, saw no impiety or presumption in making God subject to the physical laws of the universe. As Imlac urges in Chapter 48 of *Rasselas*, 'it is no limitation of omnipotence . . . to suppose that one thing is not consistent with another, that the same proposition cannot be at once true and false, that the same number cannot be even and odd, that cogitation cannot be conferred on that which is created incapable of cogitation'.[38] Similarly, Johnson's defence of the Trinity acknowledged that even an omnipotent Deity cannot be one Being and three Beings at the same time: this would be contrary to reason and the laws of nature. His point was apparently that there were two different ways of expressing the nature of God, the first as a unity and the second as the Trinity.

Yet this argument does not necessarily solve the problems raised by the unitarians. Although Johnson may have avoided the charge that the doctrine of the Trinity is contradictory, he may also have stumbled into the heresy of Sabellianism. As it was interpreted by eighteenth-century writers, the Sabellian heresy dictated that the persons of the Godhead were simply three different expressions for the same individual Being. This destroyed the individuality of Christ and the Holy Spirit, and, the unitarians claimed, essentially upheld their position that the Trinity did not exist. In order to avoid this heresy, some orthodox writers verged towards the opposite heresy of tritheism—that the Godhead was comprised of three distinct substances. This was the heresy charged by Robert South and others against William Sherlock's well-intentioned *A Vindication of the Doctrine of the Holy and Ever Blessed Trinity* (1690). In short, in their anxiety to avoid the charge of contradiction, Anglicans were forced to veer away from what was strictly orthodox. Those such as Edward Stillingfleet who attempted to maintain the Trinity in all its traditional purity, arguing that the three persons of the Godhead belong to the same indivisible substance, resorted to the most convoluted logic in order to show that this doctrine was 'above' and not 'contrary' to reason.[39]

---

[38] *Rasselas*, p. 120.

[39] See Edward Stillingfleet, *A Discourse in Vindication of the Doctrine of the Trinity* (London, 1697). The preface to this treatise, which was published at the end of the

This perplexity aside, Johnson generally upheld the definition of 'faith' given by Locke in Book 4 of *An Essay Concerning Human Understanding*: '*Faith* is the Assent to any Proposition; not thus made out by the Deductions of Reason; but upon the Credit of the Proposer, as coming from GOD.'[40] Johnson's own definition of 'faith' in the *Dictionary*—'Belief of the revealed truths of religion'—is too broad to suggest much about his personal opinions on this quality. His *Dictionary* definition is, however, more specifically Christian than the definitions proposed by writers who gave a wider and more important role to reason in creating 'faith'. In a sermon 'Of a Religious and Divine Faith', for example, John Tillotson used a three-part Scholastic definition of 'faith', arguing that it was not only 'A Persuasion of things supernatural and reveal'd', but also 'A Persuasion of the Principles of natural Religion'.[41] For Johnson, as for Locke, faith could not be equated with the philosophical deductions of natural religion.

In order to provide Scriptural foundation for this idea of faith, orthodox writers relied heavily on Paul's definition of faith in Hebrews 11: 1—'Faith is the substance of things hoped for, the evidence of things not seen'. The reference to 'evidence' was particularly pleasing to eighteenth-century divines. Yet the idea of faith as a 'rational assent' was, at best, barely in accordance with the larger tradition of Christian orthodoxy and, in particular, the characteristic teachings of Protestantism. Luther, for example, held that faith and reason were entirely distinct. He was not afraid of arguing that 'Faith must believe against reason, against its own feeling, and against the reality only of that which is empirical.'[42] Moreover, Luther gave supreme importance not to knowledge or assent, but to 'trust' (*fiducia*) in the saving mercies of the atonement, a supernaturally bestowed condition that in itself 'justified' the sinner (that is, released him from inherited guilt through the imputed righteousness of Christ). In Johnson's time the most

Trinitarian controversy, provides a useful overview of the major points of debate, and the current interpretation of the heresies that I have mentioned.

40 Locke, *Human Understanding*, IV, xviii, 689.

41 Tillotson, *Works*, iii. 319.

42 As cited by P. Althaus, in *The Theology of Martin Luther*, trans. R. C. Schultz (Philadelphia, 1966), 57. Althaus provides a good summary of Luther's doctrine on faith, pp. 43–71.

forceful proponent of justification by faith was John Wesley. In
An Earnest Appeal to Men of Reason and Religion (1743) Wesley
denied that faith could ever 'contradict' reason, but he did
insist on the entire helplessness of reason without preliminary
faith. With the supernatural gift of faith, 'you have a new class
of senses opened in your soul, not depending on organs of flesh
and blood, to be "the evidence of things not seen" . . . to
discern spiritual objects, and to furnish you with ideas of what
the outward "eye hath not seen, neither the ear heard"'.[43]
Supported by faith, we can gaze directly into the mysteries of
salvation. Like Luther, Wesley also preached that faith
cleansed the individual of all sin and all perplexity: 'the
moment a man receives faith . . . he is saved from doubt and
fear, and sorrow of heart . . . and from his sins of whatsoever
kind they were.'[44]

The first question which this background raises is this: did
Johnson's theology make faith, as opposed to all acts of moral
goodness, a condition of salvation? Most of his statements
suggest that he placed very little importance on faith itself, as
distinguished from the far more crucial objective of works. In
1781, for example, Boswell mentioned the opinion 'as to there
being merit in religious faith'. Johnson answered, 'Why, yes,
Sir, the most licentious man, were hell open before him, would
not take the most beautiful strumpet to his arms. We must, as
the Apostle says, live by faith, not by sight.'[45] This statement is
consistent with Johnson's remarks on faith in Sermon 10: 'to
live religiously, is to walk, not by sight, but by faith; to act in
confidence of things unseen, in hope of future recompence, and
in fear of future punishment' (xiv. 110). St Paul's 'things not
unseen', which for Wesley and others meant the great mysteries
of God and heaven, was here used to mean specifically the
rewards and punishments of the hereafter. And as Johnson
indicated to Boswell, the rewards and punishments were
important primarily as they strengthened the motives to good
works. In Sermon 22 Johnson suggested that the primary

---

[43] John Wesley, *An Earnest Appeal to Men of Reason and Religion* (1743), ed. G. R.
Cragg, *The Works of John Wesley*, gen. ed. F. Baker (Oxford and Nashville, 1975–), xi.
56–7.

[44] Wesley, *Earnest Appeal*, in *Works* (1975), xi. 53.

[45] *Life*, iv. 123, Johnson is citing 2 Cor. 5: 7.

question concerning our faith was 'whether it regularly influences our conduct' (xiv. 235). In Sermon 14 he seemed to turn Luther's or Wesley's formula on its head: Johnson argued that 'trust in God', by which he roughly meant faith, was achievable only through good works.[46] Whereas Luther and Wesley argued that faith gave birth to good works, Johnson suggested that good works gave birth to faith.

These opinions were by no means unusual in Johnson's time, but they represent an understanding of faith which belonged particularly to contemporary Anglicanism, and had been accepted only after considerable controversy. Johnson's treatment of faith is comparable in some respects with the idea of faith described by Locke in *The Reasonableness of Christianity* (1695). This treatise helped to create an impression that still endures today—that Locke was a deist, and entertained certain heresies. Like Johnson, Locke reduced the subject of faith to an extremely narrow range of 'mysteries' (in the sense of articles which could not be determined by reason). Whereas Johnson tended to describe faith as belief in future rewards and punishments, Locke argued that the sum of faith was only 'believing that Christ was the Messiah',[47] a conviction which also implied belief in the resurrection, and the possibility of salvation. Yet, as Locke went on to point out, devils may firmly believe in these articles as well as the most devout Christian. The only real difference between the faithful Christian and the devil was that the Christian combined mere belief with repentance and obedience. According to some contemporary divines, Locke's doctrine was really a disguised attack on faith as this doctrine was understood in its more traditional sense. Anxious to find some label for Locke's heresy, they called him a Socinian, the sect which exemplified a thoroughly legalistic understanding of Christianity bereft of any supernatural mysteries.[48] By

---

[46] See Sermon 14, xiv. 157-8.

[47] Locke, *The Reasonableness of Christianity* (London, 1695), 26-7.

[48] See John Edwards, *Socinianism Unmask'd: A Discourse Shewing the Unreasonableness of a Late Writers Opinion Concerning the Necessity of Only One Article of Faith* (London, 1696); anon., *Animadversions on a Late Book, Entituled the Reasonableness of Christianity* (Oxford, 1697), 1. Because Toland had used Locke's philosophy in *Christianity not Mysterious*, Locke was widely blamed for Toland's heterodoxies. Such allegations seemed to astonish Locke, who finally declared that he was ready 'presently to condemn and quit any Opinion of mine, as soon as I am shewn that it is contrary to any Revelation' (*A Letter to the Right Reverend Edward [Stillingfleet] Ld. Bishop of Worcester, Concerning Some*

Johnson's time, few bothered to raise the charge of Socinianism, for what was once seen as vaguely heretical was increasingly accepted as orthodox.

Orthodox writers of the eighteenth century had both narrowed the subject of faith to extremely few essential articles, and allotted this quality such secondary importance that it could hardly be described as a condition of salvation. It would be ridiculous to claim that an individual had achieved anything more than the first, basic step towards piety merely by accepting that Christ was the Messiah or that there really were rewards and punishments in the hereafter. Moreover, while Luther and Wesley had insisted that faith was entirely the gift of God, orthodox writers threatened to deprive God of even the most secondary role in its creation. Faith was the product of individual study, and seemed little different from any type of educated conviction. Nevertheless, eighteenth-century divines could not entirely remove God from the creation of faith without an utter breach from the established doctrines of the Christian Church. They were under a considerable obligation to combine their essentially empirical notion of faith with some conception of the participation of Divine grace in its achievement.

This was done by insisting that a serious examination of the evidences was itself impossible without the help of grace. As Henry Stebbing wrote in the major Anglican treatise on grace, *A Treatise Concerning the Operations of the Holy Spirit* (1719), 'This Assistance of the Spirit is necessary to *prepare* Men's Hearts, and put them into *a fit Temper* and *Disposition* to embrace the Gospel, when proposed to them with sufficient *Evidence*.'[49] Rational assent would be achieved only if the individual were *willing* to be convinced by the strength of the evidence for belief in Christianity—and such a willingness could be created only by God.

Passages Relating to Mr. Locke's Essay of Human Understanding (London, 1697), 226–7). Stephen reviewed the nature of the charges against Locke in *English Thought*, i. 93–4. For the opinion of some modern scholars that Locke was a deist or unitarian, see, e.g., Wilbur, *History of Unitarianism*, pp. 232–5; Franks, *Trinity*, p. 147; I. T. Ramsay's introduction to his edition of *Reasonableness of Christianity* (London, 1958), 16–19.

[49] Henry Stebbing, *A Treatise Concerning the Operations of the Holy Spirit* (London, 1719), 16. Stebbing's work was actually an abridgement, with numerous additions and adjustments, of a 1678 tract by William Clagett.

This reconciliation between reason and grace provided some basis for refuting the suggestion by Henry Dodwell that orthodox divines had entirely omitted the participation of God in creating faith. Dodwell contended in *Christianity not Founded in Argument* (1741) that reason could produce nothing better than an unstable belief in Christianity; each individual should pray for 'a constant and particular Revelation imparted separately and supernaturally to every Individual'.[50] Dodwell's stipulation rendered Scripture entirely useless, and can hardly have been inspired by very pious intentions. Yet his case was insidious: like Hume's declaration that 'our most holy Religion is founded on *Faith*, not Reason',[51] his arguments seemed to support the doctrine that was being widely preached by the Methodists. Wesley himself admitted that he had picked up Dodwell's treatise with high expectations, and, though he immediately recognized its profane ironies, he remarked that many of his followers had been taken in.[52] The same mistake was made by certain mystic Christians such as William Law's friend, John Byrom.[53] It is not surprising that the mainstream of 'rational' divines was not so easily impressed, yet conventional apologists were faced with a difficult problem of their own. They had to refute Dodwell while avoiding the danger of praising reason too highly, a mistake which had led to heterodoxy in the opposite extreme in the writings of Toland and Tindal. For this reason, the apologist George Benson adopted Stebbing's middle way, suggesting that grace was necessary to prepare the reasoning faculties for the sincere, unbiased examination of the Christian evidences:

Lord, preserve us in the right use of our faculties, continue to us our reasonable powers, and the means of knowledge and conviction which we already have, that we may examine more carefully the nature and evidence of all true religion, and more clearly perceive their force and excellence . . . Deliver us from all criminal prejudices, from all biasse of wrong affections . . . And may we continually be growing in this virtuous and amiable disposition of mind, 'till at last we attain the end of our Faith, even the salvation of our souls.[54]

[50] See Henry Dodwell, *Christianity not Founded in Argument* (London, 1741), 110–12.
[51] Hume, 'Of Miracles', in *Philosophical Works*, iv. 107.
[52] See Wesley, *Earnest Appeal*, in *Works* (1975), xi. 58.
[53] See Stephen, *English Thought*, i. 140.
[54] Benson, *The Reasonablenesse of the Christian Religion*, pp. 114–15.

Johnson's 'Prayer on the Study of Religion' even more strongly suggested the individual's dependence on Divine Grace to ensure the success of his studies into the truth of religion: 'Almighty God, our heavenly Father, without whose light search is vain, invigorate my studies and direct my enquiries, that I may, by due diligence and right discernment establish myself and others in thy holy Faith' (i. 62). Throughout his religious and moral writings, Johnson insisted on the enormous difficulty of cleansing one's mind of prejudice and keeping it focused on the important subject at hand. Good men, he argued in Sermon 7, had even gone into retirement so that 'the chain of reasoning may be preserved unbroken, and the mind perform its operations without any hindrance from foreign objects' (xiv. 81). For this reason, grace played a crucial role in the creation of faith by permitting the mind to examine the evidences with the 'due diligence and right discernment' necessary to achieve a sincere 'rational assent'. In addition, it is probable that this conception of faith would have increased his unwillingness to accept the reasonings against the truth of revelation. According to the doctrine set forth by Stebbing, an inability to recognize the truth of Christianity was the natural result of a heart deprived of grace. To see the strength of the evidences was a sign that God had permitted the reasoning faculties to function properly; to admit a lack of conviction after a study of the evidences was practically to admit that one had been denied grace.

As we will consider more fully in Chapter 7, grace played an important role in Johnson's theology and personal devotion. Yet an increasing number of Christian groups, such as the Methodists, were attempting to re-establish the doctrine that grace did more than prepare the mind for rational enquiry; faith was the essential and all-encompassing condition of salvation. Nor were all Protestants happy with a doctrine which narrowed faith to a firm belief in Christ's divinity or, as seems to have been the case with Johnson, in the reality of future rewards and punishments. Moreover, orthodox writers were heading into a contradiction. Their idea of faith so strongly focused on the duty of individual study that it is difficult to reconcile with their formulaic repetition of the conventional defence of religion. On the one hand, orthodox

Christians were relying on the authority of tradition and disparaging a reliance on individual judgement; on the other hand, they were making the individual act of study among the most important acts in the religious life. There is an inconsistency here—or, at least, this was the allegation of eighteenth-century free-thinkers. According to the principles of 'free-thinking', the act of studying religion was meaningless if the individual did not have the right to question approved beliefs. Johnson's contemporaries were faced with the difficult task of explaining how any individual could be said to 'assent' to evidence if the strength of that evidence could never be challenged or doubted.

3. *Free-thinking and 'Scoffers' at Religion*

It was characteristic of eighteenth-century infidels to claim that they were simply extending the principles held by orthodox writers themselves. It is this claim, for example, which supplied Anthony Collins's *A Discourse of Free-thinking* (1713) with much of its rhetorical force. It is likely that the really important influences on Collins were Bayle and Shaftesbury, writers who had argued explicitly that intellectual progress would occur only if men were free to question the most sacred and traditional doctrines. But Collins hardly mentioned these writers, and instead filled his treatise with citations from recent and contemporary divines. Reviewing orthodox writings on many of Christianity's most important doctrines—original sin, the Trinity, baptism, the resurrection—he came to the inevitable conclusion that the divines freely disagreed about almost everything that was held sacred. Most of the eminent reasoners of the past decades had been charged by someone with serious heresies: Chillingworth, Cudworth, Tillotson, Locke, Clarke, and Bold had all been called Socinians and even atheists. Moreover, all the great writers of classical and Christian literature had been, in certain important respects, rebels against the established authorities and opinions. The Reformation was a great outburst of 'free-thinking'. Lord Bacon, and what we call the 'New Science', epitomized the principles of 'free-thinking'. In all these respects, Collins's case was quite defensible: contemporary orthodoxy was the heir of certain important revolutions in intellectual history. Besides being Protestants and benefactors of the New Science, Anglicans had been strongly influenced by the doctrinal 'latitude' of Tillotson, Locke, and Clarke; the spokesmen for the old order, such as the nonjurors and Calvinists who supplied Collins with his most provocative allegations, had increasingly become voices in the wilderness.

For all that, the reaction to Collins's *Discourse* was extremely hostile. And, as we have seen, the orthodoxy of the following decades was dominated by a new order of intellectual authorities who were cited with a loyalty that was far more scholastic than Baconian. As Collins's treatise had showed, the fundamental doctrines of religion were thrown into doubt simply by assuming that they could be the subject of serious debate. The problem for orthodox writers was to disparage such 'free-thinking' on sacred matters without exposing themselves to the charge of 'bigotry'—the unreasoning reliance on tradition which they were supposed to abhor.

The best solution was to allege that it was the 'free-thinkers', not orthodox Christians, who had really betrayed the principles of free and unrestrained enquiry into religious truth. This was not, as we shall see, a charge that was easy to maintain without taking considerable liberties with the facts. But the apologists were greatly helped in their case by a doctrine that gained close associations with the whole free-thinking movement—Shaftesbury's 'test of ridicule'. As described in 'A Letter Concerning Enthusiasm' (1708), later published in the collection *Characteristics of Men, Manners, Opinions, Times etc.* (1711), the 'test of ridicule' postulates that the most solemn truths of morality and religion can never be made the subject of laughter; the ridicule will rebound on the individual who attempts it.[55] This position is not so preposterous as it might at first appear, and it was possible to advocate Shaftesbury's precept in a spirit of morality and seriousness. Fielding's Joseph Andrews, for example, defies 'the wisest man in the world to turn a true good action into ridicule. I defy him to do it. He

[55] See Anthony Ashley Cooper, Earl of Shaftesbury, 'A Letter Concerning Enthusiasm', in *Characteristics of Men, Manners, Opinions, Times etc.* (1711), ed. J. M. Robertson (2 vols.; London, 1900), i. 10. Defences of the 'test of ridicule' include Anthony Collins, *A Discourse Concerning Ridicule and Irony in Writing* (London, 1729); Charles Bulkley, *A Vindication of My Lord Shaftesbury, on the Subject of Ridicule* (London, 1751).

who should endeavour it, would be laughed at himself, instead
of making others laugh.'[56] This principle is immediately tested
when a local gentleman plays a series of practical jokes on the
benevolent Parson Adams (III, vii). Many readers will agree
that Fielding successfully illustrates Shaftesbury's real point:
the local gentleman emerges from this episode looking far more
ridiculous than Adams, who is comically bespattered without
losing any of his dignity as a good man.

According to most apologists, however, Shaftesbury's 'test
of ridicule' justified an entire abandonment of reason and
truth. Formal refutations of the test, such as the first chapter of
John Brown's *Essays on the Characteristics* (1751), strictly
distinguished between reason and ridicule, which was described
as fundamentally irrational and arbitrary:

> as the Object of every excited Passion must be examined by Reason ere
> we can determine whether it be proper or improper, real or fictitious;
> so, every Object that excites Contempt must fall under this general
> Rule. Thus, before it can be determined whether our Contempt be
> *just*, Reason alone must *examine* Circumstances, separate Ideas,
> distinguish Truth from its Appearances, decide upon, restrain, and
> *correct the Passion.*[57]

Johnson owned Brown's *Essays on the Characteristics*, and it is not
implausible that it influenced his own critique of the test of
ridicule in the 'Life of Akenside': 'If ridicule be applied to any
position as the test of truth, it will then become a question
whether such ridicule be just; and this can only be decided by
the application of truth as the test of ridicule.'[58] What this
response illustrates is a more fundamental disagreement on the
nature of our moral judgements. Shaftesbury and Fielding
placed a great deal of confidence in our emotional response to
an event, which must be the basis for our decision concerning
the 'justice' of an opinion or action even when the facts are fully
known. Brown and Johnson saw ridicule and contempt as
superficial and impulsive responses which must be subject to
reason's conclusions concerning the strength or weakness
of evidence. Because they placed little confidence in our

---

56 Henry Fielding, *Joseph Andrews* (1742), ed. D. Brooks (London, 1970), 209.
57 John Brown, *Essays on the Characteristics* (London, 1751), 42–3.
58 *Lives of the Poets*, iii. 413.

emotional reactions, they condemned the test of ridicule as a betrayal rather than an exercise in free-thought.

The test of ridicule became an important issue in apologetic literature not only as the result of Shaftesbury's influence on the principles of free-thinking, but also because orthodox writers were acutely sensitive to any trace of impious mirth in heterodox writing. Sometimes they were correct to perceive ridicule against Christianity. Collins, for example, laced *A Discourse of Free-thinking* with lewd jests on the priesthood. Tracts by Blount, Toland, and Dodwell are also more profane than at first appears, though it cannot be said that they make systematic use of ridicule. According to many apologetic tracts, however, the case for infidelity was based almost entirely on ridicule. And, as George Berkeley insisted in *Alciphron, or the Minute Philosopher* (1732), the free-thinkers turned to ridicule in order to disguise a genuine ignorance and carelessness for truth:

I have often observed the Conduct of Minute Philosophers, When one of them has got a ring of Disciples round him, his method is to exclaim against Prejudice, and recommend thinking and reasoning, giving us to understand that he himself is a Man of deep Researches and close Argument, one who examines impartially and concludes warily. The same Man in other Company, if he chance to be pressed with Reason, shall laugh at Logic and assume the lazy supine Airs of a fine Gentleman, a Wit, a Railleur, to avoid the dryness of a regular and exact Inquiry.[59]

This was what Berkeley called 'the double Face of the Minute Philosopher',[60] on the one hand espousing the principles of free enquiry, and on the other hiding his incapacity for dispute behind wit and insolence. As a description of the entire movement of sceptics and free-thinkers, it was grossly over-generalized. Nor did it have the least relevance to the genuine and often incisive arguments advanced by sceptical writers. Yet it had the advantage of deflecting the charge of 'prejudice' away from orthodox writers and on to the free-thinkers themselves. The apologists, it was claimed, were the genuine advocates of an orderly, unbiased enquiry into religious truth

---

[59] George Berkeley, *Alciphron, or the Minute Philosopher* (2 vols.; London, 1732), i. 236.

[60] Ibid.

which the free-thinkers, despite all their proclaimed ideals of sincerity and diligence, were doing everything to avoid.

Shaftesbury's 'test of ridicule' also had the convenience of roughly fulfilling a Scriptural prophecy: 'there shall come in the last days scoffers, walking after their own lusts' (2 Peter 3: 3). This became the text for a large group of sermons, including Johnson's Sermon 20, against the modern 'scoffers' at religion.[61] Johnson's sermon owes a great deal to this homiletic background, but perhaps even more to the treatment of free-thinkers in apologetic tracts and pamphlets. Like most apologists he made the 'test of ridicule' the tenet of not only Shaftesbury but the entire movement of free-thinkers: 'It is an established maxim among them, that he who ridicules an opinion confutes it' (xiv. 220). And this alleged consensus on the 'test of ridicule' revealed that the free-thinkers, despite all their pretensions 'to carry the art of reasoning to its greatest height' (xiv. 219), were really intent on avoiding the irrefutable reasoning of Christian apologetics:

This method of controversy is indeed the general refuge of those whose idleness or incapacity disable them from producing any thing solid or convincing. They, who are certain of being confuted and exposed in a sober dispute, imagine that by returning scurrility for reason, and by laughing most loudly, when they have least to say, they shall shelter their ignorance from detection, and supply with impudence what they want in knowledge (xiv. 221).

Sermon 20 thus elaborates on what Berkeley and many other Christians alleged was the hypocrisy of the free-thinking movement. It is significant that Johnson did not simply assert that the free-thinkers had no right to question the truths of Christianity. This would make him guilty of a fault which he himself, in theory, condemned: 'bigotry, that voluntary blindness, that slavish submission to the notions of others' (xiv. 219). Sermon 20 therefore upholds the basic virtues of a free enquiry into any religious question, no matter how sacred. Johnson focused his attack on the supposed unwillingness of all infidels to undertake precisely that investigation.

---

[61] Edward Stillingfleet's 'The Folly of Scoffing at Religion', James Foster's 'The Nature, Folly and Sin of Scoffing at Religion', and William Warburton's 'Iniquity the Cause of Disbelief' are a few of those sermons especially close to Sermon 20 in argument and structure.

Nevertheless, it is difficult to avoid the suspicion that Johnson, like the tradition of Christian writers he followed, was not being entirely sincere. Johnson's argument is far too distant from the real nature of the eighteenth-century debates on Christianity to have any strong claim to a genuine desire to uphold the principles of free-enquiry. Like most of his writing and conversation on infidelity, this sermon rehearses a series of arguments that had become thoroughly routine, and defames the free-thinking movement without much regard to the theoretical legitimacy of their ideals and methods. It was this objective of disgracing the infidels which became the overriding concern of much apologetic literature.

Despite their claim that ridicule was unsuitable to an enlightened debate on religious truth, many apologists had shown little hesitation to rely on this technique themselves. Collins's *A Discourse of Free-thinking* may have contained a great deal of covert scurrilousness, but it had none of the almost Swiftian ridicule launched against him by Richard Bentley. Bentley asked where Collins's '*Brains* were', commended his 'mighty Learning', and recommended that all the free-thinkers be shipped to Madagascar to join their 'Kindred . . . the *Monkeys* and *Drills*'.[62] More generally, the apologists rehearsed a series of allegations against the character and motives of infidel writers. They were arrogant, vain men who, as George Benson charged in 1741, 'scorn to think in the common track, or believe as the *vulgar do*'. Above all, 'they must be in fashion; they dread the censure of some of their acquaintance'.[63] The infidels were also debauched men, who did not want religion to be true because this would oblige them to give up their favourite vices. Alternatively, they had been led to a genuine disbelief in religion through what John Rogers called the 'easy, natural Process of our Corruption'.[64] This process began with minor deviations from the strict rule of virtue and piety which the individual justified to himself through various errors and delusions—mitigating interpretations of Scripture, the reliance on single virtues to excuse general corruption, promises of

[62] Richard Bentley, *Remarks upon a Late Discourse of Free-thinking, in a Letter to F.H.D.D. by Phileleutherus Lipsiensis* (London, 1713), 37, 43, and 47.
[63] Benson, *The Reasonablenesse of the Christian Religion*, p. 11.
[64] Rogers, *The Necessity of Divine Revelation*, p. 190.

future repentance. As these delusions accumulated, the sinner
gradually lost sight of religious truth. As Rogers concluded,
'the Sinner will go on from one Degree of Blindness and
Impiety to another, till at last he takes up with the Persuasion
of the Fool, and says in his Heart there is no God'.[65]

There were some attempts to substantiate these charges with
evidence from the lives of modern infidels. Charles Blount, it
was often related, shot himself when prohibited from marrying
his mistress; Matthew Tindal's *Christianity as Old as the Creation*
(1730) was followed by an extraordinary pamphlet describing
his dreadful table manners at All Souls, Oxford, where he was
a fellow.[66] But the charge of moral corruption was largely *a
priori*—justified by the Scriptural prophecy that the 'scoffers' at
religion would 'walk after their own lusts' and by assumptions
concerning what was *supposed* to be the character of irreligious
men. The impossible task faced by free-thinking authors was to
convince their opponents that there was no necessary connection
between infidelity and vicious inclinations. In *Miscellaneous
Reflexions, Occasion'd by the Comet which appear'd in December 1680*
(1683; trans. 1708) Pierre Bayle contended that 'speculative
Opinions' such as religious belief were 'not the true Springs of
our Actions'. After all, it would be preposterous to argue that
'Christians, who don't walk according to the Principles of their
Religion, . . . are so many conceal'd Atheists.' Why then was
it any less preposterous to claim that all atheists were vicious
men?[67]

Bayle's argument is interesting because it is based on
reasoning that was often used by Johnson himself. Johnson
often condemned those 'so grossly ignorant of human nature,
as to know that a man may be very sincere in good principles,
without having good practice'.[68] As Bayle had urged, there is
no direct connection between speculative belief and moral
conduct. In *Rambler*, No. 70, Johnson argued with some
passion that it was grossly unfair to attribute immoral conduct
to a scorn for religion: men usually sinned because they were

[65] Ibid. 190–1. Rogers is alluding the Psalms 14: 1.

[66] See anon., *The Religious, Rational and Moral Conduct of Matthew Tindal, LLD., Late
Fellow of All Souls College in Oxford. In a Letter to a Friend* (London, 1735).

[67] See Pierre Bayle, *Miscellaneous Reflexions, Occasion'd by the Comet which appear'd in
December 1680* (1683) (trans., 2 vols.; London, 1708), i. 272–326.

[68] *Life*, v. 259–60.

weak, not because they were abandoned infidels. Yet perhaps Johnson's most characteristic response to infidelity was to charge these writers with depravity and arrogance. 'No honest man could be a Deist', he told Boswell, 'for no man could be so after a fair examination of the proofs of Christianity.'[69] Elsewhere in the *Life* he alleged that 'Hume, and other sceptical innovators, are vain men, and will gratify themselves at any expense.'[70] In Sermon 20 he rehearsed the standard charges of vanity and corruption in great detail. Like Rogers, he described the process by which the vicious man 'justifies one crime by another; invents wicked principles to support wicked practices' (xiv. 216), until finally the sinner learns 'not only to neglect, but to insult religion' (xiv. 217). Like Benson, he argued that the 'scoffers' were really intent on 'following the fashion of a corrupt and licentious age, or gaining the friendship of the great, or the applause of the gay' (xiv. 225).

Like all of Johnson's homiletic writing, Sermon 20 is organized very formally, and moves with systematic precision from one argument to the next. It is worthy of a lexicographer. Yet this feature of the discourse may induce us to believe that his allegations were more reasonable and accurate than they really were. Although there can be no question that Johnson did believe that irreligion promoted vice, Sermon 20 sweeps aside the difficult question raised by Collins and other free-thinkers—whether orthodoxy was protecting its most important beliefs with bigotry and displays of solemn outrage rather than reason. Like the apologetic tracts it summarizes, Sermon 20 illustrates a tendency in debate which Johnson himself condemned in Sermon 7: 'how readily the antagonists deviate into personal invectives, and, instead of confuting the arguments, defame the lives of those, whose doctrine they disapprove' (xiv. 78).

This is not to deny that Johnson and other orthodox writers held reasoned opinions concerning how far it was the duty of the individual to abide by the opinion of society or tradition. Although very little of his more balanced understanding of this question is apparent in either apologetic literature or Sermon 20, Johnson's conservatism, his strict conformity to the conventional defence of Christianity, his appeal to the

[69] Ibid. ii. 9.   [70] See Ibid. i. 444.

convictions of 'great men', were supported by more than an emotional antipathy to free-thinkers and a fear that infidelity would corrupt morals. Even on questions quite distant from the defence of Christianity and its evidence, Johnson deemed that 'The mental disease of the present generation, is impatience of study, contempt of the great masters of ancient wisdom, and a disposition to rely wholly upon unassisted genius and natural sagacity' (v. 55). This was his argument in *Rambler*, No. 154, an essay on artistic and scientific endeavour. But he also went on to reproach mere imitation. *Rambler*, No. 154, outlines a more considered ideal of rational enquiry which balances strictures on the modern contempt for tradition with a recognition that learning must be permitted to progress beyond its past models.

Perhaps the most famous illustration of that ideal is found in the opening paragraphs of the preface to his edition of Shakespeare. On the one hand he censured those who 'hope for eminence from the heresies of paradox' (vii. 59), a remark that will recall his charge of vanity against 'Hume and other sceptical innovators'. But Johnson also made an admission that would have elicited strong approval from free-thinkers: 'Antiquity, like every other quality that attracts the notice of mankind, has undoubtedly votaries that reverence it, not from reason, but from prejudice' (vii. 59). He relied on the consensus of tradition to prove the greatness of Shakespeare, but admitted that this method was applicable only 'to works not raised upon principles demonstrative and scientifick, but appealing wholly to observation and experience' (vii. 59). This distinction is interesting. Artistic judgements were, apparently, based entirely on 'observation and experience', and therefore referable to traditional opinions. There is every indication, however, that he believed that religious faith was 'raised upon principles demonstrative and scientifick' and, for that reason, not subject to the type of strict reliance on the past consensus that is admissible in art. In other words, the arguments of the preface are theoretically consistent with the free-thinkers' claim that the consensus of tradition was irrelevant to the enquiry concerning the truth or falseness of religious beliefs.

Taken together, however, *Rambler*, No. 154, and the preface to Shakespeare leave us with the general impression that a responsible enquiry into truth must balance the objective of progress with a due respect for the authority of tradition. What Johnson disliked in all forms of learning was an entire reliance on one's own judgements and an irrational aversion to authority. As Johnson's biographer Arthur Murphy commented, Johnson's writings exemplify his own more conservative idea of a truly responsible 'originality': 'He had what Locke calls a roundabout view of his subject,' Murphy concluded, 'and, though he was never tainted, like many modern wits, with the ambition of shining in paradox, he may be fairly called an ORIGINAL THINKER.'[71] As we shall see in the course of this study, Johnson's sometimes subtle developments on traditional ideas fulfilled an ideal of originality which may have seemed 'prejudice' to the free-thinkers of his age (and our own), but which was widely shared by orthodox moralists and theologians.

[71] *Miscellanies*, i. 467.

2

The Decline of Natural Religion

1. *'True' Deism: The Ambiguity of Apologetics*

One of the most common terms in the philosophical and religious writing of the eighteenth century is also among the most difficult to define–'deism'. In modern historical studies this term is often used without much attention to its strict meaning. Yet this is not surprising: eighteenth-century writers were themselves careless in their use of the word, tending to rely on 'deism' as a vague label for a whole gambit of free-thinking and heterodox teachings. Moreover, the word generally became more vague as the century wore on. Early in the century 'deism' was more consistently confined to what was considered the least dangerous form of infidelity. Samuel Clarke, for example, distinguished between 'true deists' and those who called themselves 'deists' to disguise more sweeping and vicious forms of infidelity: while the pretended deists believed in little more than the existence of God, 'true deists' acknowledged all the theological and moral doctrines of natural religion, rejecting only the truth of Christianity.[1] Nathaniel Bailey seemed to have 'true deists' in mind when he defined this sect in the *Dictionarium Britannicum* (1721). 'Deists' were those who 'believe there is one God, a Providence, the Immortality of the Soul, Virtue and Vice, Rewards and Punishments; but reject Revelation; and believe no more than what natural Light discovers to them'.[2] In Johnson's *Dictionary*, on the other hand, 'deist' denoted a far more profound scepticism: 'A man who follows no particular religion, but only acknowledges the existence of God, without any other article of faith.' According to Johnson, a 'deist' not only rejected Christianity, but also most of natural religion. This is more like the creed of the

---

[1] See Samuel Clarke, *A Discourse Concerning the Unchangeable Obligations of Natural Religion and the Truth and Certainty of the Christian Revelation* (London, 1706), 22–34.

[2] A recent article has indicated that Bailey may have been thinking of the definition of deism given by Lord Herbert of Cherbury (1583–1648). See T. C. Blackburne, 'Friday's Religion: Its Nature and Importance in *Robinson Crusoe*', *Eighteenth-century Studies*, 18 (1985), 360–82, n. 31.

pretended deists who, according to Clarke, did not deserve that title at all.

While we cannot be sure why Johnson defined 'deist' in this way, he probably wished to remove the relatively positive connotations which, as Bailey's definition indicates, had originally adhered to this word. Apologetic tracts of the 1730s and 1740s leave little doubt that, by mid-century, Clarke's 'true deists' were perceived to be as much a threat to orthodoxy as those who denied the major truths of natural religion. The major influence on this change of perception was Matthew Tindal's *Christianity as Old as the Creation* (1730). Before Tindal the primary thrust of infidelity had been to challenge the truth of orthodox Christian beliefs rather than to promote the doctrines of natural religion. For example, Charles Blount's *The Oracles of Reason* (1693) outlined roughly the same scheme of natural religion later adopted by Tindal, yet it also contained a treatise against the immateriality of the soul and an attack on the philosophical proofs for the existence of God. Little wonder that Clarke considered Blount's 'deism' to be a mere pretext for a more dangerous scepticism.[3] Tindal, however, challenged not the truth, but the value of Christianity. He did not deny that the Scriptures revealed the true will of God, but claimed only that '*Natural* Religion differs not from *Reveal'd*, except in the manner of its communication'.[4] Not only was it unnecessary to be a Christian, but it seemed better to avoid the Scriptures, since priestcraft had added so many doctrines that had either corrupted or needlessly complicated the pure will of God as revealed by reason. This point was more fully elaborated in Thomas Chubb's *The True Gospel of Jesus Christ Asserted* (1786). Moreover, Christian writers saw that Tindal, for all his claims to the contrary, had implicitly cast doubt on the truth of the revelation. Why would a rational God reveal what was unnecessary? As Joseph Butler admitted in *The Analogy of Religion, Natural and Reveal'd* (1736), 'it is certain, there would have been [no Revelation], had the Light of Nature been sufficient in such a Sense, as to render a Revelation not wanting and useless'.[5]

---

[3] Clarke includes Blount among the recent atheists on the title-page of *A Discourse Concerning the Being and Attributes of God* (London, 1705).

[4] Matthew Tindal, *Christianity as Old as the Creation* (London, 1730), 3.

[5] Butler, *Analogy*, II, i, 141–2.

Johnson, of course, vigorously opposed the arguments of Tindal and Chubb, yet there has been little agreement among modern scholars regarding his precise attitudes on natural religion and its associated moral doctrine, natural law.[6] Nor is this disagreement surprising in the light of the great complexity and ambiguity of his opinions on this subject. This ambiguity reflects the general failure of apologetic literature to achieve any consensus on the way the deists should be answered. As we have seen, the apologists produced a defence of the Christian evidences that was repeated with formulaic precision by one writer after another. But on the question of what exactly Christianity had added to moral and religious knowledge, of why mankind could not do without the Christian revelation, the apologists were divided and inconsistent.

If the apologists were able to achieve such a consensus on the Christian evidences, then why were they not similarly united on the question of what Christianity had contributed? We have already touched on one explanation. The great heresy of the seventeenth and early eighteenth centuries was not deism (in Clarke's or Bailey's sense), but atheism and scepticism with the fundamental doctrines of both revealed and natural religion. Assuming that the primary threat lay there, not in an excessive reliance on natural religion, eminent Christian writers such as Cudworth, Cumberland, and Clarke did not hesitate to erect massive systems which provided philosophical demonstrations for all the truths of morality and religion. By inciting a wave of confidence in the reasonableness of believing in God and moral truth, they gave birth to a problem in the opposite extreme. Significantly, Tindal was able to substantiate his case against

---

[6] Modern scholarship has spanned the full range of possible opinions on whether Johnson accepted or rejected natural law and religion. D. J. Greene argued, in 'Samuel Johnson and "Natural Law" ', *Journal of British Studies*, 2 (1963), 59–75 and 84–7, that Johnson entirely rejected the belief that 'man can somehow, through the use of his "divine spark" of reason, deduce that knowledge of God's plan, of absolute good and evil' (p. 73). In *Religious Thought*, on the other hand, C. F. Chapin contended that the Christian revelation was 'not a matter of one set of virtues replacing another radically different set. . . . It is Christian eschatology, not the greater purity of Christian ethics, which is the *primary* service of revelation to mankind' (p. 94). More recently, James Gray adopted a position between Greene's opinion that Johnson entirely rejected natural law, and Chapin's that Johnson placed little importance on Christianity's moral contribution: in *Johnson's Sermons: A Study* (Oxford, 1972), Gray argued that Johnson concurred with Samuel Clarke that moral truths had only been understood imperfectly before the Christian revelation (pp. 65–92).

the necessity of a Christian revelation by quoting at great length from the most admired theologians of the age. As Philip Skelton complained in *Ophiomaches, or Deism Reveal'd* (1748), '*Cumberland, Tillotson, Scot, Clarke* & c. . . . were weak enough to run up their apologetic systems to extremes; drawing all their forces to oppose the assault made on one side of the garrison, while they were inattentive to the sap on the other.'[7] In other words, these writers had worked so hard to refute atheism, that they had paved the way for a religion which rejected Scripture in favour of reason.

More than any other infidel before Hume, Tindal's challenge roused the best orthodox writers of the age; among many others, Waterland, Sykes, Stebbing, and Law all replied. And in order to refute Tindal, these apologists were forced to dismantle the systems which had dominated orthodox thought only a few decades before. This outpouring of scepticism against natural religion undoubtedly had its effect: thereafter, Christian writers seemed far more cautious not to praise reason too highly. This was one important influence on the decline of 'the Age of Reason'. Yet orthodox writers, no less than the deists, were the inheritors of a humanist tradition which had sought to harmonize piety with the noblest achievements of learning and reason. They also had to remember that too violent an attack on reason might expose orthodoxy to atheism and the other extreme forms of infidelity. These were some of the factors which contributed to hesitance and dissension among apologists concerning the best way to refute Tindal. They could not agree on how far it was necessary and safe to cast doubt on reason in order to vindicate the contribution of Christianity.

Let us consider, for instance, the defence of Christianity's moral doctrines. Apologetic literature may be roughly divided into three groups on the issue of what Christianity had contributed to the knowledge of virtue. Some apologists such as Arthur Ashley Sykes, John Jackson, and James Foster refused to qualify their reliance on natural religion and conceded to the deists that Christianity had introduced no moral truths of any importance. They contended that the benefit of Christianity lay

---

[7] Philip Skelton, *Ophiomaches, or Deism Reveal'd* (1748) (2 vols.; 2nd edn.; London, 1749), ii. 380.

entirely in the motives it provided to virtuous conduct.[8] At the other extreme were Philip Skelton, Thomas Rutherforth, and a group of apologists and moralists who became increasingly influential at mid-century. These writers culminated the reaction against seventeenth-century orthodoxy by arguing that men possessed no natural ability to distinguish between right and wrong.

Most apologists, however, fell somewhere between these extremes into the wide and ambivalent mainstream of orthodox opinion. They wished neither entirely to reject the moral teachings of philosophy nor to reduce Christianity to a reassertion of these teachings. They admitted on the one hand that, as Samuel Chandler wrote, 'there have been some who, by the mere light of nature, have made notable discoveries with reference to God and moral goodness'. They also insisted, however, that 'the number of such persons hath been always very few'.[9] Moral truths could be deduced only through a complex chain of reasoning far above the capacities of ordinary men. This was Johnson's major criticism of natural law in the Oxford Vinerian lectures he wrote for Robert Chambers. Such an enquiry, Johnson argued, 'demands such an Acquaintance with the divine Attributes, such a thorough and clear Conception of the Relationships in w[hi]ch Creatures stand to the Creator, and of those that subsist between the Creatures themselves, as belongs to few even of those enlighten'd Reasoners in the most enlighten'd Ages'.[10] This approach took account of a few great reasoners such as Socrates and Plato whose moral teachings were, admittedly, quite close to Christianity's. But even by insisting on the rareness of such moralists, the apologists had still failed to answer a major objection. Why was Christianity necessary to impart truths that could have been discovered just as easily in the writings of the few enlightened reasoners? For the mainstream of apologists, therefore, the question was not so much what had been revealed by Christianity, but, more importantly, the effectiveness of Scripture as a means of popular instruction.

---

[8] See, e.g., Arthur Ashley Sykes, *The Principles and Connexion of Natural and Revealed Religion Distinctly Considered* (London, 1740), 108 and 244.

[9] Samuel Chandler, *A Vindication of the Christian Religion* (London, 1725), 64–5.

[10] Reprinted in Greene, 'Samuel Johnson and "Natural Law" ', p. 72.

As Samuel Chandler went on to argue, even 'an uniform system of truth, and a perfect system of morals' would fail to reform the world: 'For all, that know any thing of mankind, know, that there are but few capable of abstracted reasonings, and that bare lectures of morality and virtue are likely to have but little success, unless attended with proper motives and encouragements.'[11] Men would pay little attention to moral teachings delivered in the form of philosophical lectures. 'Are not Men, in such Cases, apt to reflect,' asked John Conybeare, 'That no one Man, merely as such, hath any Authority to dictate or prescribe to others?'[12] Christianity provided, as Chandler explained, 'motives and encouragements' to practise virtue, and also special marks of divine authority which would persuade ordinary men to adopt the teachings they had previously ignored. While much of Christianity was, Joseph Butler admitted, 'a Promulgation of the Law of Nature', it was more importantly 'an authoritative Promulgation of it'.[13] In Sermon 25 Johnson elaborated on the problem of authority with reference to the immortality of the soul:

it is plain, that the constitution of mankind is such, that abstruse and intellectual truths can be taught no otherwise than by positive assertion, supported by some sensible evidence, by which the assertor is secured from the suspicion of falsehood; and that, if it should please God to inspire a teacher with some demonstration of the immortality of the soul, it would far less avail him for general instruction, than the power of working a miracle in its vindication, unless God should, at the same time, inspire all the hearers with docility and apprehension, and turn, at once, all the sensual, the giddy, the lazy, the busy, the corrupt and the proud, into humble, abstracted and diligent philosophers (xiv. 265).

Roughly the same argument, that the revelation spares men 'the labour of tedious enquiries' (xiv. 40) by lending a visible and miraculous authority to its propositions, was repeated in Sermon 4 with application to moral truths. Central to this defence was the assumption that men would not understand moral and religious truths even when they were proposed to them by an enlightened reasoner. The common people required

[11] Chandler, *Vindication*, pp. 72–3.
[12] John Conybeare, *A Defence of Reveal'd Religion* (London, 1732), 43.
[13] Butler, *Analogy*, II, i, 149.

miracles and other signs of divine authority to stir them from their indifference and sensuality, and to persuade them to adopt ideas that they were otherwise incapable of recognizing as the truth.

This had basically been Samuel Clarke's defence of revelation in a work which greatly influenced eighteenth-century apologetics, *a Discourse Concerning the Unchangeable Obligations of Natural Religion and the Truth and Certainty of the Christian Revelation* (1706).[14] But Matthew Tindal found a contradiction in Clarke's argument that reflects a similar inconsistency throughout the mainstream of apologetics. Tindal asked how Clarke could portray moral truth as entirely above the comprehension of all but the most enlightened reasoners, yet, throughout the first half of his treatise, argue that 'the eternal differences of Good and Evil, the unalterable rule of Right and Equity, do necessarily and unavoidably determine the Judgment, and force the Assent of all Men that use any Consideration'.[15] Clarke's moral philosophy centred on the claim that all men possessed an intuitive understanding of moral truths. But he was attempting, at the same time, to argue that all the authority of a Divine revelation was necessary to make these truths apparent to ordinary men.

This is a serious inconsistency. None the less, it persisted in apologetic literature even after Tindal pointed it out in the work of Clarke. John Leland attacked Tindal's argument that moral knowledge 'needs no Reflection or Consideration, but the most illiterate Rustick may as easily and certainly know it, as a Man that has made the deepest Inquiries'.[16] Yet Leland admitted in the same treatise that 'there is a kind of natural Sense of Right and Wrong, of the moral Beauty and Fitness of Things'.[17] This contradiction is also evident in Johnson's moral thought. Although Johnson seemed highly sceptical of reason in the Vinerian lectures and in Sermons 4 and 25, his periodical essays frequently attest to a confidence in the moral

[14] See Clarke, *Natural Religion*, pp. 243–4.
[15] Ibid. 70. See Tindal, *Christianity as Old as the Creation*, pp. 239–40.
[16] John Leland, *An Answer to a Late Book, Intituled Christianity as Old as the Creation* (2 vols.; Dublin, 1733), i. 112.
[17] Ibid. 16.

judgements of even the most uneducated and common men. In
Rambler, No. 68, for instance, he observed:

The highest panegyrick . . . that private virtue can receive is the
praise of servants. For, however vanity or insolence may look down
with contempt on the suffrage of men, undignified by wealth, and
unenlightened by education, it very seldom happens that they
commend or blame without justice. Vice and virtue are easily distinguished. Oppression, according to Harrington's aphorism, will be
felt by those that cannot see it; and, perhaps, it falls out very often
that, in moral questions, the philosophers in the gown, and in the
livery, differ not so much in their sentiments, as in their language,
and have equal power of discerning right, though they cannot point it
out to others with equal address (iii. 361).

How could Johnson give this praise to the moral judgement
of servants, yet argue elsewhere that moral truths were far
above the comprehension of all but the most enlightened
reasoners? Nor is *Rambler*, No. 68, the only essay which
suggests that a popular assent to basic moral truths is easily
attained without all the authority of a Divine revelation. In
Rambler, No. 31, he argued that writers who wickedly attempt
to confuse the distinction between good and evil (probably
Mandeville) will ultimately be unable to diminish the authority
which moral truth *naturally* exercises over society. 'The cause of
virtue requires so little art to defend it,' Johnson wrote, 'and
good and evil, when they have been once shewn, are so easily
distinguished, that such apologists [for vice] seldom gain
proselytes to their party' (iii. 172).

There were some attempts after Tindal's attack to make
sense of this apparent contradiction in the writings of Clarke
and the apologists. Clarke's admirers attempted to distinguish
between the ordinary man's recognition of virtue and vice, and
the actual discovery of moral truths, which remained far above
his capacities. As Thomas Broughton wrote, 'whenever God
gives his Creatures any command, the nature of things will
shew it to be fit,' yet 'it will not follow, that therefore the nature
of things will point out to us *a priori*, everything that is fit to be
the subject of God's command'.[18] This was precisely the

[18] Thomas Broughton, *Christianity Distinct from the Religion of Nature* (3 pts.; London,
1732), I. 35–6.

distinction which Johnson tried to point out in his one work designed primarily to refute the deists, the allegorical *The Vision of Theodore: The Hermit of Teneriffe* (1748):

I looked then upon the Road of *Reason*, which was indeed, so far as it reached, the same with that of *Religion*, nor had Reason discovered it but by her Instructions. Yet when she had once been taught it she clearly saw it was right; and *Pride* had sometimes incited her to declare that she discovered it herself, and persuaded her to offer herself as a Guide to *Religion*; whom after many vain Experiments, she found it her highest Privilege to follow.[19]

The deists, according to this defence, believed they had deduced moral truths which, in fact, they had originally learned from Scripture and had only *seen* to be right. Roughly the same distinction between the discovery and mere recognition of moral truth is held with fair consistency throughout Johnson's work: he usually maintained, as in *Rambler*, No. 31, that good and evil were easily distinguished only 'when they have been once shewn'.

But this does not rescue Johnson's defence of Christianity from the charge of inconsistency. Like others, he had claimed that men would not accept moral truths even when they were shown to them by the few enlightened philosophers of past ages. Yet, according to the view he takes throughout his periodical essays, men would have immediately recognized that these truths were right. In many of the *Ramblers* it was clearly advantageous to Johnson's moral lesson that he accept the ease and universality of basic ethical distinctions. The belief that even 'the meanest Capacity' immediately recognizes good and evil will encourage masters to be honest with their servants and check the designs of wicked 'apologists' for vice.

Indeed, it may be suspected that Johnson's expressed opinions on 'natural law' vary according to the objective of a particular work. As a moral essayist Johnson showed no particular scepticism with the power of unassisted reason. But in his direct responses to deism, such as the discussion of natural law in the Vinerian lectures or *Vision of Theodore*, he drew far sharper distinctions between revealed and natural religion, sometimes tending to the extreme view of apologists

[19] *Vision of Theodore*, ii. 524–5.

who denied that reason could attain any knowledge of virtue. *Vision of Theodore* does not go that far, but Johnson did suggest one unusually harsh restriction on the power of reason: he denied that the unenlightened intellect possessed a 'conscience', the feeling of guilt associated with an immoral act.[20] Skelton's *Ophiomaches, or Deism Reveal'd* (1748) published the same year as *Vision of Theodore*, and Thomas Rutherforth's *An Essay on the Nature and Obligations of Virtue* (1744), were among the very few orthodox works to make the same claim.[21] To deny that men naturally felt regret upon the commission of a crime was an extreme view which, as recently as the controversy aroused by Mandeville's *The Fable of the Bees* (1724), had been associated with moral profligacy and even atheism.[22]

But Johnson did not hesitate to write in *Rambler*, No. 76, that 'No man yet was ever wicked without secret discontent' (iv. 35), a virtual admission that conscience *was* natural to mankind. And this was precisely the type of claim which, developed in the works of Samuel Clarke and innumerable other orthodox writers, prepared the way for the deistic argument that even 'the most illiterate Rustick' had no need for the moral directions of Christianity. In other areas of moral doctrine, such as the question of how virtuous acts were motivated, Johnson's views on the contribution of Christianity were reasonably consistent and coherent. But on the question of what Christianity had contributed to moral knowledge, his attitudes strongly reflect the general ambivalence and uncertainty of apologetic literature. In particular, it is the failure of both Johnson and the majority of apologists to elucidate the distinction between the arduous process of deduction and the intuitive recognition of moral truths, the unclarity of their claim that all the miraculous authority of the revelation was needed to persuade men of propositions which were immediately seen to be right, which so greatly frustrates the efforts of

---

[20] See ibid. 522.

[21] See Skelton, *Ophiomaches*, i. 289–90; Thomas Rutherforth, *An Essay on the Nature and Obligations of Virtue* (Cambridge, 1744), 95–100.

[22] Mandeville, like Hobbes, suggested that the conscience was created entirely by the internalization of the standards of approval and censure imposed by an individual's education. A feeling of guilt, for instance, represented no more than the fear of castigation if one's crime were made public. See Bernard Mandeville, *The Fable of the Bees* (1724), ed. F. B. Kaye (2 vols.; Oxford, 1924), i. 68–9. Freud's 'superego' is a more sophisticated variation on the same idea.

modern scholarship to determine the precise nature of their case against the moral doctrines of deism.

2. *The Being and Attributes of God*

The question of the contribution of Christianity to moral knowledge occupied only half of the debate between the deists and apologists. The second half concerned the capacity of reason to achieve, without the assistance of revelation, just ideas concerning the nature of God. In this area of debate the apologists seldom denied that non-Christians could attain adequate ideas concerning certain fundamental truths such as the existence of a single, benevolent Creator. To dispute reason's capacity to discover these truths would recall the arguments of atheism which seventeenth-century orthodoxy had so diligently resisted. Nevertheless, all the questions debated by the deists and apologists were so tightly inter-connected that the apologists could not show scepticism with reason's capacities in one area of knowledge without weakening the philosophical proofs in all other areas. Even on the question of God's being and goodness, eighteenth-century apologetics were led into the same type of inconsistencies and contradic-tions which characterized their defence of Scripture's moral truths.

Seventeenth-century and Restoration tracts against atheism had left eighteenth-century religion with an enormously complex defence of God's being and goodness. Ralph Cudworth's *The True Intellectual System of the Universe* (1678) and Samuel Clarke's *A Discourse Concerning the Being and Attributes of God* (1705) are, for example, notable for a sophistication of argument which at times seems needlessly fine and ostentatious. Yet there seemed little question early in the century that such high reasoning was necessary to check the advance of atheism—nor was this belief without foundation. In *The Oracles of Reason* (1693) Charles Blount charged that Richard Bentley's Boyle lectures against atheism (1692–3) had needlessly displayed that divine's vast (and tedious) scholarship for no purpose, since the existence of God was obvious to common sense. But Blount then went on to contend that Bentley's arguments 'could not hold', raising the suspicion that this truth was not so obvious after all. [23] As the result of such duplicity, apologists adhered to the advice of 1 Peter 3: 15, and declared their duty to 'instruct you in such Questions as relate to the Fundamentals of our Faith, and enable you to give an Answer to all who shall oppose them'. [24] It was apparently expected that even ordinary people should be familiar with the most intricate and difficult questions debated with the infidels.

It was this expectation which, during the major eighteenth-century debates with deism, exposed the orthodox position to serious question. On the one hand, the apologists expected an ordinary Christian to defend himself against objections which had required all the skill and erudition of a Samuel Clarke to refute. In their answers to Tindal, however, they charged the deists with absurdly overrating the intelligence and philosophical abilities of the common man. This was the inconsistency brought to light by Dodwell's *Christianity not Founded in Argument* (1741): Dodwell alleged that since the common man was so incapable of reasoning he must rely entirely on the direct inspiration of God in order to preserve his faith. Once again trapped by their own attacks on reason, the apologists were forced to reassess the advice of 1 Peter 3: 15. It was decided in most answers to Dodwell that the common man did not, in fact, need to know anything about the controversy with the atheists. His own unassisted speculations were at least sufficient to create a stable belief in religion's most basic doctrine—the existence of God and His benevolent government over the world. John Leland, for example, had been strongly critical of the 'illiterate Rustick' in his answer to Tindal, but against Dodwell he declared,

Nor is it necessary to a rational Belief, to enter into a particular Examination of every Difficulty and every Objection. A Man may firmly and upon good solid grounds believe a God and a Providence, without knowing the several atheistical Schemes that have been advanced, or so much as any one of them. [25]

The great Christian theoreticians of natural religion again

[23] See Charles Blount, *The Oracles of Reason* (London, 1693), 80-2.

[24] Rogers, *The Necessity of Divine Revelation*, p. 57.

[25] Leland, *Remarks on a Late Pamphlet, Entitled Christianity not Founded on Argument* (London, 1744), 53-4. See Benson, *The Reasonablenesse of the Christian Religion*, p. 149; Randolph, *Rational Assent*, pp. 122-3.

took part of the blame for creating the difficulties now encountered by Christianity. But while Cudworth, Cumberland,
Clarke, and others were rebuked elsewhere for making the
knowledge of moral truths seem too easy, they were now
blamed for making belief in a single, benevolent Creator seem
too hard. As Thomas Randolph complained in 1744, 'even
upon the plainest Question in Nature, the Existence of a Deity
himself, all the labour'd Productions of *Dr. Clarke* himself
have rather contributed to make for the other Side of the
Question, and rais'd a thousand new Difficulties in the
Reader's Mind, which would never else have occur'd to
him'.[26] There was, therefore, a reversion away from the
difficult philosophical proofs for God's being and goodness,
and back towards a confidence in the basic common sense of
the ordinary man.

Boswell was recalling the old advice of 1 Peter 3: 15 when, in
conversation with Johnson, he 'expressed a wish to have the
arguments for Christianity always in readiness, that my
religious faith might be as firm and clear as any proposition
whatever, so that I need not be under the least uneasiness,
when it should be attacked'.[27] But Johnson's reply reflected the
reconsideration of this advice that was undertaken especially
following Dodwell's 1741 attack on the difficulty of the
orthodox defence: 'Sir, you cannot answer all objections. You
have demonstration for a First Cause: you see he must be good
as well as powerful, because there is nothing to make him
otherwise, and goodness of itself is preferable.'[28] Johnson's
argument for a 'First Cause' has been attributed by Stuart
Gerry Brown and later critics to demonstrations for the
existence of God by John Pearson and Samuel Clarke.[29] It is
likely, however, that Johnson agreed with Leland and
Randolph that the being and goodness of God were evident
without the complex philosophical systems of these writers.
Although Johnson often insisted on the difficulty of the
reasoning necessary to understand moral truths, on the
question of the Divine attributes it was in the best interests of

[26] Randolph, *Rational Assent*, p. 122.
[27] *Life*, iii. 316.
[28] Ibid. 316–17.
[29] See S. G. Brown, 'Dr. Johnson and the Religious Problem', *English Studies*, 20
(1938), 1–17; Pierce, *Religious Life*, p. 35.

orthodoxy that he affirm the ease with which most men could avoid the pitfalls of atheism.

Such a reliance on common sense was not, however, so straightforward as it first appeared. Johnson went on in the same conversation with Boswell to suggest that belief in God's existence and goodness was really far more complex than the apologists were claiming: 'Yet you have against this, what is very certain, the unhappiness of human life. This, however, gives us reason to hope for a future state of compensation, that there may be a perfect system. But of that we were not sure, till we had a positive revelation.'[30] Despite the claim that easy, common-sense reasoning was sufficient to deduce the existence and goodness of God, the unjust distribution of happiness in life presented a serious difficulty which had traditionally formed the basis for the attacks of atheism. In order to solve this problem Johnson turned to a slightly more sophisticated chain of reasoning—the 'moral argument' for immortality. This argument went as follows: God is a just and benevolent Being who would never allow virtue to remain unrewarded, the evident fate of many good men in this life. Therefore, we may deduce the existence of a happy afterlife to compensate good men who have suffered in the present world. Johnson could claim on the grounds of the 'moral argument' that the 'unhappiness of human life . . . gives us reason to hope for a future state of compensation, that there may be a perfect system'.

It is evident, however, that Johnson is arguing in a circle. As Hume pointed out in 'Of a Particular Providence and of a Future State' (1748), belief in the goodness of God is based entirely on the evidence of life's goodness. One cannot first admit the unhappiness of life and then use the supposed benevolence of God, which is contradicted by the first admission, to reason that everything will be happy in the end. Johnson, in fact, made precisely this objection to Soame Jenyns's assertion at the beginning of *A Free Inquiry into the Nature and Origin of Evil* (1757) that it was needless to debate a truth so self-evident as the benevolence of God.[31] By assuming

---

[30] *Life*, iii. 317.
[31] See review of *A Free Inquiry into the Nature and Origin of Evil* (1757), repr. in R. B. Schwartz, *Samuel Johnson and the Problem of Evil* (Madison, Wis., 1975), 99.

that God is benevolent in his discussion with Boswell, Johnson is ignoring a problem which he himself had pointed out. Moreover, how can Johnson rely on the 'moral argument' for immortality in his comments to Boswell when in *Vision of Theodore*, Sermon 25, and elsewhere he denied that unassisted reason had any power to deduce the existence of a happy afterlife? Johnson seems aware that he has contradicted his arguments against the deists, and adds that mankind was not sure of a future state of compensation, 'till we had a positive revelation'. Hence, in an argument which was originally intended to show Boswell that the existence and benevolence of God could be assumed without answering all the objections to these truths, Johnson must ultimately turn to revealed religion as the only escape from the difficulties that spring up naturally from his arguments. So far from showing that it is only common sense to believe in a benevolent Creator, Johnson's final position is that reason is incapable of satisfactory knowledge in this area without Christianity.

But the apologists did not wish to argue that unassisted reason was incapable of this knowledge: this would make belief in a single benevolent Creator dependent on the proofs for Scripture, yet evidences for the truth of Christianity, such as the miracles, were in turn dependent on belief in a benevolent God. Only a benevolent God, as we have considered, would miraculously interrupt the course of nature to benefit man. For this reason, Hume's 'Of a Particular Providence and of a Future State', which refuted the natural proofs for a benevolent God, also weakened the proofs for revealed religion. Such was the labyrinth of interdependencies which the apologists encountered in their defence of religion's most fundamental idea—the existence of a benevolent God.

It is not surprising that God's other major attributes, His mercy and justice, were the subject of an equally complex debate. The orthodox position on these attributes, however, changed according to the more regular pattern of eighteenth-century thought: the decline of reason as the central support of orthodox faith. The issue of God's mercy—His willingness to forgive repentant sinners—provides an especially good illustration of how the confidence in the powers of reason expressed by orthodox writers early in the age was sharply diminished by the rise of Christian apologetics. In the Restoration and early eighteenth century this doctrine of Divine mercy was seldom denied to natural religion. As Stephen Nye wrote in *A Discourse Concerning Natural and Revealed Religion* (1698), 'I affirm, it is an Article of natural Religion, that Forgiveness does certainly follow Repentance. If God be a merciful and benign Being, he will accept the Payment we are able to make.'[32] But after Tindal used this opinion to support his case for the sufficiency of natural religion,[33] the orthodox position generally changed. It was increasingly argued that sinners could have no assurance, without Christianity, that they could appease the just wrath of God.

The task of denying this knowledge to reason was complicated not only by the number of eminent Christian authorities who had furnished the deists with their arguments for God's mercy, but also by the evidence of propitiatory ceremonies such as sacrifice in numerous cultures and religions. Even primitive societies had apparently held that sacrifice would win Divine forgiveness. Indeed, the extensiveness of this belief among all mankind continued to be used by orthodox writers, including Johnson, to show that God was acting in accordance with generally accepted standards of wisdom when he accepted the sacrifice of His Son.[34] It was, then, futile to deny that mankind had often believed in God's willingness to forgive repentant sinners. Most apologists insisted instead that this 'belief' was not the same as 'knowledge'. Men could certainly hope that God would forgive their sins. Indeed, such a hope was essential to the preservation of religion and, since all men have sinned, the continuation of virtuous conduct. Without a belief in the placability of Divine nature, wrote Duncan Forbes, man, 'would remain in the same gloomy state of despair, without the least glimpse of hope, or encouragement to pray, to praise, to love, or to rejoice in the mercy and salvation of God; which would have left him a prey to his terrors and his lusts, and must

[32] Stephen Nye, *A Discourse Concerning Natural and Revealed Religion* (London, 1698), 85–6. See also Clarke, *Natural Religion*, pp. 277–8.

[33] See Tindal, *Christianity as Old as the Creation*, p. 392.

[34] See Johnson's discussion of the atonement in *Life*, iv. 124. For a more detailed discussion of the background to Johnson's idea of the atonement, see Gray, *Johnson's Sermons*, pp. 76–83; N. J. Hudson, 'Johnson, Socinianism and the Meaning of Christ's Sacrifice', *Notes and Queries*, NS 32 (1985), 238–40.

have determined him to have shut out all thought of the Deity'.[35] It was good, therefore, that men continued to hope for forgiveness. But this did not change Forbes's opinion that the mercy of God 'is not deducible from nature'.[36] As John Conybeare summarized, 'Hope is One Thing, and Certainty is another.'[37] Men could hope that they would be forgiven, but they could have no real knowledge or assurance of Divine mercy until the promise of redemption through Christ.

Although Johnson's statements on natural religion usually reflect the eighteenth-century's attacks on reason, on this one question of God's mercy he remained close to the attitude of orthodox writers earlier in the century. There was, as usual, some ambiguity. In Sermon 2 he returned to the standard formula used to defend Christianity's moral teachings: the mercy of God was deducible only by a complex chain of reasoning and Christianity's revelation of this attribute was necessary 'for the sake of those that are incapable of philosophic enquiries' (iv. 17). *Rambler*, No. 110, however, is a strong statement of the view that, as the customs of propitiation demonstrated, men had always known that God would forgive repentant sinners:

The various methods of propitiation and atonement which fear and folly have dictated, or artifice and interest tolerated in the different parts of the world, however they may sometimes reproach or degrade humanity, at least shew the general consent of all ages and nations in their opinion of the placability of the divine nature. That God will forgive, may, indeed, be established as the first and fundamental truth of religion; for though the knowledge of his existence is the origin of philosophy, yet, without the belief of his mercy, it would have little influence upon our moral conduct. There could be no prospect of enjoying the protection or regard of him, whom the least deviation from rectitude made inexorable for ever; and every man would naturally withdraw his thoughts from the contemplation of a Creator, whom he must consider as a governor too pure to be pleased, and too severe to be pacified (iv. 221).

[35] Duncan Forbes, *Some Thoughts Concerning Religion, Natural and Revealed* (Edinburgh, 1750), 17.

[36] Ibid. 13. According to Henry Stebbing, pagan sacrifices were 'originally God's own Appointment', directly revealed in some unidentified manner at an unspecified time. But Stebbing had no real evidence for this claim. See Stebbing, *A Discourse Concerning the Use and Advantages of the Gospel Revelation* (London, 1730), 32–3. Joseph Butler later used a similar argument in *Analogy*, II, v, 199–201.

[37] Conybeare, *Reveal'd Religion*, p. 116.

'Where there is no hope,' Johnson wrote in the same essay, 'there can be no endeavour' (iv. 221). He agreed with Forbes and other apologists that belief in the efficacy of repentance was necessary to sustain the individual's love of God and efforts to be virtuous. But Johnson did not try to discriminate between this belief and a genuine knowledge of the mercy of God. *Rambler*, No. 110, leaves little doubt that most religions, whatever their inadequacies, have given men sufficient assurance that God will forgive repentant sinners.

There was, however, one further twist to this issue. Even when God's mercy was established, natural religion could never fully satisfy the individual that he himself would be forgiven. This was because the Divine attribute of mercy was limited by the opposite attribute of justice. It was one of the most difficult problems of natural religion to determine how far God would be just, by punishing the sinner, and how far he would be merciful, by accepting repentance. The very idea of God, it was agreed, was predicated on the notion that He was a 'perfect' Being. But how could He be perfectly forgiving and perfectly just at the same time? This difficulty led theoreticians of natural religion such as John Tillotson to speculate obscurely on the 'degrees of perfection' to which God's mercy and justice attain, but never surpass.[38]

This was not an explanation which later satisfied all Christian apologists. In Skelton's *Ophiomaches*, for instance, a deistic and a Christian character engage in a debate on the Divine attributes. The deist argues that 'God, who is infinitely gracious, will accept of repentance as an atonement.'[39] The Christian, however, maintains that reason can never properly reconcile God's conflicting attributes of infinite mercy and infinite justice:

Surely, you forget. God, as the Judge and Governor of the world, acts for the good of all his subjects; and altho' *his mercy is over all his works*, yet his justice also presides as extensively over his whole universal empire. God can, and would, always forgive, were it not that his wisdom and justice, taking place as well as his mercy, make the punishment of particulars conducive to the general good.[40]

[38] See John Tillotson, 'Concerning the Perfections of God', in *Works*, ii. 491.
[39] Skelton, *Ophiomaches*, i. 319.
[40] Ibid. 318–19.

As Skelton's spokesman goes on to argue, the atonement of
Christ had resolved a dilemma that had previously confined
even God himself. Before Christianity, God's perfect mercy
was always cancelled by his perfect justice: all sinners were
damned. But Christ satisfied the justice of God, so that His
attribute of mercy could come into effect and sinners could be
pardoned. This argument is a rather welcome addition to
the controversy: the atonement, surprisingly, was rarely
introduced as a feature of the distinctive contribution of
Christianity.

Yet it cannot be said that the atonement truly resolved the
individual's uncertainty concerning his forgiveness. Skelton's
deist makes an objection which, perhaps, Skelton himself is
unable to remove entirely. 'The application of *Christ's* merit,'
the deist resumes, 'if it were granted, must be a thing of great
uncertainty: for who can tell whether he is within the terms, on
which it is to be expected?'[41] The Christian answers that 'it is
better to have even the lowest hopes of pardon, than to be sure
of condemnation'.[42] Yet few would agree with Skelton that
natural religion, even if it gave no more than a weak assurance
of forgiveness, absolutely affirmed a man's damnation. The
atonement, as it is used by Skelton, seems to provide no more
assurance of pardon than was usually granted to natural
religion by the apologists.

At least on this issue, Johnson was far from the extreme
scepticism of Skelton: he believed that reason did provide good
evidence of God's mercy to sinners. Nevertheless, according to
one famous exchange in Boswell's *Life*, he was also perplexed
by the conflict between God's attributes of infinite mercy and
infinite justice. During his last visit to Oxford in 1784, Johnson
mentioned that he was afraid of death. William Adams, who
was in his company, reminded him that 'GOD was infinitely
good', but Johnson refused to be consoled:

That he is infinitely good, as far as the perfection of his nature will
allow, I certainly believe; but it is necessary for good upon the whole,
that individuals should be punished. As to an *individual*, therefore, he
is not infinitely good; and as I cannot be *sure* that I have fulfilled the
conditions on which salvation is granted, I am afraid I may be one of
those who shall be damned.'[43]

[41] Ibid. 342.   [42] Ibid. 342.   [43] *Life*, iv. 299.

Like many writers of the age, Johnson saw no impiety in assuming that God was limited by physical laws governing the universe and His own nature. God could not be infinitely good and infinitely just at the same time: 'the perfection of his nature' allowed only—however we make sense of this idea— certain degrees of infinite mercy. But Johnson gave no indication that the atonement had done much to relieve the individual's anxieties concerning the conditions of forgiveness. It was still necessary for 'the general good', as Skelton had put it, that some sinners be punished. Christianity, for all its emphasis on atonement and mercy, in fact provided no more assurance than natural religion that the individual could be rescued from Divine justice.

Both natural religion and Christianity, therefore, reached a stalemate on the question of what could be known about the Divine attributes. Indeed, this stalemate reflects the lack of resolution on most of the issues debated by the deists and apologists. There were no winners in this controversy. The apologists never organized a consistent position on the relationship between natural and revealed religion. And deism faded considerably during the second half of the century, at least as a doctrine of any force and originality. There remained some self-proclaimed 'deists', but their ideas had ceased to generate much interest in England. For example, Bolingbroke's *Philosophical Works*, posthumously released in 1754, upheld many of Tindal's claims for natural religion, yet they prompted the derision rather than the outrage of the few orthodox writers who bothered replying. William Warburton and Thomas Church had little trouble dismissing Bolingbroke's philosophy as not only clumsy, but also highly derivative of deistic notions that had been adequately explored by previous infidels.[44] Surely the infidels, they implied, could contrive some more interesting allegations against orthodoxy. Yet perhaps only a polemicist of Voltaire's skill could breathe new fire into the old tenets of English deism.

Johnson's attitudes on natural religion strongly reflect the ambiguities and contradictions of the apologists' case as it

---

[44] See William Warburton, *A View of Lord Bolingbroke's Philosophy* (1754) (3rd edn.; London, 1756); Thomas Church, *An Analysis of the Philosophical Works of Lord Bolingbroke* (London, 1755).

developed during the height of the deistic controversy in the 1730s and 1740s. This was a time of increasing scepticism among orthodox writers concerning the powers of reason, a scepticism that probably resulted more from a desire to protect Christianity than from any genuinely new insights into the problems of natural religion. Johnson's replies to deism cover a wide range of opinions, and it is difficult to place him with any particular group of apologists. On the question of the Divine attributes, Johnson was generally less sceptical of natural religion than most apologists. On the contribution of Christianity to moral knowledge, Johnson was ambivalent but, if anything, slightly more sceptical of man's unassisted powers. This scepticism was perhaps most marked in an area which we have still to consider. This was the issue of the contribution of Christianity to the doctrine of charity. While our consideration of this question will lead us away from the central controversy with the deists, Johnson's views of the nature of Christian charity represent one of his major defences of revealed religion.

3. *Charity as a Virtue Exclusive to Christianity*

Although Johnson's defence of the contribution made by Christianity to ethical knowledge is not always clear, he did state categorically that, 'Charity, or tenderness to the poor . . . is, I think, known only to those who enjoy, either immediately or by transmission, the light of revelation' (*Idler*, No. 4, ii. 12–13). As on most moral and religious issues, such an unqualified restriction on man's unenlightened intellect was not accepted even by many prominent apologists. Arthur Ashley Sykes, for instance, flatly denied the uniqueness of Christian charity: 'Take the Expressions of the Gospel in a reasonable Sense and Latitude only, and it will appear that our Saviour did not design . . . to enlarge the common Principles of Benevolence and Charity; but only to fix them in such a manner as Truth and Justice do require.'[45] Most apologists, however, agreed that Christianity had contributed a unique understanding of charity. They could not deny that generosity and kindness existed in some form outside Christianity: this would contradict both the evidence of classical literature and

---

[45] Sykes, *Principles and Connexion*, pp. 409–10.

what was generally acknowledged to be mankind's innate capacity for love and sympathy. But the apologists could redefine 'charity' in specifically Christian terms. While conceding to the deists that compassion and alms-giving were possible among non-Christians, they insisted that, as Thomas Yalden wrote in a 1728 charity sermon, only Christianity was 'capable of infusing the generous Passion of universal Love into our Hearts, by the strong Obligations of a necessary and essential Duty'.[46] It is likely that Johnson, despite his sweeping assertion in *Idler*, No. 4, that charity was an exclusively Christian virtue, generally shared Yalden's more qualified and specific understanding of revelation's contribution. Only Christianity made 'universal Love' a 'Duty'.

The idea of universal love is very complex and was then, as it has always been, the subject of many different and even contradictory interpretations. Nevertheless, it had long been conventional to illustrate the greatness of universal love by indicating how it had expanded and improved the classical virtue of friendship. As Jeremy Taylor wrote in *A Treatise of Friendship* (1657):

Christian charity is friendship to all the world; and when friendships were the noblest things to all the world, charity was little, like the sun drawn in at a chink, or his beams drawn into the centre of a burning-glass; but christian charity is friendship, expanded like the face of the sun when it mounts above the eastern hills.[47]

Christianity has extended the duties of friendship to all of mankind. But it was questioned, most notably by Lord Shaftesbury in his *Characteristics* (1711), whether this was really an improvement on classical philosophy. Shaftesbury objected that Christianity had apparently eliminated forms of limited benevolence such as friendship and patriotism that were both useful and natural to man.[48] The same objection was raised by Shaftesbury's admirer, Anthony Collins, who cited Taylor's

[46] Thomas Yalden, 'The Education of Poor Children, the most Excellent Kind of Charity', in *Twenty-five Sermons Preached at the Anniversary Meetings of the Children Educated in Charity-schools in and about the Cities of London and Westminster* (London, 1729), 555–6. (This collection of sermons by various divines hereafter referred to as *Twenty-five Sermons*.)

[47] Jeremy Taylor, *The Whole Works*, ed. Charles Eden (10 vols.; London, 1848), i. 72.

[48] See Shaftesbury, *Characteristics*, i, 67–8.

opinion that Scripture never uses the word 'friendship' in the classical sense of a special love between individuals.[49] In response to Shaftesbury, however, James Foster argued that friendship and patriotism remained valid categories of universal love.[50] And some writers argued that there was even Scriptural authority for retaining friendship as a Christian virtue. In *A Companion for the Festivals and Fasts of the Church of England* (1705), one of the most popular books of the eighteenth century, Robert Nelson noted that St John the Evangelist was 'the Disciple whom Jesus loved' (John 13: 23). 'Our Saviour has by his Example and Authority', Nelson concluded, 'sanctified the Relation of *Friendship*.'[51]

Johnson's comments on this issue are characterized by predictable inconsistency. In a 1778 discussion with the Quaker Mary Knowles, he submitted, not unlike Shaftesbury, that 'Christianity recommends universal benevolence . . . which is contrary to the virtue of friendship, as described by the ancient philosophers.'[52] When Mrs Knowles retorted by citing 'the disciple whom Jesus loved', Johnson conceded, '(with eyes sparkling benignantly,) "Very well, indeed, Madam. You have said very well." BOSWELL. "A fine application. Pray, Sir, had you ever thought of it?" JOHNSON. "I had not, Sir."'[53] This exchange is peculiar because Johnson almost certainly would have seen Mrs Knowles's application of John 13: 23 in Nelson's *Festivals and Fasts*, a work which he often consulted. Moreover, in Sermon 27 he suggested that there was no necessary contradiction between universal and private benevolence:

The religion of Jesus has . . . not abolish'd friendship, but superadded charity; we are not commanded to extinguish particular affections, but not to suffer them, wholly to engross us; we are not, while we are studying the gratifications of our friends, to neglect the universal happiness of mankind; but, at once, to attend to private and general duties, as the sun, at the same time, gives the day by one motion, and the year by another (xiv. 289).

---

[49] See Anthony Collins, *A Discourse of Free-thinking* (London, 1713), 129–31.

[50] See James Foster, 'The Perfection of the Christian Scheme of Benevolence', in *Sermons* (4 vols.; London, 1733), i. 67.

[51] Robert Nelson, *A Companion for the Festivals and Fasts of the Church of England* (London, 1705), 87.

[52] *Life*, iii. 289–90.

[53] Ibid. 290.

This was the position of most orthodox writers: Christianity had extended the duty of love to all men, yet it had also retained the limited forms of benevolence described in classical philosophy.[54]

The second great contribution of Christianity to charity, as described by Thomas Yalden, was that it had made universal love 'a necessary and essential Duty', a principle of conduct required for the individual's salvation. This represented an important improvement on the obligations to charity imposed by natural compassion or pity. Despite what is often assumed, few of the century's moralists and theologians considered man's innate sentiments of love and benevolence to be an adequate basis for Christian charity, even if they acknowledged that such sentiments existed. Johnson was not, as has been sometimes suggested, an isolated sceptic against a rising tide of benevolism.[55] His views on this, as on most issues, were solidly endorsed by Christian orthodoxy.

The doctrine of mankind's instinctive goodness and compassion was the central moral doctrine of Lord Shaftesbury, whose ideas were developed with greater sophistication by Francis Hutcheson, Lord Kames, and Adam Smith. But there was an alternative view of human nature which was almost equally prevalent in the eighteenth century—Hobbes's doctrine of man's essential selfishness and cruelty. This doctrine endured in the form of satirical attacks on human nature by La Rochefoucault, Swift, and Mandeville. It also gained a strongly Christian orientation in works such as Jacques Esprit's popular *Discourses on the Deceitfulness of Humane Virtues* (1691; trans. 1706). Esprit alleged that natural pity was nothing but 'the Effeminacy of the Soul', an uncontrollable reflex at the sight of misery.[56] Since it was involuntary, pity possessed no moral value. Mandeville, who was strongly influenced

---

[54] This question was in fact far more complicated than this simple relationship between classical and Christian ethics implies. Though divines praised the ideal of universal love in order to demonstrate the superiority of Christianity to deism, their internal debates on this issue often questioned whether universal love was a realistic standard of human compassion. Forms of limited benevolence such as friendship and patriotism became the basis for a rather less idealistic understanding of Christian charity. We will turn to this debate in ch. 6, sec. 1.

[55] See, e.g., Voitle, *Johnson the Moralist*, pp. 27–8.

[56] Jacques Esprit, *Discourses on the Deceitfulness of Humane Virtues* (1691), trans. William Beauvoir (London, 1706), 134.

by Esprit, similarly denigrated pity as merely 'a Frailty of our Nature' like anger or fear.[57] But Mandeville wished primarily to humiliate man's pride in his compassionate feelings. He did not, like Esprit, go on to describe a Christian alternative to the involuntary impulse of pity. Esprit had argued that Christian charity, unlike natural pity, was a steady and forcible rule of action which 'gives us always a sense of the Calamities of others . . . even of those that are absent; and makes us receive them as well as we can; whereas Pity inclines us to assist them no more than present Objects excite us to it'.[58] We could depend 'but little on the Assistance of those who relieve their Neighbour by a mere impulse of natural Compassion', but the principles instilled by Christianity were effectual and consistent.[59]

Johnson's claim in *Idler*, No. 4, that charity was known 'only by those who enjoy, immediately, or by transmission, the light of revelation', was based on reasonings very similar to Esprit's. 'Compassion', he wrote in *Idler*, No. 4, 'is by some reasoners, on whom the name of philosophers has been too easily conferred, resolved into an affection merely selfish, an involuntary perception of pain at the involuntary sight of a being like ourselves languishing in misery' (ii. 13). Johnson's major 'reasoner' was probably Mandeville, who did not attempt to define a Christian idea of compassion which surpassed the mere reflex of pity. Like Esprit, Johnson's primary intention in *Idler*, No. 4, was to describe the advantages of the exclusively Christian notion of steady, dependable principles of charity. He argued that the involuntary impulse of pity, 'if ever it be felt at all from the brute instinct of uninstructed nature, will only produce effects desultory and transient; it will never settle into a principle of action, or extend relief to calamities unseen, in generations not yet in being' (ii. 13). Christian charity was not confined to sudden impulses and incentives: it made alms, as Yalden wrote, a 'necessary and essential Duty' which applied even to distresses that could have little effect on our immediate feelings. In English sermons on alms-giving, the need for consistent and active charity was

---

57 See Mandeville, *Fable of the Bees*, i. 56.
58 Esprit, *Deceitfulness of Humane Virtues*, pp. 137–8.
59 Ibid. 135.

frequently noted. Joseph Watson, Samuel Chandler, and Thomas Secker, the Archbishop of Canterbury, all urged Christians to 'Act upon deliberate Conviction, Act from a settled Principle', not 'a sudden Warmth of affection . . . serving a present Turn'.[60]

One did not have to be a Hobbesian, therefore, to argue that man's instinctive compassion was inadequate as a basis for charity. This was a contention of Christian apologetics and of most eighteenth-century divines. Yet *Idler*, No. 4, does express some curiously sceptical opinions on human nature. In particular, Johnson's view that compassion may not be felt at all by 'the brute instinct of uninstructed nature' was unusual even among the strongest opponents to Shaftesbury and 'natural benevolence': pessimists such as Mandeville and Esprit accepted that natural pity did exist in some form. And other statements by Johnson on the cruelty of man in a natural state have led many scholars to conclude that his view of human nature was dark and Hobbesian, much akin, though more compassionate, to the misanthropy of Swift. But Johnson never wished simply to make his audience recognize the essential cruelty of their nature. His remarks on human nature were not uniformly pessimistic and, even at their darkest, were dictated by the purpose of showing each man's freedom and responsibility to make himself compassionate and charitable.

'Children are always cruel. Savages are always cruel. Pity is acquired and improved by the cultivation of reason.'[61] This well-known statement from Boswell's *Life* does far more than express a particularly cynical view of life. Johnson has chosen his examples with a specific purpose: children and savages both represent a state of human nature before eduction, and the need for an education in Christian morality was the fundamental issue between deists and apologists. Shaftesbury had outraged orthodox writers by denying the need for moral

---

[60] Thomas Secker, 'Preached before the Right Honourable the Lord Mayor, etc., on Monday in Easter Week, 1738', in *Fourteen Sermons on Several Occasions* (London, 1766), 88. See Joseph Watson, 'Preventative Charity the Best Method of doing Good', in *Twenty-five Sermons*, p. 532; Samuel Chandler, 'The Nature of Charity', in *Sermons* (4 vols.; London, 1759), 308.

[61] *Life*, i. 437. This statement has no necessary connection with the doctrine of original sin which, for most eighteenth-century writers, was a quite distinct issue treated in a separate controversy. See ch. 7, sec. 2, below.

education, and his follower Francis Hutcheson appealed to the supposed compassion of children to prove that all men possessed a 'moral sense'—a natural love of compassion and kindness 'antecedent to *Instruction*'.[62] It is not surprising that some apologists subsequently remarked on the ill nature of children. 'The irregular and untoward dispositions of children', wrote Philip Skelton in *Ophiomaches*, 'are but the natural prognostics of those vices, into which, if good education and discipline do not prevent it, they never fail to ripen with age.'[63] This statement refuted Hutcheson and upheld the need for a Christian education; it would be quite unreasonable to attribute it to a deeply pessimistic attitude to human nature.

Nor are we really in less danger of reading too much into Johnson's statements against natural benevolence. He could seem pessimistic about human nature when confronted with the doctrines of Shaftesbury and Hutcheson, but he was not so theoretically committed to the doctrine of man's innate cruelty that he refused to appeal to the belief in man's instinctive compassion when, as in Sermon 4, it was of some benefit to the moral instruction of his audience. Sermon 4 is a charity sermon which warns that 'unreasonable self-love' could, as Shaftesbury explained in a lengthy section of his *Characteristics*, destroy one's natural sense of compassion. 'How wretched must it be', Shaftesbury wrote of this consequence, '. . . for man, of all other creatures, to lose that sense and feeling which is proper to him as a man, and suitable to his character and genius?'[64] Johnson drew a similar picture of the man who had lost his natural compassion:

Let every one, that considers this state of obdurate wickedness, that is struck with horrour at the mention of a man void of pity, that feels resentment at the name of oppression, and melts with sorrow at the voice of misery, remember that those, who have now lost all these sentiments, were originally formed with passions, and instincts, and reason, like his own: . . . let him be warned by their example, to avoid the original causes of depravity, and repel the first attacks of unreasonable self-love (xiv. 41–2).

[62] Francis Hutcheson, *An Inquiry into the Original of Our Ideas of Beauty and Virtue* (1725) (3rd edn.; London, 1729), 216–17. For Shaftesbury's views on education, see *Characteristics*, i. 199.

[63] Skelton, *Ophiomaches*, i. 148.

[64] Shaftesbury, *Characteristics*, i. 315.

Was Johnson, the alleged pessimist who has been compared to Swift, endorsing the benevolist teachings of Shaftesbury? Probably not. Sermon 4 belongs to a large group of homiletic writings which similarly warned against the 'irregular self-love' by which, as John Conybeare wrote in 1738, 'the Sentiments both of Generosity and Compassion are almost entirely extinguish'd'.[65] These sermons were not designed to make a theoretical point about human nature. They were intended primarily to persuade the congregation to avoid selfishness: Shaftesbury's teachings on the destruction of natural benevolence provided a well-known, rather fashionable model for such a lesson. The same practical consideration was probably uppermost in Johnson's mind when he reminded men of their natural goodness in Sermon 4.

But Sermon 4 does at least show that Johnson was not so antagonistic to the theory of man's instinctive compassion that he was unwilling to use it for some useful moral or religious end. As so often in Johnson's work, theory is utilized primarily to advance practical objectives such as the protection of Christianity and the moral improvement of his audience. He opposed Shaftesbury's benevolism so far as it denied the need for a stronger and more consistent basis for charity than immediate sensations of pity and kindness. Like most of those who instructed Christians on alms-giving, he believed that revelation had greatly served mankind by supplying such a basis in the 'necessary and essential Duty' of 'universal Love'.

[65] John Conybeare, *A Sermon Preach'd in the Parish-church of Christ-Church, London* (London, 1738), 18–19. The same danger is identified in Andrew Snape's *A Sermon Preach'd before the Right Honourable the Lord Mayor* (London, 1731), 8.

3

New Trends in Ethics

1. *Johnson's Moral Doctrine: 'Christian Epicureanism'*

As we have seen, much can be learned about Johnson's moral thought by considering how he defended the contribution of Christianity to the knowledge of virtue: deism forced Christian writers to undertake an important re-evaluation of many central tenets of ethical philosophy. And, even when we turn to an examination of Johnson's moral thought independent of the controversy with the deists, we find that the issue of Christianity's role in moral conduct is never far removed from Johnson's mind. Indeed, one of his most consistent and important vindications of Christianity concerns an issue debated primarily among Christian moralists, not the deists and apologists. This was the issue of moral 'obligation'—the reason why an individual 'ought' to choose virtue rather than vice. By reviewing Johnson's opinions on this question we will be able to place him with a small group of ethical philosophers who came into prominence during the 1750s, the major decade of Johnson's own moral writing. This group revived ideas on 'obligation' which may be roughly aligned with the classical school of epicureanism. But they also gave Christianity a new and fundamental place in the psychology of virtue. For this reason, I have called their doctrine, which Johnson generally advocated, 'Christian epicureanism'.

I will be most concerned in this chapter to show how 'Christian epicureanism' is different from other doctrines both before and after the eighteenth century. Of particular significance to the study of Johnson is how this doctrine differs from an associated school which emerged late in the eighteenth century—utilitarianism. Recent scholarship has closely associated Johnson with utilitarianism,[1] yet he really held an earlier and, in important respects, quite different theory.

---

[1] See Voitle, *Johnson the Moralist*, pp. 59–72; Greene, 'Samuel Johnson and "Natural Law"', p. 69.

The first fifty years of the eighteenth century were a time of widespread interest in ethical philosophy; moral questions divided not only philosophers, but even novelists and poets into various ethical schools. There were the followers of Shaftesbury and Hutcheson who claimed that mankind possessed an instinctive 'moral sense'—a passionate love for virtue and aversion to iniquity antecedent to all education. This group was especially interested in the similarity between aesthetic and moral judgements, and characteristically spoke of the 'beauty' of virtue. Followers of Samuel Clarke such as John Balguy and the blue-stocking Catherine Cockburn agreed that the love of moral truth was natural, but placed its perception in the reason, not the passions. Clarke borrowed the stoic terminology of the 'fitness' and 'relations' of virtue as a part of his effort, considered brilliant by his many admirers, to give ethical reasoning the same mathematical precision that Newton had given to physics and astronomy. William Wollaston's *The Religion of Nature Delineated* (1722) generated a smaller band of admirers who equated virtue with 'truth'.

Moralists of the 1740s and 1750s such as Thomas Rutherforth, John Brown, Lord Bolingbroke, and Adam Smith attempted, as part of a general mid-century review of ethical philosophy, to categorize the major groups and their founders according to the divisions of classical philosophy. They were especially interested in aligning modern philosophers with either the stoics or peripatetics, and frequently cited Cicero's distinction between these sects in Book III of *De officiis:*

For whether moral goodness is the only good, as the Stoics believe, or whether, as you Peripatetics think, moral goodness is in so far the highest good that everything else gathered together into the opposing scale would scarcely have the slightest weight, it is beyond question that expediency can never conflict with moral rectitude.[2]

That this classical division was of only limited accuracy in describing contemporary philosophy may be surmised from the almost total lack of agreement on how the classifications should be allotted. Rutherforth, for example, placed both Shaftesbury and Clarke with the stoics, while Adam Smith thought that

---

[2] Cicero, *De officiis*, trans. W. Miller (London and Cambridge, Mass., 1913), III, iii, 279.

both were peripatetics.[3] The problem was partly that, as Cicero had remarked, there was little basic disagreement between the stoics and the peripatetics. Both held that *utilitas*—the 'expediency', 'advantage', or 'utility' of an act—could never conflict with moral goodness. For the stoics, there were no advantageous choices besides virtue: desires of all sorts were opposed to the individual's true happiness. For the peripatetics, friendship, esteem, and freedom from pain did represent real advantages, but they could never outweigh the happiness of virtue. The stoics and peripatetics both, in effect, raised virtue to a special class of 'happiness' distinct from and far superior to all pleasures. Virtue was a 'good' to be followed for its own sake, regardless of all pains or sacrifices.

There was, however, a third and more distinct group of classical thinkers who, even as late as the eighteenth century, were regarded as the heretics of ethical philosophy—the epicureans. The followers of Epicurus held that pleasure, not virtue, was 'the highest good'. As Adam Smith summarized in *The Theory of Moral Sentiments* (1759): 'Virtue . . . according to Epicurus, did not deserve to be pursued for its own sake, nor was itself one of the ultimate objects of natural appetite, but was eligible only upon account of its tendency to prevent pain and to procure ease and pleasure.'[4] The epicureans refused to assign virtue to a special class of 'good' or 'happiness'. The 'good' or 'happiness' was nothing more than the maximum pleasure obtainable by any course of action. Epicurus did not deny that virtue was, ultimately, the surest means to pleasure in the enlightened sense of health and freedom from anxiety. But he would never accept that the individual was under any obligation to sacrifice his ultimate ease and advantage in the name of moral rectitude.

The stoics and peripatetics objected to epicureanism because it was used by some of its corrupt followers to justify a debauched life-style—'eat, drink and be merry'. The epicureans objected to the stoics and peripatetics because, they contended, it made no sense to claim that virtue should be pursued 'for its

---

[3] Rutherforth, *Nature and Obligations of Virtue*, pp. 182–206; Adam Smith, *The Theory of Moral Sentiments* (London, 1759), 438–9. See also Henry St John, Lord Bolingbroke, *Philosophical Works* (5 vols.; London, 1754), v. 12–13.

[4] Smith, *Moral Sentiments*, p. 454.

own sake'. Was not the pleasure of a good conscience what was really sought in performing the most heroic and selflessly virtuous act? In the eighteenth century this debate was revived. The epicurean charges against the stoics and peripatetics were taken up by a group of moralists highly sceptical of the claim by Shaftesbury, Wollaston, and, in particular, Samuel Clarke that virtue ought to be chosen 'for its own sake'.

Samuel Clarke was the special focus of this controversy because he was so widely respected by Christian writers and because he had written specifically on the question of 'obligation'. Johnson himself was well known to be an admirer of Clarke and, as our discussion of apologetics has already indicated, there were numerous similarities between their moral and religious ideas. According to Sir John Hawkins, Johnson's agreement with Clarke extended to the issue of moral obligation: 'Dr. Clarke supposes all rational agents as under an obligation to act agreeably to the relations that subsist between such, or according to what he calls the fitness of things. Johnson was ever an admirer of Clarke, and agreed with him in this and most other opinions.'[5] It was precisely this theory that was attacked by the eighteenth century's counterpart to epicureanism. A variation of this classical doctrine first became a strong force in the century's moral thought with an attack on Samuel Clarke by a Hull schoolmaster, John Clarke, in his 1726 treatise, *The Foundation of Morality in Theory and Practice Considered*. In response to Samuel Clarke's notion that men were obliged to act morally from the very 'fitness' of virtue, John Clarke retorted, not unlike Epicurus, 'where any Conduct is said to be reasonable, and fit for Man, it is always upon the Supposition, that sooner or later it will make more for his Interest and Advantage than the contrary; it is always with Reference to the Happiness, or Welfare of the Agent, that those Terms are applied to human Actions'.[6] This doctrine reflected a general conception of human nature as motivated entirely by self-interest. 'There neither is, nor can be,' John Clarke argued, 'any other Principle of human Conduct than

---

[5] Sir John Hawkins, *The Life of Samuel Johnson* (1787) (2nd edn.; London, 1787), 253.

[6] John Clarke, *The Foundation of Morality in Theory and Practice Considered* (London, 1726), 14–15.

Self-love, or a general regard to Interest in this Life, or a future.'[7] For this reason it really made no sense to say that men should follow virtue for its own sake or because it was merely 'fit': men were obliged to act virtuously only so far as virtue was seen to be in their best interest.

John Clarke's case immediately found the approval of conservative divines such as Daniel Waterland who were apprehensive of Samuel Clarke's large concessions to natural religion and the deists.[8] It also influenced a group of moralists, including Thomas Johnson, John Gay, John Brown, and Thomas Rutherforth, in a general reaction against all the 'metaphysical' systems of ethics which had flourished early in the century. The following passage from John Brown's generally unfavourable reassessment of Shaftesbury, *Essays on the Characteristics* (1751), reflects this group's special impatience with, as they argued, the essentially meaningless idea of obligation common to all these systems. 'One asserts', wrote Brown, 'that we are obliged to *love* and *pursue* Virtue, because *she* is *beautiful*; another, because Virtue is *good*; another, because Virtue is . . . agreeable to the *Relations of Things*.' Against all 'these *amusing* Expressions', Brown affirmed that 'the only *Reason* or *Motive*, by which Individuals can possibly be *induced* or *obliged* to the Practice of Virtue, must be the *Feeling* immediate, or the *Prospect* of future *private Happiness*'.[9] Brown and the other moralists who followed John Clarke were intolerant of abstractions. The ethical teachings of Epicurus were tough and practical, seeking their ratification not in *a priori* deductions, but in the experience of real life. By favouring this doctrine, John Clarke, John Brown, and others reflected the general mood of scepticism which was typical of much apologetic literature at the same time and which became a very evident part of orthodox thought by the 1750s.

Johnson's definition of 'obligation' in the *Dictionary*, 'an act which binds any man to some performance', would seem to give little indication of the controversy that then surrounded this word. Nevertheless, he was a great pragmatist who

---

[7] Ibid. 15.

[8] See Waterland's praise for John Clarke in *The Nature, Obligation, and Efficacy of the Christian Sacrament* (London, 1730), 16–17.

[9] John Brown, *Essays on the Characteristics*, p. 159.

generally demanded that speculative theory withstand the test of experience: it is not surprising that the Christian revival of epicurean moral theory should have appealed to him. As usual, there are ambiguities. Hawkins's testimony that Johnson agreed with Samuel Clarke on the problem of obligation cannot be ignored: Johnson did admire Clarke a great deal. But in Sermon 14 Johnson ratified the position of John Clarke and others that human nature was entirely motivated by, as John Brown put it, 'the *Feeling* immediate, or the *Prospect* of future *private Happiness*': 'Every man is conscious, that he neither performs, nor forbears upon any other motive than the prospect, either of an immediate gratification, or a distant reward' (xiv. 149). In addition, in his review of Soame Jenyns's *A Free Inquiry into the Nature and Origin of Evil* (1757), Johnson cited a lengthy passage describing Jenyns's moral doctrine. Jenyns had reiterated the increasingly influential stand of Christian epicureans on the speciousness of the metaphysical ideas of moral obligation:

Some have placed [virtue] in the conformity to truth, some to the fitness of things, and others to the will of God. But all this is merely superficial: they resolve us not, why truth, or the fitness of things, are either eligible or obligatory, or why God, should require us to act in some manner rather than another. The true reason of which can possibly be no other than this, because some actions produce happiness, and others misery. . . . They who extol the truth, beauty, and harmony of virtue, exclusive of its consequences, deal but in pompous nonsense. [10]

Johnson highly praised Jenyns's moral system, calling it 'a criterion of action, an account of virtue and vice, for which I have often contended, and which might be embraced by all who are willing to know why they act, or why they forbear'. [11] Although it is not clear where Johnson had 'contended' for this view, it should be noted that he owned both Brown's *Essays on the Characteristics* and Rutherforth's *Essay on the Nature and Obligations of Virtue* (1744). [12] He was certainly familiar with this

[10] Review of *Free Inquiry* in Schwartz, *Evil*, p. 109.
[11] Ibid.
[12] In the sale of Johnson's library, Brown's *Essays on the Characteristics* was Sale Lot No. 50 and Rutherforth's *Essay on the Nature and Obligations of Virtue* was Sale Lot No. 61.

group of moralists, and his praise for Jenyns's statement, combined with his assertion in Sermon 14 on the necessary self-interest of all human actions, strongly suggests that he supported its position on the nature of moral 'obligation'.

Establishing Johnson's position on the issue of moral 'obligation' does help to locate him in a tradition of ethical philosophy which would achieve its best-known form in the utilitarianism of Bentham and Mill. Just as John Clarke and those who followed him were aligned by eighteenth-century writers with the epicureans, John Stuart Mill recognized his own links with this classical sect. There was, Mill observed, a direct tradition 'from Epicurus to Bentham'.[13] Utilitarianism, like epicureanism, insisted that the desire for happiness was the sole end of all human actions. But Johnson and contemporary writers who shared his views on obligation were no more 'utilitarians' than they were, in the strict classical sense, epicureans. Johnson certainly was not, like Epicurus, a materialist who denied the immortality of the soul and the influence of God on human affairs. Mainly because of these epicurean doctrines, he would have agreed with the stoics and peripatetics that epicureanism, literally followed, would ultimately justify moral corruption. But similarly, Johnson cannot, without considerable inaccuracy, be aligned with Bentham or Mill's 'Greatest Happiness Principle' that 'actions are right in proportion as they tend to promote happiness, wrong as they tend to produce the reverse of happiness'.[14] To understand why this connection cannot be made, we must turn our attention to one of the most complex questions of eighteenth-century ethics—the precise meaning and existence of 'natural law'.

Both 'natural law' and 'utilitarianism' are ways to understand the origin or basis of the distinction between good and evil. In the eighteenth century there were three general theories on the origin of moral truth. First, the highest and purest form of 'natural law' postulated that good and evil were determined entirely by the transcendent moral order of the universe or 'nature' which governed God Himself. Second, it was argued against this view that the 'will of God' was unconfined by any superior order of nature and that His command was the only

---

[13] John Stuart Mill, *Utilitarianism* (London, 1863), 8.   [14] Ibid. 9–10.

source of moral truth. Third, it was postulated by a small group of heterodox moralists, such as Hobbes and Mandeville, that the distinction between good and evil had nothing to do with God or 'nature', but was entirely a man-made principle of social order: this was essentially the belief adopted by Bentham and Mill.

The first theory, that the universe possessed an immutable moral harmony antecedent even to God's will, was upheld without apparent hesitation by many important Christian writers of the seventeenth century such as Grotius and Cudworth.[15] It survived in the eighteenth century among writers such as Arthur Ashley Sykes who, despite the rise of deism, remained sympathetic to the speculative 'natural philosophy' of Christians in the previous century. 'The Will of God does not make the Relations of Things,' wrote Sykes, '. . . but conforms his Will, and requires that we should conform ours, to Truth.'[16] Although this theory placed restrictions on the freedom of the Divine will, it was used to uphold belief in human freedom against both the Calvinist doctrine of predestination and the philosophical arguments for necessity. In *The Body of Divinity* (1718), a textbook for the direction of Anglican ministers, Richard Fiddes contended against the Calvinists that 'as a wise and holy God can do nothing irreconcilable with the character of a just and good God, it is directly contrary to all our notions, both of goodness and justice, that any creature should be treated as criminal, upon the charge of a crime, which it has not, in fact, committed'.[17] The Calvinists maintained that those subject to the predestined sentence of reprobation would be damned regardless of their works; Fiddes answered that God, confined by the law of justice, could punish only voluntary acts of sin. This represents a distinctly legalistic variant of a position adopted by Arminius in his famous reply to the English Calvinist, William Perkins, at the turn of the seventeenth century.[18] It also recalled Cudworth's attack on

[15] See Hugo Grotius, *The Rights of War and Peace* (1625), trans. William Evats (London, 1682), 5; Cudworth, *True Intellectual System*, pp. 896–7.

[16] Sykes, *Principles and Connexion*, p. 18.

[17] Richard Fiddes, *The Body of Divinity* (2 pts.; Dublin, 1718), I. 227–8. This work was owned and consulted by Johnson. See *Yale Edition*, i. 226.

[18] For a description of Arminius' answer to Perkins, see C. Bangs, *Arminius: A Study in the Dutch Reformation* (Nashville and New York, 1971), 213–15.

the philosophical doctrine of necessity in *The True Intellectual System of the Universe* (1678). Cudworth contended that unless 'God's *Will* is *Ruled* by his Justice' then the moral law represented no more than the arbitrary mandate of 'brute Force'. Man would be without any liberty to choose goodness for the sake of its intrinsic worth, and would be virtuous only under the compulsion of Divine wrath.[19] As some philosophers had viewed this issue, therefore, man could be free only if God's will was, in certain important ways, confined.

It is not surprising, however, that this willingness to circumscribe the power of God was frequently rejected as impious and presumptuous. In *The Law of Nature and Nations* (1672; trans. 1749), Samuel Pufendorf criticized Grotius' use of this theory, contending that 'without doubt those imperious Terms, *God ought necessarily*, are very unsuitable to the Majesty of an Omnipotent Legislator'.[20] The same objection was raised by the High-Church divine, Daniel Waterland, in a 1730 controversy with Arthur Ashley Sykes. According to Waterland, virtue and vice were entirely the product of God's unbounded will. There was nothing 'immutable' or 'eternal' about moral truth; what God had made right today he could make wrong tomorrow.[21]

Waterland's position represents the second theory—that moral distinctions derive entirely from the 'Will of God'—in its most extreme and unusual form. Most writers who wished to vindicate the liberty of God did not deny that moral truth reflected the 'external' and 'immutable' order of the universe. 'Nature' could always be our guide. But these writers argued that God was not Himself subject to this natural order because, indeed, it was He who had created the universe and established its moral truths in their present form. Just as God was eternal and immutable, so were the moral distinctions which He had formed through an entirely arbitrary act of will. This had roughly been the position of the first great Christian theoretician of natural law, St Thomas Aquinas, and it was

---

[19] Cudworth, *True Intellectual System*, p. 897.

[20] Samuel Pufendorf, *The Law of Nature and Nations* (1672), trans. Basil Kennet (London, 1749), 121.

[21] See Waterland, *Christian Sacraments*, pp. 16–17, and *A Supplement to the Treatise, Entituled, The Nature, Obligation, and Efficacy of the Christian Sacraments* (London, 1730), 20.

also the argument of Samuel Clarke in *A Discourse Concerning the Unchangeable Obligations of Natural Religion* (1706):

The Nature indeed and Relations, the Proportions and Disproportions, the Fitness and Unfitness of Things, are eternal and in themselves absolutely unalterable; But this is only upon Supposition that the Things Exist, and that they Exist in such manner as they at present do: Now that things Exist in such manner as they do, or that they Exist at all, depends entirely on the Arbitrary Will and good Pleasure of God.[22]

Sykes, who adopted the vocabulary of 'the eternal and immutable fitness of things', was considered to be a follower of Samuel Clarke. Yet the issue of Divine liberty was one of many upon which Clarke's disciples adopted a position far different from that of their master. Clarke wished to combine his theory of natural law with the idea that God was solely responsible for the distinction between good and evil. It might be said that he bridged the first two theories on the origin of moral truth— virtue was both 'eternal and immutable' and freely willed by God.

Johnson's statements on the origin of moral truth are not entirely clear, and the complexity of the issue should warn us against incautious conclusions. Nevertheless, the following observations by Boswell suggest that Johnson at least rejected the extreme form of 'natural law' which made God Himself the subject of a transcendental 'fitness':

His profound admiration of the GREAT FIRST CAUSE was such as to set him above that 'Philosophy and vain deceit' with which men of narrower conceptions have been infected. I have heard him strongly maintain that 'what is right is not so from any natural fitness, but because GOD wills it to be right,' and it is certainly so, because He had predisposed the relations of things so as that which He wills must be right.[23]

Johnson might seem to be advocating Waterland's position that moral truth was entirely the product of God's arbitrary will: what was virtue today, could be made vice tomorrow. According to Boswell, however, Johnson was objecting only to the view that the Divine will was itself bound by the immutable

---

[22] Samuel Clarke, *Natural Religion*, p. 150.
[23] *Life*, iv. 31 n. 1.

order of the universe. Samuel Clarke and other theoreticians of natural law agreed with this objection for the reason cited by Boswell—it was God who had originally predisposed the immutable relations and fitness of things.

It is likely, in fact, that this was close to Johnson's true opinion. His writings contain strong evidence that he believed that virtue was 'eternal and immutable', the reflection of a universal order rather than a temporary injunction of the Divine will. 'Truth, indeed, is always truth,' he wrote in the 'Life of Cowley', 'and reason is always reason; they have an intrinsick and unalterable value, and constitute the intellectual gold which defies destruction.'[24] As Jean H. Hagstrum has shown in an article on 'The Nature of Johnson's Rationalism', Johnson did not hesitate to write of the 'settled and unalterable nature of things' (*Rambler*, No. 140, iv. 377).[25] These passages provide good evidence that Johnson was not, as has been often suggested, uniformly hostile to 'natural law': indeed, he conceded a central tenet of natural law that the universe possessed an invariable moral order, even if that order was originally willed by God. Most important, this belief in the eternal and immutable nature of moral truth distinguishes his doctrine from the third major theory on the origin of moral truth—that virtue and vice are principles originally agreed upon between men to promote the common good of society.

This was Epicurus' theory. The following passage from Walter Charleton's 1655 translation of Epicurus' *Morals* suggests how close the classical formulation of this doctrine was to its variants in English philosophy:

To speak plainly and properly, therefore; Right or Just Natural, is nothing else but *Tessera Utilitatis*, the Symbol of Utility, proposed and agreed upon by the concurrent votes of all the Society, to the end, that they may be kept from mutually harming each other, and that each one may live securely; which as it is a Good, so doth every man, by the direction of Nature, desire it.[26]

It would be difficult to cite a passage from classical philosophy which has had such an enormous influence on British ethics.

[24] *Lives of the Poets*, i. 59.
[25] See J. H. Hagstrum, 'The Nature of Dr. Johnson's Rationalism', *ELH* 17 (1950), 191–205.
[26] Epicurus, *Morals*, trans. Walter Charleton (London, 1655; repr. London, 1926), 91.

For example, Epicurus' theory that the social contract was made to protect individuals from harming each other would receive its classic elaboration in Hobbes's *Leviathan* (1651). Mandeville's famous statement that the moral virtues were first 'broach'd by skilfull Politicians, to render Men useful to each other as well as tractable'[27] also originates with Epicurus. And Hobbes and Mandeville in some ways anticipated the utilitarianism of Bentham and Mill. By making virtue exactly proportionate to the greatest happiness of society, the utilitarians ratified Epicurus' argument that moral truth did not reflect any immutable order of 'Nature' but was simply an agreed standard of mutual support and protection among individuals. This might be called 'natural law' so far as it is 'natural' for all men to desire their own happiness as ensured by the good of society. But this moral theory depended on no particular conception of the universe or God: virtue and vice were essentially man-made and altered according to the conveniences of man.

It is this belief that virtue and vice derive from a social consensus or covenant, rather than from a higher order of nature, which properly distinguishes utilitarianism from 'natural law'. It is sometimes mistakenly assumed that it is the connection between virtue and the 'common good' which characterizes utilitarianism. But there is nothing peculiarly 'utilitarian' about the doctrine that virtue promotes the 'greatest happiness' of man and society. The most abstracted theoreticians of natural law in the eighteenth century postulated that the 'fitness', 'beauty', or 'truth' of virtue coincided with the greatest happiness. As Samuel Clarke wrote, 'whatever tends directly and certainly to promote the Good and Happiness of the Whole . . . must needs be agreeable to the *Will of God*'.[28] John Clarke's position on the origin and basis of morality, which was probably shared by Johnson, differed from Samuel Clarke's only so far as John Clarke made happiness, rather than 'fitness', the prime object of God's will in creating the universal order. 'By Actions *morally good*', wrote John Clarke, 'are meant such as have a Natural Tendency or Fitness to promote the Well-being and Happiness of Mankind,

---

[27] Mandeville, *Fable of the Bees*, i. 51.
[28] Samuel Clarke, *Natural Religion*, p. 151.

and are for that reason enjoined by God, and the Practice of them enforced upon Mankind by a Sanction of future Rewards and Punishments.'[29] This again is different from the utilitarianism of Bentham and Mill because it presupposed the existence of an immutable order established by God. It is, in effect, a special form of 'natural law'. Neither John Clarke nor Johnson would agree that moral truth could vary from culture to culture, according to what was there agreed to facilitate the common good.[30]

In theory this distinction may seem slight, but in practice it led to crucial differences between the way John Clarke and the utilitarians understood the moral duties of mankind. First, John Clarke and his adherents would disagree that mankind could ever arrive at a complete understanding of the 'greatest happiness' on their own: men should obey the expression of God's eternal will in Scripture, even if it was not always apparent, in a particular society or at a particular time, how the Bible's commands promoted the common good. Second, John Clarke and Johnson were particularly concerned to point out that the individual was under no obligation to promote the common good without the prospect of rewards and punishments in the hereafter. In this way they differed from both utilitarianism and classical epicureanism, for they stressed that virtue or the promotion of the common good did not always coincide with the best interests of the individual. Only the promises and threats of the Christian revelation imposed any real obligation on the individual to practise virtue at all times, even at the expense of his present happiness.

Scepticism among eighteenth-century Christian writers concerning, first, the ability of men to achieve a complete under-

---

[29] John Clarke, *An Examination of what has been Advanced Relating to Moral Obligation, in a late Pamphlet, Entitled, A Defence of the Answer, &c.* (London, 1730), 39–40.

[30] The discourse of the natural philosopher in *Rasselas*, ch. 22, might occur to some readers as an example of Johnson's hostility to all doctrines of natural law. But this passage specifically satirizes the claim that 'the way to be happy is to follow nature': very few eighteenth-century writers on natural law would agree that absolute happiness was assured through the practice of virtue, even if they contended that virtue was worth pursuing 'for its own sake'. This observation applies particularly to Samuel Clarke. Though Clarke has often been included among those satirized in this portrait, he was strongly associated in the eighteenth century with the belief that natural law did *not* provide the way to temporal happiness. This point is discussed in more detail in ch. 4, sec. 1, below.

standing of the common good resulted partly from the rise of deism. And deism had derived its confidence concerning man's knowledge of the common good from, again, Christian writers of the seventeenth century. Among the most respected orthodox works of the previous century was Richard Cumberland's 1672 reply to Hobbes, *De legibus naturae*. Cumberland had contrived an elaborate argument for a position which we have already noted in the works of eighteenth-century moralists such as Samuel Clarke—that acts which promote the common good correspond to the law of nature. 'The Dictates of all true Wisdom,' wrote Cumberland, 'which are to direct human Acts at all Times and in all Places, in producing the Publick Good, (that is the common Good of all Rational Beings) are no other Dictates than the very Laws of Nature themselves.'[31] Robert Voitle has remarked on the similarity between some of Johnson's statements and Cumberland's thesis, and concluded that Johnson owed an important debt to *De legibus naturae*, which he owned in a 1750 translation from the original Latin. As Donald Greene later pointed out, the similarity between Cumberland and Johnson is particularly evident in Johnson's discussion of natural law in the Vinerian lectures.[32] But Cumberland's system represented an extreme claim for the view that men could achieve, without Christianity, a just notion of the 'common good'. Not surprisingly, Cumberland's theory was widely used by Matthew Tindal.

Cumberland's system was also becoming outdated by new issues and problems surrounding the nature of the 'common good'. Cumberland had argued that any act which benefited mankind reflected the law of nature, but, as Mandeville pointed out in *The Fable of the Bees* (1724), many 'Private Vices' are 'Public Benefits'. Greed, aggression, and vanity, Mandeville argued, are the foundation of economic prosperity: does this mean that such qualities correspond to the law of nature? Partly to offset this type of difficulty, Francis Hutcheson contended in *An Inquiry into the Original of Our Ideas of Beauty and Virtue* (1725) that, to achieve a just idea of the moral worth of an action, we

[31] Richard Cumberland, *A Philosophical Enquiry into the Laws of Nature* (Dublin, 1750), 307.

[32] Voitle, *Johnson the Moralist*, pp. 59–72; Greene, 'Samuel Johnson and "Natural Law"', p. 69.

must balance its possible benefits against its harm: 'When the *Consequences* of Actions are of a *mix'd* Nature, partly *Advantageous*, and partly *Pernicious*; *that Action* is *good*, whose *good* Effects preponderate the *evil*, by being useful to many and pernicious to few; and *that, Evil*, which is *otherwise*.'[33] Hutcheson's criterion might be used in this way: greed may benefit society in economic ways, but, if those benefits are outweighed by, for example, the number of serious crimes incited by this drive, it does not qualify as a virtue. Johnson cited roughly the same principle of utility in his 1778 remarks on Mandeville in Boswell's *Life*. 'This is the way to try what is vicious', he argued, 'by ascertaining whether more evil than good is produced by it upon the whole, which is the case in all vice. It may happen that good is produced by vice; but not as vice.'[34] Bentham's intricate calculations of the 'greatest Happiness' in *An Introduction to the Principles of Morals and Legislation* (1789) were founded on similar reasoning.

When, however, Tindal claimed that 'there is none of the Questions, whether relating to God or Man, but what may be easily determined by considering, which side of the Question carries with it, the greatest Goodness',[35] Christian apologists insisted on the great difficulty of this calculation. In his reply to Tindal, John Leland cited Mandeville as an example of how men could be led into the most pernicious errors in their speculations on what qualities benefited society:

there have not been wanting Men, and those too admir'd in this discerning Age, this Age of Liberty and Free-Thought, that have made no scruple to assert, and have endeavour'd to prove, that Vice itself is for the general Good of the Community, and *that private Vices are publick Benefits*. . . . It must therefore be a great Advantage not to have our Duty left thus at large, but particularly determin'd by God, who is a far better Judge than Man can pretend to be of what tends to the general Good, as he takes in the Whole Compass of Things. And it must be a great Satisfaction, and of signal Benefit, to be inform'd by a Revelation from him what does so.[36]

Leland's position was that men must rely on the teachings of Scripture whatever their beliefs concerning the common good.

---

[33] Hutcheson, *Beauty and Virtue*, p. 180.   [34] *Life*, iii. 292.
[35] Tindal, *Christianity as Old as the Creation*, p. 75.
[36] Leland, *Answer to Christianity as Old as the Creation*, i. 158–9.

We could always trust that the law of God would ultimately support his benevolent plan for mankind.

In his statement on morals in *A Free Inquiry*, Soame Jenyns had also considered the difficulty raised by Mandeville—that certain vicious actions seem to promote the common good. Jenyns explained that vice has beneficial effects only 'by force of accidental circumstances'.[37] In his review of the *Free Inquiry*, however, Johnson was not satisfied. He qualified his praise for Jenyns's system by contending, like Leland, that it is extremely difficult to calculate the greatest happiness. For this reason men must rely implicitly on the teachings of Scripture:

To this account of the essence of vice and virtue, it is only necessary to add, that the consequences of human actions being sometimes uncertain and sometimes remote, it is not possible in many cases for most men, nor in all cases for any man to determine what actions will ultimately produce happiness, and therefore it was proper that *Revelation* should lay down a rule to be followed invariably in opposition to appearances, and in every change of circumstances, by which we may be certain to promote the general felicity, and be set free from the dangerous temptation of *doing evil that good may come*.[38]

As we shall consider in the next section, Johnson's opinion that men could not properly determine the consequences of their actions was relevant to his understanding of human liberty. The importance of this opinion to our present subject was that he made the 'common good' unviable as an objective or criterion of moral conduct. As Johnson remarked to Boswell, men 'have no business with consequences'.[39] He believed that men should rely on either Scripture or, alternatively, their own intuitive recognition of moral truth. He did not believe that the individual should, in the regular course of moral action, determine the effects of his acts on the general good. Men were to perform their moral duty and leave the common good to God.

This, clearly, was not the position advocated by the utilitarians. The doctrine of Bentham and Mill differs in no significant way from all the various eighteenth-century theories on the 'general good' if it does not make the consequences of actions an immediate consideration for the individual.

[37] Review of *Free Inquiry*, in Schwartz, *Evil*, p. 110.
[38] Ibid. 110–11.
[39] See *Life*, iv. 306.

Bentham explained in *An Introduction to the Principles of Morals and Legislation*:

A man may be said to be a partisan of the principle of utility, when the approbation or disapprobation he annexes to any action, or to any measure, is determined by and proportioned to the tendency which he conceives it to have to augment or to diminish the happiness of the community: or in other words, to its conformity or unconformity to the laws or dictates of utility.[40]

Mill, of course, made this doctrine far more sophisticated and far more in keeping with the way we really make moral decisions. He argued that we are often guided to serve the general good not by formal calculations of what action will most augment public happiness, but by 'a subjective feeling in our minds' instilled by education.[41] But he agreed with Bentham that 'The principle of utility neither requires nor admits any regulator than itself.'[42] There was no question of adhering to some written standard of duty such as Scripture, regardless of its perceived consequences.

This is a significant practical difference between utilitarianism and the doctrine of Johnson and John Clarke: they made the word of God, natural and revealed, the standard of moral duty without reference to its perceived benefits or harm. But, even more important, these eighteenth-century writers did not believe that the individual was under any consistent or even frequent obligation to promote the common good without the rewards and punishments of Christianity. This position was originally adopted against the view, attributed to Samuel Clarke, that 'Man is not to make his own Happiness, but that of others, his Chief and Supreme End.'[43] Because Samuel

---

[40] Jeremy Bentham, *An Introduction to the Principles of Morals and Legislation* (London, 1789), 3–4.

[41] Mill, *Utilitarianism*, p. 41.

[42] Bentham, *Principles of Morals*, p. 20.

[43] John Clarke, *Foundation of Morality*, p. 23. John Clarke was actually not being entirely fair to Samuel Clarke by suggesting that he expected benevolence without any consideration of self-interest. Samuel Clarke did admit that, 'though Virtue is unquestionably *worthy to be chosen for its own sake* . . . yet it does not follow that it is therefore entirely *Self-sufficient*, and able to support a Man, under all kinds of suffering, and even Death itself, for its sake' (*Natural Religion*, pp. 116–17). At this point Samuel Clarke's argument is not easy to follow, yet he is very insistent that the rewards and punishments of Christianity are necessary to support the frailties of human nature.

Clarke believed that we are obliged to practise virtue 'for its own sake', such a selfless dedication to the happiness of others was quite consistent with his general thesis. A doctrine which, on the other hand, made private advantage the only ground of moral obligation could not admit that men should promote the common good for its own sake. Therefore, as John Clarke answered,

God, who knows human Nature best, expects no such Conduct from us, as to prefer the Happiness of others to our own Absolutely and Finally, but has made a Steady Adherence to Virtue under all Extremities, or the Preference of the Public, to his own private Good, a Man's truest Interest, by a Promise of endless and unspeakable Happiness hereafter for it. [44]

In his qualifying remarks on Jenyns's moral system, Johnson similarly argued that a future state of rewards and punishments was absolutely necessary to encourage the pursuit of the general good:

it may easily happen, and, in effect, will happen very frequently, that our own private happiness may be promoted by an act injurious to others, when yet no man can be obliged by nature to prefer ultimately the happiness of others to his own. Therefore, to the instructions of infinite wisdom, it was necessary that infinite power should add penal sanctions. That every man, to whom these instructions shall be imparted may know, that he can never ultimately injure himself by benefiting others, or ultimately by injuring others benefit himself. [45]

John Clarke and Johnson were addressing a problem which would later confront utilitarianism. The utilitarians would agree that the sacrifice of personal ease for the good of society is an act of outstanding virtue. But the utilitarians also believed, in accordance with the whole epicurean tradition, that the acts of an individual are motivated entirely by the desire for personal happiness. How, then, can this doctrine explain even the existence of acts of heroic sacrifice? Does this not show that virtue really is, as the stoics and peripatetics taught, a good to be pursued for its own sake?

Although he was sometimes associated with stoicism, there is no question that he acknowledged the reality of physical suffering.

[44] John Clarke, *Foundation of Morality*, p. 23.
[45] Review of *Free Inquiry*, in Schwartz, *Evil*, p. 111.

John Clarke and Johnson introduced a future state of rewards and punishments to bridge this gap between the interests of the individual and the greatest happiness of mankind. For them, the happiness of the individual included not only this world, but also the next; similarly, they conceived of the 'general good' not as the happiness of a single society or even of the present world, but as the happiness represented by God's eternal plan for mankind. Utilitarianism, on the other hand, is a strictly secular ethic which, as Mill admitted, makes little sense if happiness is not available in the present life.[46] Mill admitted that 'external sanctions' such as eternal rewards and punishments could help motivate virtuous acts, but there was no question of relying entirely on this prospect. Mill's 'ultimate sanction' was 'the subjective feeling of the mind', a sense of dignity and self-congratulation instilled by education. The happiness of this 'subjective feeling' conceivably outweighed even the most dreadful tortures.[47] This argument, as Mill himself was conscious, was drawing close to the doctrine that virtue was the 'highest good' to be chosen 'for its own sake'.

Johnson was not, then, a utilitarian. He represented a specific eighteenth-century doctrine which, though it generally belongs to the epicurean tradition of ethics, differs in significant ways from both its classical predecessor and the doctrine developed by Bentham and Mill. Indeed, Johnson holds a rather interesting place in the history of ethics as perhaps the best-known spokesman for this small movement of English moralists. Certain key aspects of his doctrine come to light through contrast with classical epicureanism and, even more especially, utilitarianism. The eighteenth-century doctrine was, first and foremost, strongly Christian. It really evolved as a means of showing man's absolute dependency on the law of Scripture and the rewards and punishments of the hereafter. It was, perhaps, Johnson's most consistent basis for defending the need for the Christian revelation. Yet 'Christian epicureanism' did not necessarily reject many of the central claims of 'natural law': Johnson was not primarily concerned to dispute the claim that virtue was 'immutable' or even that it possessed an intrinsic 'beauty', 'truth', or 'fitness'. His major

---

[46] See Mill, *Utilitarianism*, p. 18.
[47] Ibid., ch. 3, 'Of the Ultimate Sanction of the Principle of Utility'.

argument was that men were under no obligation to be virtuous unless the happiness promised by virtue outbalanced the temptations to vice. Since virtue, however understood, was not always the greatest happiness of this life, men depended absolutely on the prospect of a future existence.

2. *Free Will*

By aligning Johnson with Christian epicureanism we are directed towards some unexpected conclusions concerning his position on free will. Johnson has usually been seen as a strong supporter of the view that man is free. Yet his view that actions are necessarily founded on self-interest, that a man 'neither performs, nor forebears upon any other motive than the prospect, either of an immediate gratification, or a distant reward', was widely condemned by orthodox writers as deterministic. Neither Johnson, nor writers such as John Clarke or John Brown, would concede this charge; they adopted their own understanding of true freedom. Nevertheless, Johnson made no effort to disguise his links with a highly controversial view of the will. This is one issue on which he struck out against a position that was held by most orthodox Christians of his age.

The debate on free will centred on two questions. The first question, which I will discuss later in this section, concerned the possibility of freedom in a universe governed by inexorable physical laws (such as cause and effect) or by an omniscient creator who knew every action of every individual from the beginning of time. This was known as the issue of 'extrinsic' necessity. The second question concerned 'antecedent' necessity—whether individuals were motivated entirely by the desire for happiness, as Johnson believed, or by an independent faculty called the 'will'. Hobbes had incited a famous debate in the seventeenth century by arguing that the actions of an individual were determined entirely by 'the *last* opinion or *judgment* immediately preceding the *action*, concerning whether it be good to do or not'.[48] 'The last judgment of the understanding', which became a key phrase among advocates

---

[48] Thomas Hobbes, 'Of Liberty and Necessity' (1654), in *English Works*, ed. Sir William Molesworth (11 vols.; London, 1839; repr. Scientia Verlaag Aalen, 1962), iv. 268.

for Hobbes's position, meant the individual's perception of which course of action would best promote his own interests. Hobbes thought of the mind as a mechanism like a scale which balanced the possible advantage of alternative actions. 'The understanding of a convenience or inconvenience is the pressure of those weights', Hobbes explained, 'which incline him now one way, now another; and that inclination is the will.'[49]

It is easy to see how alike this is to Johnson's belief that man always acts for personal advantage. As Hobbes's major eighteenth-century advocate, Anthony Collins, wrote in *A Philosophical Inquiry Concerning Human Liberty* (1717): 'To suppose a sensible being capable of willing or preferring, or chusing (call it as you please) misery, and refusing good, is to deny it to be really sensible; for every Man, while he has his senses, aims at pleasure and happiness, and avoids pain and misery.'[50] Johnson seems to have agreed with Hobbes and Collins that self-interest could be the only source of human action. According to most orthodox writers of the seventeenth and early eighteenth century, this view imposed a dangerous restriction on human freedom by suggesting, it was thought, that a man had no choice but to follow strong temptations to vice. The rebuttal used in the most famous answer to Hobbes, Bishop John Bramhall's *A Defence of True Liberty from Antecedent and Extrinsecall Necessity* (1655), and later by the eighteenth century's foremost opponent to necessity, Samuel Clarke, was sometimes entitled 'the Doctrine of the self-determination Power of the Will'.[51] This doctrine postulated that the will was a faculty which operated with indifference to the relative advantage of alternative courses of action.

This position may seem rather distant from the real experience of human action, yet its advocates were able to point out that we are often forced to act without a clear opinion concerning the possible advantage of our choices. This is particularly true of trivial, domestic actions; a favourite example

---

[49] Hobbes, 'The Questions concerning Liberty, Necessity, and Chance, Clearly Stated and Debated' (1656), in *English Works*, v. 326.

[50] Anthony Collins, *A Philosophical Inquiry Concerning Human Liberty* (London, 1717), 42–3.

[51] This title, or variations on it, was used in eighteenth-century tracts on liberty such as anon., *An Essay on the Freedom of Will in God and in Creatures* (London, 1732), 56.

was the choice of which egg to eat for a meal. As Bramhall replied to Hobbes, 'I do not believe that a man is bound to weigh the expedience or inexpedience of every ordinary, triviall action to the least grain of the understanding.'[52] On this point, Johnson seems to have sided with Bramhall. We have already considered his rejection of the belief that an individual could always determine which moral choice would result in the greatest happiness for himself and others. And in Chapter 29 of *Rasselas* Nekayah makes an observation on daily experience which strongly recalls Bramhall's reply to Hobbes: 'how few can be supposed to act upon any occasions, whether small or great, with all the reasons of action present to their minds. Wretched would be the pair above all names of wretchedness, who should be doomed to adjust by reason every morning all the minute details of a domestic day.'[53] Since we often act without 'all the reasons of action' present to the understanding, it is difficult to conceive how we can form any 'judgement' concerning which action will lead to the greatest happiness. This, at least, was what Bramhall concluded on the basis of a similar observation on human experience.

Nor was this the only point of apparent agreement between Johnson and the opponents to Hobbes's doctrine of necessity. Bramhall and later advocates of his position also pointed out that men perform actions in *contradiction* to what they know is their best interest. For example, men often commit vices despite their conviction that only virtue can lead to ultimate happiness. This argument was summarized by the anonymous author of *An Essay on the Freedom of Will in God and in Creatures* (1732):

there are many Persons convinced that future Happiness pursued in a way of Piety and Virtue is really the greatest *natural* Good: this appears very plain to their *Understanding*, yet their Will chuses present Sensualities and vicious Pleasures, and pursues these in opposition to this greatest apparent Good, and the last Dictate of their Understanding about it.[54]

This was consistent with one of Johnson's most common observations on human conduct. He was convinced that only

[52] John Bramhall, *A Defence of True Liberty from Antecedent and Extrinsecall Necessity* (London, 1655), 182–3.
[53] *Rasselas*, p. 71.   [54] Anon., *Freedom of Will*, p. 19.

the 'grossly ignorant' did not know that 'a man may be very sincere in good principles, without having good practice'.[55] As he wrote in *Rambler*, No. 155:

Nothing surely can be more unworthy of a reasonable nature, than to continue in a state so opposite to real happiness, as that all the peace of solitude and felicity of meditation, must arise from resolutions of foresaking it. Yet the world will often afford examples of men, who pass months and years in a continual war with their own convictions, and are daily dragged by habit or betrayed by passion into practices, which they closed and opened their eyes with purposes to avoid; purposes which, though settled in conviction, the first impulse of momentary desire totally overthrows (v. 63).

We are confronted, therefore, with a peculiarity in the way Johnson treated the nature of the will. On the one hand, he asserted like Hobbes or Collins that the will was regulated entirely by self-interest. On the other hand, he agreed with Bramhall and other advocates for liberty that men very often act without clear reasons, or even in direct opposition to their 'last judgement' concerning the greatest good. Nevertheless, Johnson almost certainly did not concur with Bramhall that these admissions implied the existence of an independent faculty called the 'will'. As some recent scholarship has suggested, he was probably following the model of the will proposed in John Locke's chapter 'Of Power' in *An Essay Concerning Human Understanding* (1690).[56]

Locke had originally held Hobbes's position that the will was determined by the 'last judgment of the understanding', but he too was interested in the problem of why men often acted against their judgement of the greatest good. In the last edition of *An Essay Concerning Human Understanding*, therefore, he retreated from his original position and admitted that 'upon a stricter enquiry, I am forced to conclude, that *good*, the *greater good*, though apprehended and acknowledged to be so, does not determine the *will*, until our desire, raised proportionally to it, makes us *uneasy* in the want of it'.[57] This revision exposed

---

[55] *Life*, v. 259–60.

[56] See esp. C. L. Johnson, 'Samuel Johnson's Moral Psychology and Locke's "Of Power"', *SEL* 24 (1984), 563–82, which continues the discussion of Locke and Johnson on free will by P. K. Alkon, *Samuel Johnson and Moral Discipline* (Evanston, Ill., 1967), 80–3.

[57] Locke, *Human Understanding*, II, xxi, 253.

Locke to the charge of 'absolute Contradiction' from advocates for free will such as Samuel Strutt.[58] Locke had not, however, really abandoned his view that all actions were determined by the desire for happiness: his term 'uneasiness' only signified that the desire for good was based entirely in the passions, not in the judgement or understanding. He explained that the understanding was itself powerless to choose one action over another without giving the desire for an approved good sufficient force to overwhelm conflicting impulses towards forms of happiness known to be vicious or deluded. Because actions were the product not of reason, but of strong desires achieving superiority over weaker desires, a man might easily act against his convictions. Moreover, the performance of trivial actions did not require that we have 'reasons' for choosing one alternative rather than another.

Despite his links with Hobbes, Locke denied that he was propounding a doctrine of antecedent necessity. According to Locke, we possess a great deal of power over our acts: 'By a due consideration and examining any good proposed, it is in our power to raise our desires, in due proportion to the value of that good, whereby in its turn, and place, it may come to work upon the *will* and be pursued.'[59] Because the individual, according to Locke, did have this power to strengthen a chosen desire through contemplation, he claimed that men were, properly speaking, free, 'the very end of our Freedom being, that we may attain the good we chuse'.[60] It might be noted that Locke seems to have assumed the existence of some further power in the mind which, for example, can freely initiate the decision to contemplate or not to contemplate a course of action. As Collins suggested in *A Philosophical Inquiry Concerning Human Liberty*, Locke had not considered the true origin of volition, but only the connection, between the will and physical acts.[61] But this feature of Locke's argument was usually overlooked, and his position condemned as no less deterministic than Hobbes's. Just as Hobbes had portrayed the mind as a

[58] See Samuel Strutt, *A Defence of the Late Learned Dr. Clarke's Notion of Natural Liberty* (London, 1730), 46–7.

[59] Locke, *Human Understanding*, II, xxi, 262.

[60] Ibid. 264.

[61] See Collins, *Human Liberty*, p. 15. Collins criticized Locke's habit of regarding liberty as simply freedom from 'outward impediments'.

balance, an image later used by Samuel Clarke to describe
Leibniz's alleged determinism, Samuel Strutt argued that
Locke had made man 'as necessary as a Machine moved by
Weights and Ballances'.[62] So far as this charge aligned Locke
with those who generally agreed with Hobbes's understanding
of the will, it was reasonably accurate. Locke had not so much
broken with Hobbes as attempted to revise Hobbes's basic
notions in the light of the difficulties raised by Bramhall.

This is what makes Johnson's affinities with Locke's theory
of the will so interesting. Boswell seemed convinced that
Johnson was so deeply disturbed by the case for necessity that
he was unwilling to face the question squarely.[63] This inference
has led to some modern conjectures on Johnson's secret
agreement with Hobbes.[64] But, in fact, Johnson's writings
almost invite comparison between his view of the mind and, as
it was widely thought, the mechanical and deterministic view of
Hobbes and Locke. In *Rambler*, No. 7, for example, he
described the will with a metaphor widely associated with
determinism: 'the balance is put into our own hands, and we
have power to transfer the weight to either side' (iii. 39).
According to this essay, action derived not from an
independent faculty of will, but from the proportionate
strength or weakness of desires which, as Locke had urged,
could be adjusted through contemplation and other religious
exercises:

The great art therefore of piety, and the end for which all the rites of
religion seem to be instituted, is the perpetual renovation of the
motives to virtue, by a voluntary employment of our mind in the
contemplation of its excellence, its importance, and its necessity,
which, in proportion as they are more frequently and more willingly
revolved, gain a more forcible and permanent influence, 'till in time
they become the reigning ideas, the standing principles of action, and
the test by which every thing proposed to the judgment is rejected or
approved (iii. 40).

Johnson was, more often than not, the very embodiment of
conservative orthodox doctrine, a writer who was usually

---

[62] Strutt, *Defence of Clarke*, p. 45. See Samuel Clarke and Gottfried von Leibniz, *A Collection of Papers Relating to the Principles of Natural Philosophy and Religion* (London, 1717), 121.   [63] See *Life*, ii. 104.
[64] See Chapin, *Religious Thought*, pp. 115–16; Pierce, *Religious Life*, pp. 39–42.

willing to defend the approved position of the Church against all theories which might compromise moral responsibility or religious conviction. Indeed, when repeatedly pressed by Boswell on the issue of free will, Johnson told him to read Bramhall and Samuel Clarke.[65] But evidence suggests that Johnson himself did not agree with these advocates for a full and unrestrained liberty. His view of the will was essentially that of Hobbes, probably as revised by Locke. It was a view which, it should be noted, departed from the traditional understanding of moral conduct as a simple conflict between the reason and the passions: virtue did not, strictly speaking, consist of raising the reason or judgement into a position of control over wayward desires, but of strengthening or weakening the desires themselves in accordance with some reasonable objective.

This was Johnson's position on the issue of 'antecedent necessity'—whether human actions were determined entirely by self-interested judgements and affections. The importance of this issue lay partly in its connection with the question of 'extrinsic necessity'—that is, the possibility of human freedom in a universe ruled by inexorable physical laws or God's omnipotent decree. Our consideration of 'extrinsic necessity' is complicated by the similarities between the philosophical treatment of this problem and the theological issue of predestination. In the Reformation both Calvin and Arminius were concerned to keep the debate on predestination focused on Scripture, as free as possible from the philosophical arguments for necessity. But the distinction was sometimes difficult to preserve. In the eighteenth century natural and revealed religion became so intertwined that the distinction threatened to disappear completely. Consider, for example, Augustus Toplady's sermon, 'The Doctrine of Absolute Predestination Stated and Asserted' (1775). Toplady noted that it had 'been not unusual with the Arminian writers to tax us with adopting the fate of the ancient Stoics'. The stoics were usually regarded as the founders of the philosophical case for necessity, but Toplady made no objection to being called 'stoic' on account of his Calvinism: 'I frankly confess that, as far as the coincidence

[65] See *Life*, ii. 104.

of the Stoical fate with the Bible predestination holds good; I see no reason why we should be ashamed to acknowledge it.'[66]

In fact, there are important differences between necessity and Calvinism, and we are under some obligation to keep this distinction much clearer than was often the case in the eighteenth century. Our full discussion of Calvinism will be deferred until we consider the doctrinal controversy on original sin and grace, since predestination is most easily, and best approached by way of these doctrines. Nevertheless, it is useful to keep in mind that Johnson's arguments against philosophical necessity could and, in the eighteenth century, often were used against predestination.

In philosophical writings on the Divine attributes, it was debated whether God's omniscience implied that all human actions had been predetermined from the beginning of time. According to Leibniz, for example, all human actions must occur in their present form in order to actualize the best possible universe as selected by God. Though this universe is not itself 'necessary', for it is only one of infinite possibilities, its choice must determine all events and actions that occur within it.[67] Opponents to Leibniz, such as Samuel Clarke, retorted that God had only foreseen actions and events that were in themselves contingent.[68] In order to make sense of this notion, however, they were forced to turn to somewhat whimsical speculations on the Divine attributes. In *A Discourse Concerning the Being and Attributes of God* (1705), Clarke argued that Divine foreknowledge possibly represented God's perfection of mankind's familiar capacity to predict how an individual will behave under given conditions. As Chester F. Chapin noted, Johnson mused on the same possibility in a discussion recorded by Boswell.[69] This argument exemplifies a tendency among many orthodox writers, including Johnson, to view God anthropomorphically as an 'infinitely wise' legislator

[66] Augustus Toplady, *Works* (London, 1853), 688.

[67] Leibniz's views on liberty are problematical, because he denied that he was imposing a doctrine of 'necessity'. Nevertheless, it seems justifiable to call his philosophy 'deterministic'. See C. D. Broad, *Leibniz: An Introduction*, ed. C. Levy (Cambridge, 1975), 29.

[68] See Clarke, *Being and Attributes of God*, pp. 108–9. This approach was later taken by William Wollaston, *The Religion of Nature Delineated* (1722) (5th edn.; London, 1726), 100–1.

[69] See *Life*, iii. 291; Chapin, *Religious Thought*, p. 114.

whose attributes could be discerned in an imperfect form among human beings. A writer for necessity might complain that this analogy is of no relevance to an omniscient Being, for there can be no 'prediction' when a result is already known.

Discussions of how the physical laws of the universe affect human freedom belonged to a philosophical tradition dating back to the stoics (though this issue began to infiltrate eighteenth-century discussions of Calvinism). As usually stated, the philosophical argument for necessity took advantage of the reasoning for a First Cause, a major basis of orthodox demonstrations for the existence of God. Although Hume would demonstrate the weakness of this reasoning in *A Treatise of Human Nature* (1739), it had been traditionally assumed that effects were determined absolutely by their causes. All the effects of the First Cause, therefore, followed *necessarily* in a great chain which linked all the events of the universe. We will recall that the argument for antecedent necessity postulated that the human will could not arbitrarily initiate a course of action; action was determined without exception by the individual's perception of the greater good or, alternatively, by some 'uneasiness' concerning the absence of some good. Since the external world was responsible for all impressions on the senses and the appetites, it exerted a direct causal influence on the preferences which regulated the will. The will was therefore caught up in and determined by the chain of causes and effects that followed necessarily from the First Cause. It was partly for this reason that advocates for liberty were so concerned to demonstrate that the will was independent and self-determining. This freed human motives from the necessity imposed by the physical law of cause and effect.

This summary also suggests why epicureanism had been condemned by Cudworth and others as not only atheistic, but also fatalistic. As we have seen, Johnson accepted the epicurean thesis that human choices were determined entirely by self-interest. He also held traditional notions on the relationship between cause and effect, and the validity of this relationship as a basis for proving the existence of a First Cause. How, then, could he avoid acknowledging the validity of the philosophical arguments for necessity? It is not too unfair, I think, to suggest that his objections to necessity were

largely practical rather than philosophical: he was concerned
that belief in necessity would destroy the incentives to virtuous
conduct by dictating that an individual could not have avoided
committing vice. If no actions were truly free, it would be of no
purpose to blame men for their wickedness. Although these
considerations really had nothing to do with the philosophical
issue, they were arguably the mainstay of the orthodox case
against the large number of free-thinking authors—Hobbes,
Bayle, Collins—who openly espoused the logic of determinism.

In *An Essay Concerning Liberty, Grace, and Prescience* (1729), for
example, Samuel Fancourt warned of 'the innumerable
temporal advantages that particular persons, private families,
or more publick societies may lose; or the temporal evils they
may suffer, by the unvirtuous activity, or vicious compliances,
which the belief of such a mechanick, passive principle, as the
want of liberty in the creature, may introduce into the rational
world'.[70] It is worth noting that Fancourt levelled this charge
against both deterministic philosophers and Calvinists, whom
he felt were equally guilty of diminishing moral responsibility.
In *Rambler*, No. 113, a similar concern causes Hymenaeus to end
his courtship with Misothea when she 'endeavoured to demonstrate the folly of attributing choice and self-direction to any
human being':

> It was not difficult to discover the danger of committing myself for
> ever to the arms of one who might at any time mistake the dictates of
> passion, or the calls of appetite, for the decree of fate; or consider
> cuckoldom as necessary to the general system, as a link in the ever-
> lasting chain of successive causes. I therefore told her, that destiny
> had ordained us to part; and that nothing should have torn me from
> her but the talons of necessity (iv. 239).

Hymenaeus expresses the gist of the philosophical argument
for necessity which we have just summarized. The passage
undoubtedly reflects a real concern on Johnson's part that men
could use determinism to justify their vicious actions. Yet we
might also notice something else. It is significant that Johnson
makes one of his very few written comments on philosophical
necessity through a fictional correspondent in a ludicrous tale

---

[70] Samuel Fancourt, *An Essay Concerning Liberty, Grace, and Prescience* (London,
1729), 31.

on marriage. *Rambler*, No. 113, suggests, despite the seriousness of the debate on liberty, that there was something absurd about this issue as well.

Hymenaeus' ironic apology for parting with Misothea recalls an anecdote from the stoic philosopher Zeno which Bishop Bramhall had cited against Hobbes, and which was reiterated in many subsequent attacks on determinism. A servant, recalled Bramhall, 'had committed some petty larceny, and the master cudgelling him well for it; The servent [*sic*] thinks to creep under his master's blind-side, and pleads for him; That *the necessity of destiny did compell him to steal*. The master answers, *the same necessity of destiny compells me to beat thee*.'[71] The joke for both Hymenaeus and Zeno's master was that belief in the doctrine of necessity really made no difference to their own decision to act as they wished: the claim of 'destiny' could be attributed to any action and was of no relevance to the experience of choosing freely. Indeed, this type of observation strongly influenced the way most eighteenth-century opponents to determinism treated this issue. Although there was some fear that the doctrine of necessity might compromise the belief that men were responsible for their acts, it was also felt that every man was fully convinced that he was free to act as he chose, regardless of all the philosophical proofs for determinism.

There was, in other words, an unbridgeable gap between the experience of free agency and the *a priori* evidence that human acts were necessitated. This contradiction between experience and speculation led to many different conclusions. For some writers it represented a major dilemma that blocked further progress in this area of philosophy. John Locke, for instance, admitted in a famous letter to Molyneux that he could not reconcile his assent to the philosophical proofs for necessity with his firm empirical conviction that he was free.[72] Other writers such as Bramhall and Samuel Clarke tried to use the experience of free will as at least a partial demonstration

---

[71] See Bramhall, *True Liberty*, p. 88. This anecdote is also cited by Henry Grove as a part of his defence of free will in *A System of Moral Philosophy* (2 vols.; London, 1749), i. 184.

[72] 20 Jan. 1693, in *The Correspondence of John Locke*, ed. E. S. de Beer (8 vols.; Oxford, 1979), iv. 625–6.

against philosophical determinism. As Clarke wrote in answer to Anthony Collins:

All our Actions do Now in experience *Seem* to us to be *Free*, exactly in the *Same Manner*, as they *would* do upon *supposition* of our being really *Free* Agents: And consequently, though This alone does not indeed amount to a *strict Demonstration* of our being Free; yet it leaves on the other side of the Question nothing but a *bare Possibility* of our being so framed by the Author of Nature, as to be unavoidably deceived in the matter by every experience of every Action we perform.[73]

The proponents of determinism were not always very successful in their attempts to counter this argument. In *Essays on the Principles of Morality and Natural Religion* (1751), for example, Lord Kames attempted to solve a theological difficulty raised by Clarke's argument—why a benevolent God would deceive his creatures with the false experience of liberty. Kames explained that God had permitted the delusion of free will in order that men would not give up, and submit to their vicious appetites.[74] In *Thoughts upon Necessity* (1774) John Wesley easily showed that Kames had been led into a contradiction, for the need of such a delusion implied the possibility of free choice.[75]

A rather more acute reasoner, Anthony Collins, pointed out a contradiction in the orthodox reliance on the experience of free will. On the one hand, Collins argued, the advocates of free will appealed to the 'vulgar experience' of liberty, yet 'inconsistently therewith, contradict the vulgar experience by owning it to be an *intricate matter*, and treating it after an intricate manner'.[76] Collins's objection was particularly relevant to writers such as Bramhall and Clarke, who combined a confidence in the common sensation of free will with much

[73] Samuel Clarke, *Remarks upon a Late Book, Entituled, A Philosophical Enquiry Concerning Human Liberty* (London, 1717), 19–20. See Bramhall, *True Liberty*, p. 194.

[74] See Henry Home, Lord Kames, *Essays on the Principles of Morality and Natural Religion* (Edinburgh, 1751), 206–7.

[75] John Wesley, *Works* (14 vols.; London, 1830), x. 465–6.

[76] Collins, *Human Liberty*, p. 30. According to Collins, experience actually teaches that we cannot act without motives, which would tend to substantiate the view of the will also held by Johnson. Hume's essay 'Of Liberty and Necessity', published in *An Enquiry Concerning Human Understanding* (1748), also points out that 'however we may imagine that we feel liberty within ourselves, a spectator can commonly infer our actions from our motives and character'. We customarily assume that all human action is the product of some motive or cause, and is to a large degree predictable and controllable for that reason. See Hume, *Philosophical Works*, iv. 77 n. 1.

abstract theorizing designed to offset the objections of determinism. If the reality of free-will was so obvious, why did these writers resort to such convoluted reasoning to prove their case? Collins's argument was, however, less relevant to later advocates for free will, who largely abandoned the effort to counter the philosophical case for determinism with theorizing of their own. Late in the century, for example, Scottish 'common-sense' philosophers such as Reid and Beattie relied on the common experience of free will as an actual proof which outweighed all speculative reasonings, no matter how plausible.[77] This way of thinking takes us back to Tillotson's *Discourse against Transubstantiation*. And more generally, there was a feeling among many prominent divines that the debate on free will had reached a stalemate, would yield no fresh insights of any value, and was besides not very relevant to the moral and social issues which really mattered. As Joseph Butler remarked in his 1736 *Analogy of Religion*, 'though it were admitted that this Opinion of Necessity were speculatively true, yet, with regard to Practice it is as if it were false'.[78] Perhaps as the result of this opinion, there was extremely little written on free will by orthodox writers between Clarke at the beginning of the century and Wesley in the 1770s. Even Hume admitted in his excellent essay 'Of Liberty and Necessity' that the issue had fallen victim to 'obscure sophistry', and that 'it is no wonder if a sensible reader indulge his ease so far as to turn a deaf ear to the proposal of such a question from which he can expect neither instruction nor entertainment'.[79]

Among those who, in effect, turned a deaf ear to further speculation on this topic was Samuel Johnson. Johnson relied entirely on the 'vulgar experience' of freedom, and seemed intolerant of all theorizing: 'Sir . . . we *know* our will is free, and *there's* an end on't.'[80] Johnson's irritable rebuttals to

[77] For a detailed discussion of Johnson's affinities with Reid and Beattie, see C. F. Chapin, 'Samuel Johnson and the Scottish Common-sense School', *Eighteenth Century: Theory and Interpretation*, 20 (1979), 50–64. It should be noted that many of the principles expounded by these writers, including their views on free will, had long been used by philosophers whom we know Johnson read and admired. The common-sense philosophers capped an increasing tendency in British philosophy to move away from speculative reasoning and towards a stubborn faith in common experience. See ch. 1, sec. 1, above.

[78] Butler, *Analogy*, I, iv, 109.

[79] Hume, *Philosophical Works*, iv. 66.

[80] *Life*, iii. 82.

Boswell's proddings on the question of necessity have often been regarded as 'poetry, rather than proof',[81] an example of his colourful and quotable disdain for philosophic method. As so often, however, his conversation really expressed attitudes commonly held by orthodox writers throughout the first half of the century. What he persistently indicated to Boswell was that the question of free will presented an insoluble contradiction between experience and speculation. As he told Boswell in 1778, 'All theory is against the freedom of the will; all experience for it.'[82] This statement has strengthened the belief of some critics that Johnson secretly, and fearfully, recognized that he could not refute Hobbes's determinism. But if the most common attitude of orthodox writers can be used as a measure for Johnson's views, he felt only that Hobbes's case for necessity, no matter how sound it was in theory, held at best limited relevance to the practical matters of life. So long as men believed that they were morally accountable for their actions, he was not preoccupied with refuting every possible restriction on human liberty. Clearly he did not feel that moral responsibility was threatened by admitting that passions worked on the will like weights on a balance. And, like many others, he thought that the best demonstrations for the doctrine of necessity would never dissuade men that they could act as they chose.

The attitude exemplified by Johnson suggests again that 'the Age of Reason' was on the wane by mid-century, even among orthodox writers. In their debates on the question of free will, reason had failed orthodox writers; even by their own admission, they had been unable to make determinism appear entirely illogical. The 'common sense' which became the new mainstay of orthodoxy was, as William Law complained in 1739, often a more acceptable term for 'vulgar Prejudice':[83] the conventional assumptions and valued beliefs of eighteenth-century society had achieved the status of inviolable truth. More charitably, Johnson and his orthodox contemporaries

---

[81] B.Willey, *The English Moralists* (London, 1964), 177.

[82] *Life*, iii. 291.

[83] William Law, *Animadversions on Dr. Trapp's Late Reply* (1739), in *Works* (9 vols.; London, 1762; repr. Setley, Hants., 1892-3), vi. 181-2. This work was part of Law's exchange of pamphlets with Joseph Trapp on the issue of Christian perfection. See ch. 7, sec. 1, below.

showed a refreshing determination to keep philosophy in touch with the world of the living. While we might be forgiven for responding with irritation to Johnson's blustering illogic on the issue of free will, modern criticism has found reason to admire his intolerance of abstract speculation on other issues. It is, for example, easy to understand his impatience with the whimsical systems which some writers used to make sense of worldly affliction. As we shall see in the next chapter, Johnson's hostility to these theodicies was widely shared by other orthodox moralists and theologians.

4

Suffering and the Universal Order

1. *The Correspondence between Vice and Suffering*

Central to Johnson's ethical thought was the belief that the virtuous could have no assurance that they would be happy in this world. Since he rejected the view that men were obliged to choose virtue for its own sake, the preservation of moral conduct was dependent on the prospect of rewards and punishments in the hereafter. And even those who believed that men were obliged to choose virtue for its own sake, such as Samuel Clarke, acknowledged that virtuous men could not be expected to withstand sufferings and sacrifice without the incentive of future recompense. This, Clarke argued, was 'the Errour of the *Stoicks*', whose terminology of the 'fitness' and 'relation of things' he none the less adopted.[1] Needless to say, Clarke's position is very confusing: how can we be 'obliged' to perform acts for their own sake when we cannot be expected to perform them without future recompense? However we make sense of this, neither Clarke nor the many divines who admired his philosophy were under the delusion that virtue was a sure means to present happiness.

There was, however, a group of moralists who argued that virtue was the certain means to happiness in this world, and that the rewards and punishments of Christianity were, for this reason, unnecessary to support morality. Despite what is often assumed concerning the fatuous optimism of eighteenth-century thought, this group was really quite small. As Philip Skelton remarked in 1748, Lord Shaftesbury was considered singular in his efforts 'to strike out, and establish, a new system of morality, unhappily founded on a notorious falsehood' that the virtuous were always content, 'for good men are often miserable in this world, and bad men triumphant'.[2] Later in the century Lord Bolingbroke contended that the virtuous were as happy in this world as they could ever expect to be, and called

---

[1] Clarke, *Natural Religion*, p. 117.
[2] Skelton, *Ophiomaches*, i. 173. See Shaftesbury, *Characteristics*, i. 336.

orthodox writers 'grossly absurd, and much more impious than HOBBES' for claiming that God required a future state of compensation to vindicate his justice.[3] Against 'the doctrine which CLARKE and other divines teach',[4] Bolingbroke asserted that 'God has given us the desire of happiness, and the means of attaining it'.[5] He appealed to the 'numerous and unanswerable proofs, which are to be found in the writings of natural philosophers', who had done more service to religion than 'divines and atheists in confederacy have done it hurt'.[6]

It is likely that Bolingbroke and Shaftesbury were among Johnson's principal targets of the discourse of the natural philosopher in *Rasselas*, Chapter 22. Despite what has been conventionally observed about this satirical portrait, his target was almost certainly not Samuel Clarke, who was widely known to oppose the position which the natural philosopher expounds— that, by following 'nature' or any rule of secular morality, men could be assured of present happiness. But Johnson's attacks on this belief lead to a difficulty in understanding his treatment of another great problem of religion and philosophy. While it was advantageous that all men believe in the necessity of Christianity to sustain virtue, the worldly suffering of the virtuous was difficult to reconcile with an orthodox confidence in a just and benevolent God. As the result of this problem, Johnson and many contemporaries drifted towards yet another inconsistency.

On the one hand, Johnson ridiculed the position of Shaftesbury and Bolingbroke that the virtuous were always content. But when it was useful to exonerate God of blame for present suffering, he adopted a position very similar to theirs, arguing that only the vicious were truly and consistently afflicted. The following passage in Sermon 5, for instance, seems to come close to upholding the belief that virtue and happiness are inseparably linked even in this world:

religion shews us that physical and moral evil entered the world together, and reason and experience assure us that they continue for the most part so closely united, that, to avoid misery, we must avoid

---

[3] Bolingbroke, *Works*, v. 79.
[4] Ibid. 77.
[5] Ibid. 112.
[6] iv. 328-9.

sin, and that while it is in our power to be virtuous, it is in our power to be happy, at least to be happy to such a degree as may have little room for murmur and complaints (xiv. 55).

In his book *Samuel Johnson and the Problem of Evil* Richard B. Schwartz identified this as the explanation for temporal misery advanced by most orthodox writers since the seventeenth century.[7] It fulfilled a major objective of any theodicy by shifting the blame for suffering away from God, in this case by making man solely responsible for his misery. But it was increasingly acknowledged in the eighteenth century that the problem could not be resolved so easily. Johnson's simple connection between vice and suffering is consistent neither with real life nor with his numerous and characteristic statements—in 'The Vanity of Human Wishes' (1749), the review of Jenyns's *Free Inquiry, Rasselas*—on the apparently indiscriminate distribution of pain and affliction. Moreover, it was not only plainly inaccurate to claim that only the vicious suffered, but such a doctrine could be used to support some highly uncharitable inferences concerning the moral character of the afflicted.

The supposed correspondence between vice and suffering was related to the idea of 'natural punishments'. A long tradition of philosophers, including Hobbes and Hooker, had distinguished between legal and 'natural' punishment, the suffering which regularly followed vice and intemperance in the natural course of events.[8] As the term 'punishment' was used in Joseph Butler's *The Analogy of Religion, Natural and Revealed* (1736), it meant that wicked men should be warned by their suffering in this world of analogous wages for sin in the next. 'The natural Consequences of Vice in this Life', Butler explained, 'are doubtless to be considered as judicial Punishments inflicted by God; so likewise, for aught we know, the judicial Punishments of the future Life, may be in a like Way or a like Sense, the natural Consequence of Vice.'[9] In Sermon 16 Johnson similarly depicted the suffering which often attended a vicious or intemperate life as a 'punishment' (xiv. 174).

[7] Schwartz, pp. 23–7.
[8] See Hobbes, *Leviathan* (1651), II, xxxi, in *English Works*, iii. 356–7; Sir Richard Hooker, *Ecclesiastical Policy* (1593), I, ix, in *Works*, ed. John Keble (7th edn.; Oxford, 1888), i. 237.
[9] Butler, *Analogy*, I, iv, 70–6.

According to both Johnson and Butler, life was a state of 'trial' or 'probation' in which men should see by the tendency of vice to suffering in this world that the vicious would also be punished in the next.

The idea of suffering as a 'punishment' for vice could also, however, be used in a slightly different way. Especially in the heated sectarian polemics of the Restoration it was not unusual to characterize affliction as a Providential judgement on religious and political enemies. Robert South, an Oxford divine who (though a former Presbyterian) displayed a virulent hatred of Puritans, suggested that 'Providence, where it loves a Nation, concerns itself to own, and assert the interest of Religion, by blasting the spoilers of Religious Persons and Places.'[10] South went on to cite the dismal fate of numerous Puritans who had desecrated Anglican churches. This type of reasoning remained sufficiently prevalent that some English writers proclaimed that the 1755 Lisbon earthquake, a disaster of almost unheard of proportions, was a mark of God's displeasure with the Papists. The most prominent of these writers was John Wesley. In *Serious Thoughts Occasioned by the Late Earthquake at Lisbon* (1755) Wesley strongly suggested the possibility that the earthquake represented Divine retribution for the sins of the Inquisition:

And what shall we say of the late accounts from Portugal? That some thousand houses, and many thousand persons, are no more! that a fair city is now in ruinous heaps! Is there indeed a God that judges the world? And is he now making inquisition for blood? If so, it is not surprising, he should begin there, where so much blood has been poured on the ground like water! where so many have been murdered, in the most base and cowardly as well as barbarous manner, almost every day, as well as every night, while none regarded or laid it to heart.[11]

Although Wesley's position does seem extremely uncharitable to the Portuguese, we will see that he had good theological reasons for interpreting the earthquake in this way. Methodism revived a belief that was greatly weakened in the main Anglican Church—the belief in the closeness of God as an active

---

[10] Robert South, 'A Sermon Preached at the Consecration of a Chapel, 1667', in *Sermons Preached upon Several Occasions* (11 vols.; London, 1737–44), i. 343.

[11] Wesley, *Works* (1830), xi. 1–2.

participant in the events of the world and in the personal trials of each individual.

Largely for humanitarian reasons, most Anglican divines of the 1750s strongly rejected the view that the earthquake was a judgement on the special sins of the Portuguese. Among the numerous pamphleteers was Johnson's friend, Canon Thomas Seward of Lichfield. In a 1755 sermon on the Lisbon earthquake Seward cited the prophecy of Isaiah 53: 3 that Christ Himself would be 'a *Man of Sorrows* and *acquainted with Grief*. . . . [We] shall ill have learned of *Christ* ourselves, if after this, we interpret the *Misfortunes* of any to be Proofs of their *Guilt* or of our own *comparative Virtues.*'[12] The Lisbon earthquake provided a forum for the increasing dissatisfaction with a view of suffering that, by imputing all misfortune to vice or Divine vengeance, blocked charity and increased complacency with one's own virtues and favour with God.[13] Two years before Seward's sermon, Johnson had instructed in *Adventurer*, No. 120, that afflictions 'are no particular mark of divine displeasure; since all the distresses of persecution have been suffered by those, "of whom the world was not worthy;" and the Redeemer of mankind himself was "a man of sorrows and acquainted with grief" ' (ii. 470–1).

These writers characterized the Lisbon earthquake neither as a 'natural punishment' nor as a sign of God's direct judgement on human affairs. While it is refreshing to see such an outburst of charity, this response also had some serious theological disadvantages. Not only was there nothing 'just' about the suffering caused by the earthquake, but Anglican divines seemed determined to remove God as far as possible from the event. He was blameless, but also entirely inactive and, perhaps, uncaring.

This understanding of God had been evolving since the seventeenth century. In order to explain the existence of moral evil, divines agreed that God 'permitted' vices to flourish without retribution in order to preserve free will. If God

---

[12] Thomas Seward, *The Late Dreadful Earthquake no Proof of God's Particular Wrath against the Portuguese: A Sermon Preached at Lichfield, Sunday, December 7, 1755* (London, 1756), 12.

[13] Previous writers who inveighed against the practice of treating affliction as a sign of God's displeasure include Tillotson in his sermons 'Of Judgment', and Addison in *Spectator*, No. 483.

intervened to stop men from sinning, they would be reduced to, many writers urged, 'mere Machines'.[14] As Johnson told Boswell, 'With all the evil there is, there is no man but would rather be a free agent, than a mere machine without the evil.'[15] The same contention, that the vicious were allowed to succeed in this world in order to preserve free agency, was also used to explain why God never seemed to intervene in order to rescue good and religious men from natural or accidental calamities. The best-known statement of this argument was by William Wollaston in *The Religion of Nature Delineated* (1722):

As to the *course of nature*, if a *good* man be passing by an infirm building, just in the article of falling, can it be expected, that God should *suspend* the force of gravitation till he is gone by, in order to his deliverance? . . . In short, may we expect *miracles*: or can there be a particular providence, a providence that suits the *several cases* and prayers of individuals, without a continual *repetition* of them, and force *frequently* committed upon the laws of nature, and the freedom of intelligent agents?[16]

Wollaston's argument served to justify God's failure to protect innocent men from suffering, but it also raised some difficulties for orthodox writers. The doctrine of 'particular providences' which Wollaston questioned was a major support for a number of important Anglican beliefs. As opposed to God's 'general providence'—the universal plan originally established by God—'particular providences' manifested God's willingness to interrupt the natural courses of events in order to benefit mankind or an individual. Though particular providences were difficult to reconcile with belief in Divine omniscience (surely each particular providence had always been part of God's eternal plan), we have already seen that the evidence for the Christian miracles relied on the assumption that God would interrupt the order of nature to enlighten the world. The revelation was itself evidence of God's 'particular providence'.

[14] See, e.g. John Clarke, *An Enquiry into the Cause and Origin of Evil* (London, 1720), 75. This John Clarke (1682–1757), brother of Samuel Clarke and one time Dean of Salisbury, should be distinguished from John Clarke (1687–1734), the schoolmaster of Hull who revived epicurean ideas on moral obligation. See also Johnson's translation of Jean-Pierre Crousaz, *A Commentary on Mr. Pope's Essay on Man* (London, 1739), 224–5.

[15] *Life*, v. 117.

[16] Wollaston, *The Religion of Nature Delineated*, p. 99.

Moreover, particular providences were necessary to demonstrate the usefulness of prayer: why beseech God for a favour which He would never interrupt the course of nature to bestow?

For these reasons, attacks on the doctrine of particular providences by Hume, Thomas Chubb, John Hawkesworth, and others were diligently resisted.[17] While orthodox writers were sympathetic to Wollaston's attempt to justify the ways of God, they could not deny the possibility of a particular providence. They could only deny that God *ordinarily* interfered to correct the iniquities and undeserved afflictions of mankind. As Johnson wrote in Sermon 5:

God may indeed, by special acts of providence, sometimes hinder the designs of bad men from being successfully executed, or the execution of them from producing such consequences as it naturally tends to; but this, whenever it is done, is a real, though not always a visible miracle, and is not to be expected in the ordinary occurrences of life, or the common transactions of the world (xiv. 57).

By telling men that they could not expect God to hinder worldly affliction, orthodox divines painted a rather comfortless picture of the universe. All for the sake of free will, bad men succeeded, good men suffered, and cities were destroyed by earthquakes while God refused to interfere. Moreover, the Lisbon earthquake and similar natural disasters cast doubt on the regularity and justice of God's general plan for the universe. The 'laws of nature' did not appear to embody an ordered and beneficent scheme of creation, but instead consisted of random physical forces established but not controlled by God.

This implication was stated by Thomas Alcock in a sermon on the Lisbon earthquake. Alcock urged that the earthquake was not a sign of Divine vengeance, since 'These Misfortunes or Calamities very often arise from the generally established Laws of Nature,—they are what must happen in the necessary Course of Things—are natural Effects of plain and natural

---

[17] See Hume, 'Of a Particular Providence and of a Future State' (1748), in *Philosophical Works*, iv; Thomas Chubb, *A Short Dissertation on Providence*, added to *The True Gospel of Jesus Christ Asserted* (1738); J. L. Abbot, *John Hawkesworth: Eighteenth-century Man of Letters* (Madison, Wis., 1982), 164–7.

Causes.'[18] He went on to use the example that 'Buildings . . . consisting chiefly of Wood abounding with an oily sulphurous Principle or Resin, are composed of very combustible Materials', and, for that reason only, liable to catch fire.[19] In Sermon 5 Johnson also suggested that man was often the victim of indifferent natural forces, and used the same example of combustible building materials. Man, he wrote, 'was created susceptible of pain, but not necessarily subjected to that particular injury which he now feels, and he is therefore not to charge God with his afflictions. The materials for building are naturally combustible, but when a city is fired by incendiaries, God is not the authour of its destruction' (xiv. 57). Newton had demonstrated the wonderful regularity of the physical laws which governed creation, inspiring the vision of a 'clockwork universe' which, among some writers, persisted throughout the century. In 1751, for example, Lord Kames asserted that 'this universe is a vast machine, wound up and set a going'. Everything in the universe occurs with the perfect regularity intended by God: 'The hand advances, and the clock strikes, precisely as the artist has determined.'[20] Alcock and Johnson represented a large group of writers who basically rejected this vision, suggesting that the physical forces of the universe were far less regular than clockwork, and did not always act to the benefit of man. By admitting that the physical world possessed certain properties which might accidentally cause harm, orthodox writers could, like Alcock, justify compassion for the victims of a natural disaster, or, like Johnson, relieve God of responsibility for the afflictions of the innocent. But such a vision of the universe was not comforting, and in fact contradicted the belief in God's care and supervision of His creation. Indeed, this view was dangerously close to the materialistic doctrines of atheism.

This partly explains why Wesley insisted on the possibility that the Lisbon earthquake represented a direct judgement by God. Wesley attacked Kames's notion of the universe as a great 'machine' in *A Thought on Necessity* (1774), giving vent to the antagonism felt by many Christians towards a

---

[18] Thomas Alcock, *A Sermon on the Late Earthquakes* (Oxford, 1756), 10.
[19] Ibid. 11.
[20] Kames, *Essays*, p. 188.

theory which, by reducing man to a 'cog' in this mechanism, deprived him of free will. In *Serious Thoughts Occasioned by the Late Earthquake at Lisbon*, however, Wesley censured the position which had gained favour among the orthodox divines themselves—that 'these afflictive incidents entirely depend on the fortuitous concourse and agency of blind material causes'. Even if Wesley's own view of the earthquake was uncharitable, surely the more 'humane' view left mankind in a dismal and helpless state. If disasters were simply the effect of natural forces, then whom could men 'hope to appease? . . . Shall they intreat the famine or the pestilence to show mercy?'[21] The conventional response to the earthquake deprived man of a caring, active Deity:

But if our own wisdom and strength be not sufficient to defend us, let us not be ashamed to seek farther help. Let us even dare to own that we believe there is a God; nay, and not a lazy, indolent, epicurean deity, who sits at ease upon the circle of the heavens, and neither knows nor cares what is done below; but one who, as he created heaven and earth, and all the armies of them, as he sustains them all by the aid of his power, so cannot neglect the work of his own hands.[22]

Wesley's reference to the 'lazy, indolent, epicurean deity' reveals a significant irony in the position of contemporary Anglicans. Epicurus argued that the universe, including mankind, was comprised entirely of atoms flung into their present shape by random forces; he denied that we could attribute human qualities to the gods (if they indeed existed at all), or assume that they had any direct influence on human affairs. Although Epicurus' ethical doctrine gained new favour among some Christian moralists, this materialism and denial of providence continued to be condemned as atheistical. Epicurus was the major target of anti-atheistical tomes such as Cudworth's *True Intellectual System of the Universe* (1678); Hume and Bolingbroke were condemned for reviving some of Epicurus' notions in a new form. Yet Wesley did not need to exaggerate very much to accuse contemporary Anglicans of supporting a basically epicurean understanding of God and the physical universe.

[21] Wesley, *Works* (1830), xi. 7.
[22] Ibid. 10.

What this charge revealed was a serious dilemma raised by the conflicting objectives of orthodox theodicies. As we shall see in the next section, orthodox writers *did* wish to maintain the consoling belief that God governed the universe, but this objective was easily forgotten in their efforts to exonerate God from blame for suffering. Perhaps because he wished to avoid this dilemma, Johnson did not attempt really detailed explanations of disasters which were purely environmental or accidental. It was far easier to treat all calamities as if they were the responsibility of wicked men—the 'incendiaries' mentioned in Sermon 5. This view did not make the innocent man any less prone to evils he could not immediately prevent, but it did, at least, reaffirm some ultimate connection between vice and suffering. Men did not always suffer because they were personally guilty of any crime, but because they were victims of a corrupt society. This position also offered some potential solution to this injustice. If the world were perfectly reformed, all men would be as happy as they deserved.

Orthodox theodicies frequently deferred a just distribution of happiness and suffering to an ideal state in which all men were perfectly virtuous. 'Let us return to the Earth our Habitation,' Joseph Butler wrote in *Analogy of Religion*; 'and we shall see this happy Tendency of Virtue, by imagining an Instance not so vast and remote: by supposing a Kingdom or Society of Men upon it, perfectly virtuous, for a Succession of many ages.'[23] Butler's ideal state was one in which the virtuous were fully rewarded for all their efforts. There was absolute political harmony and 'no such thing as Faction'.[24] Moreover, this society possessed an economic prosperity unknown in the corrupt world of the present. 'Some would in a higher Way contribute,' Butler promised, 'but all would in some Way contribute, to the public Prosperity: and in it, each would enjoy the Fruits of his own Virtue.'[25] This emphasis on the economic health of the ideally virtuous state was almost certainly in response to Mandeville's *The Fable of the Bees* (1724). Mandeville's satire of orthodoxy begins when Jove miraculously fulfils the wish of the 'Grumbling Hive' for perfect virtue. But

---

[23] Butler, *Analogy*, I, iii, 63.   [24] Ibid.   [25] Ibid. 63-4.

the bees, pure of all greed and vanity, consequently lose all their wealth and power: 'private vices' are shown to be essential to prosperity. Butler made sure, therefore, that he clearly illustrated the advantage of virtue to not only religious but also material contentment.

Johnson's Sermon 5 also includes a vision of the perfectly virtuous state which would be 'opulent without luxury, and powerful without faction', and where 'every man would endeavour after merit, because merit would always be rewarded' (xiv. 61). In most respects, then, Johnson's vision follows Butler's ideal of a society where virtuous men never fall victim to undeserved sufferings, and where there is political stability and economic prosperity. Butler and Johnson disagree in only one major way. Butler, ironically like Mandeville, made clear that this society of perfect virtue could be attained only through the miraculous intervention of God: 'Our Knowledge of human Nature, and the whole History of Mankind, shew the Impossibility, without some miraculous Interpositions, that a Number of Men, here on Earth, should unite in one Society or Government, in the Fear of God, and the universal Practice of Virtue.' [26] Johnson, however, remained unwilling to rely on Divine intervention to rectify the injustice of life. Despite his usually keen awareness of human frailty, he exhorted men to struggle towards the creation of a faultlessly virtuous state: 'Let no man charge this prospect of things, with being a train of airy phantoms. . . . To effect all this, no miracle is required; men need only unite their endeavours, and exert those abilities, which God has conferred upon them, in conformity to the laws of religion' (xiv. 62). The possibility that men could unite in a reformation of society that eliminated all vice and crime does seem extremely remote. But it was only by insisting on this possibility that Johnson was able to exonerate God from responsibility for suffering in the present world. Innocent men suffered as the result of a corrupt society, but it was the task of men, not God, to create a new world of perfect virtue.

This reformation of society would represent at least a partial return to the order and justice of the pre-fallen world. As Samuel Clarke explained in his description of the virtuous

[26] Ibid. 64.

state, it was 'originally the Constitution and Order of God's Creation . . . that Virtue and Vice are by the regular *Tendency* of Things, followed with natural Rewards and Punishments'.[27] In other words, the world was originally designed so that virtue and happiness, vice and suffering, regularly corresponded. As the result of corruption, however, 'the condition of Men in the present State is plainly such, that this natural Order of things in the World is manifestly perverted'.[28] The implication of Clarke's argument seems to have been accepted by Butler, Johnson, and most other orthodox writers: the fall not only introduced suffering into the world, the well-known consequence of original sin mentioned in our initial citation from Sermon 5; the fall also disrupted the exact correspondence between vice and affliction so that now the innocent suffer as well as the wicked. The reformation of society would return the world to the moral order which, in the present world, endures only as a general but highly imperfect tendency towards the greater happiness of virtue rather than vice.

As the result of works such as Pope's *An Essay on Man* (1734), it is often assumed that the eighteenth century was characterized by a confidence in the benevolent order of the universe which no vice or suffering could disturb. But Pope and his mentor, Bolingbroke, lay quite outside the main orthodox Christian tradition. The Christian vision of the universe, which was at least as characteristic of the age as the originally stoic or Renaissance ideal of cosmic harmony, affirmed the essential disharmony of the fallen world, a disharmony that could be rectified only by the moral reformation of mankind. We have seen that there was also a tendency among orthodox writers such as Johnson to withdraw God from any direct involvement in the world. This exonerated God from responsibility for the disasters and moral atrocities that afflict mankind indiscriminately. But it was ultimately unsatisfying to portray man as the victim of random physical forces and social chaos. Further discussions of the problem of suffering, therefore, tended to draw God back into a direct governance of His creation.

[27] Clarke, *Natural Religion*, p. 165.
[28] Ibid. 165-6.

2. 'Universal Optimism' and Divine Government

There is more than one way to exonerate God of blame for suffering. Most writers, as we have seen, placed the blame for affliction entirely on mankind. But it could also be claimed that God had no choice but to allow some evils, both moral and physical. Even the omnipotent Creator could not overcome an inexorable law of the universe; though He intends the greatest possible happiness for the whole, this goal cannot be achieved without making some of his creatures less happy and less perfect than others. Because this doctrine insisted that the harmony and order of the universe was always preserved, no matter what afflictions had to be endured by particular individuals, it has been commonly entitled 'universal optimism'. Perhaps its best-known description is in A. O. Lovejoy's famous *The Great Chain of Being* (1936), which links this doctrine with a tradition of ideas originating with Aristotle and Plato. It is worth pointing out that, in fact, most eighteenth-century philosophers attributed what we call 'universal optimism' not to Platonic or Aristotelian thought, but to stoicism. According to Adam Smith's *The Theory of Moral Sentiments* (1759), for example, the stoics originated the belief that 'whatever happened, tended to the prosperity and perfection of the whole', and that 'a wise man . . . could never feel any reluctance to comply with this disposition of things'.[29] Only a year before, the same commonplaces were enunciated by the natural philosopher in Chapter 22 of *Rasselas*: 'To live according to nature is to act always with due regard to the fitness arising from the relations and qualities of causes and effects; to concur with the great and unchangeable scheme of universal felicity; to co-operate with the general disposition and tendency of the present system of things.'[30] What is not always recognized is that Johnson's satire of this doctrine was as typical of eighteenth-century thought as the optimism of Leibniz, Pope, Bolingbroke, and Soame Jenyns. Because Lovejoy's *The Great Chain of Being* has become a standard work in the history of ideas, it is often mistakenly assumed that almost all eighteenth-century writers believed that the universe was a perfectly

[29] See Smith, *Moral Sentiments*, pp. 434–8;
[30] *Rasselas*, p. 56.

ordered system of interdependencies. For this reason, Johnson's critique of Jenyns's enthusiastic exegesis of universal optimism, *A Free Inquiry into the Nature and Origin of Evil* (1757), has been applauded as an almost unprecedented attack on this doctrine. To argue that Johnson's objections to Jenyns were not entirely original or uncommon is not to deny that his review is a powerful and incisive statement of the case against universal optimism. Nevertheless, we should not allow Jenyns or Pope or Bolingbroke to create the impression that this doctrine was more generally favoured than it really was.

Jenyns's *Free Inquiry* was a particularly inept statement of a theodicy which, with the possible exception of Leibniz's philosophy, had never been able to achieve much coherence or precision. Johnson was able to catch Jenyns in confusions which had been detected by commentators on previous theodicies of this kind, and which a better writer would have been cautious to avoid. For example, much of Jenyns's argument assumed the existence of so called 'evils of imperfection'. According to some previous writers, the very act of creation implied the subordination and the imperfection of the created being; as the result of a law that bound even God Himself, all created beings were deprived of absolute perfection. Thus, as William King wrote in his popular *De origine mali* (1702; trans. 1731), 'the Evils of Imperfection . . . must be permitted in the Nature of things; and inequality of Perfections must be permitted also, since it is impossible that all the Works of God should be endowed with equal Perfections'.[31] This argument was taken up by Jenyns: 'all subordination [implies] imperfection, all imperfection evil, and all evil some kind of inconveniency or suffering: so that there must be particular inconveniences and sufferings annexed to every particular rank of created beings by the circumstances of things, and their modes of existence.'[32]

But Jenyns had added something significant to King's position—an addition which indicates how confused this form of theodicy could be. Although King had called imperfection an 'evil', he denied that subordination and imperfection

---

[31] William King, *An Essay on the Origin of Evil* (1702), trans. Edmund Law (1731; 2 vols.; 2nd edn.; London, 1732), i. 135–6.

[32] Review of *Free Inquiry*, in Schwartz, *Evil*, p. 105.

necessarily implied suffering: 'any particular Evil does not bring Misery upon us; otherwise every Creature would be miserable, as of necessity labouring under the Evils of Imperfection.'[33] The obvious objection was how the ideas of 'evil' and 'suffering' could be disconnected in this manner. Because human imperfection in comparison to God evidently did not cause suffering, many writers had denied that imperfection could even be called an 'evil'. As Samuel Clarke's brother, John, argued in *An Enquiry into the Cause and Origin of Evil* (1720), 'the *Evil* of *Imperfection*, is not properly any *Evil* at all'.[34] This objection was sufficiently prevalent that the translator and editor of King's *De origine mali*, Edmund Law, found it necessary to defend at great length the notion that 'a Privation of Good' was properly speaking an evil, even if it did not imply positive suffering.[35] With an ineptitude which is all too characteristic of his work, Jenyns skated over these problems by glibly assuming that 'evil' *did* imply suffering. Thus, Johnson was able to refute Jenyns by raising an old objection: 'Imperfection may imply privative evil, or the absence of some good, but this privation produces no suffering, but by the help of knowledge.'[36]

More important, universal optimism ran directly counter to some important assumptions and objectives in orthodox thought. We have already seen that orthodox writers conceived of the universe as badly disordered by original sin. Both King and Jenyns, on the other hand, denied that man had been perfect in the garden and that original sin had been responsible for the introduction of temporal evils. Moreover, while universal optimism instructed that men could not, or even should not, attempt to remove all forms of suffering, the orthodox majority placed an increasingly heavy burden on mankind to correct the ills of the world. Orthodox divines did need some way to assure individuals that their suffering had meaning and purpose, but a doctrine which so audaciously constrained the liberty of God and man could never gain widespread favour in the Church. The alternative was a doctrine of Divine government or

[33] King, *Evil*, i. 209.
[34] John Clarke, *Evil*, pp. 84–5.
[35] See King, *Evil*, i. 136–40.
[36] Review of *Free Inquiry*, in Schwartz, *Evil*, p. 105.

'general providence' which proclaimed God's continuing care over his creation, yet maintained the individual's responsibility to rectify his own suffering. This was the doctrine which Johnson upheld against Jenyns.

It is important to keep in mind, however, that such an understanding of providence was not entirely consistent with the tendencies in orthodox thought which we examined in the last section. Wesley had good reason to charge that divines were stressing the randomness, rather than the order, of the universe in their response to the Lisbon earthquake. In the following pages we will consider orthodox consolations which insisted that there was no randomness, and that God was in control of all events. In addition, the orthodox conception of Divine government does possess some interesting, though ultimately superficial similarities to universal optimism. It is not always easy to discern the difference between the two doctrines, and they have sometimes been confused by modern scholars.

Universal optimism assumes, as Lovejoy explained, that 'everything becomes endurable to us when we once see clearly that it never could have been otherwise'.[37] As Pope expressed it in that famous line in *An Essay on Man*, 'Whatever *is*, is right.'[38] There are no chance events or sufferings: everything supports the perfection of the benevolent scheme of the universe. This all seems to be little different from Johnson's conviction, expressed in *Rambler*, No. 184, that men should find comfort in the knowledge that all events are appointed by a benevolent Creator:

In this state of universal uncertainty, where a thousand dangers hover about us, and none can tell whether the good that he persues is not evil in disguise, or whether the next step will lead him to safety or destruction, nothing can afford any rational tranquillity, but the conviction that, however we amuse ourselves with unideal sounds, nothing in reality is governed by chance, but the universe is under the perpetual superintendence of him who created it; that our being is in the hands of omnipotent goodness, by whom what appears casual to us is directed for ends ultimately kind and merciful; and that nothing can finally hurt him who debars not himself from the divine favour (v. 205).

[37] A. O. Lovejoy, *The Great Chain of Being* (Cambridge, Mass., 1936), 210-11.
[38] *Essay on Man*, i, l. 294.

'A mighty maze! but not without a plan.'[39] Is Johnson endorsing the optimism of Pope or Jenyns? Some scholars have, indeed, viewed this and similar statements in Johnson's work as confusing and anomalous in the light of his famous attack on Jenyns. Robert Voitle, for instance, suggested that *Rambler*, No. 184, advocates an 'over-riding determinism',[40] perhaps in the style of Hobbes or the greatest philosopher of universal optimism, Leibniz. Charles E. Pierce focused on Johnson's expression of a similar idea near the end of 'The Vanity of Human Wishes'. In the final paragraph of this poem Johnson advises the reader to 'Implore [God's] aid, in his decisions rest, / Secure whate'er he gives, he gives the best' (ll. 355–6). Pierce argued that these lines 'appear to pay more than lip service to a facile conception of divinity that Johnson associated with Pope in *An Essay on Man* and that he would soon excoriate in his review of Soame Jenyns's *Free Inquiry*'.[41]

Yet Johnson was not dependent on Leibniz or Pope for any of these statements on the benevolent order of the universe. Although, as Wesley indicated, Anglicans themselves had drifted towards the view that random physical forces presided over the universe, such an 'epicurean' doctrine was traditionally associated with atheism. As William Sherlock wrote in *A Discourse Concerning the Divine Providence* (1694), 'the Dispute, Whether there be a God or no, principally resolves it self into this, Whether this World, and all things in it, is made and governed by Wisdom and Counsel, or by Chance, and a blind material Necessity and Fate'.[42] Here we find an association not between Divine intervention and the doctrine of necessity, but between chance and necessity: if man is the victim of indifferent natural forces or the moral chaos of the fallen world, can he really be said to have any freedom? This is what Johnson probably means in 'The Vanity of Human Wishes' when he asks, 'Must helpless man, in ignorance sedate, / Roll darkling down the torrent of his fate?' (ll. 345–6). The answer to this question is 'no', because man can trust in the benevolent care of his Creator. This is not Leibnizian optimism or, as is

[39] Ibid., l. 6.
[40] See Voitle, *Johnson the Moralist*, p. 36.
[41] Pierce, *Religious Life*, p. 115.
[42] William Sherlock, *A Discourse Concerning the Divine Providence* (London, 1694), 9.

sometimes assumed with relation to 'The Vanity of Human Wishes', the stoicism of Juvenal's Tenth Satire: it is sound, conventional Christian theology. As Samuel Clarke wrote in a sermon on providence, 'we may observe, that what men vulgarly call *Chance* or unforeseen *Accident*, is in Scripture always declared to be the *determinate Counsel and Providence of God*'.[43] This is the doctrine which Johnson cites in *Rambler*, No. 184, and which will be found in the writings of almost every divine of the Restoration and eighteenth century. Despite the unwillingness often expressed by these authors to admit that God ordinarily interfered with man's moral freedom, Divine providence instructed that, indeed, the Creator remained in direct control of all temporal events.

Nor is it true that Johnson denied the benevolent order of the universe in his review of Jenyns's *Free Inquiry*. Indeed, among his major criticisms of Jenyns was that he had uselessly reiterated the belief in the essential goodness of creation: 'We believed that the present system of creation was right, though we could not explain the adaptation of one part to the other, or for the whole series of causes and consequences. Where has the enquirer added to the little knowledge that we had before?'[44] Johnson's convictions cannot be distinguished from Jenyns's theodicy by arguing that, while Jenyns claimed that suffering played a significant role in a Divine plan, Johnson denied that this plan existed. The true distinction between universal optimism and Divine government is more subtle than this. First, Jenyns and other proponents of his doctrine made God Himself subject to universal laws which required the existence of suffering. 'Omnipotence cannot work contradictions,' Jenyns wrote; 'it can only effect all possible things.'[45] Johnson and most orthodox writers would agree that there were certain contradictions which even God could not perform. He could not, for instance, be one Being and three Beings at the same time.[46] But the orthodox tradition certainly would not concede

[43] Samuel Clarke, 'The Events of Things not always Answerable to Second Causes', in *Sermons* (1730) (10 vols.: 2nd. edn.; London, 1731), vi. 302. Johnson read a sermon by Clarke on the meaning of suffering during the last week of his life. See M. Quinlan, *Samuel Johnson: A Layman's Religion* (Madison Wis., 1964), 42-5; *Miscellanies*, ii. 156.

[44] Review of *Free Inquiry*, in Schwartz, *Evil*, p. 107.

[45] Ibid. 99.

[46] See ch. 1, sec. 2, above.

that the elimination of suffering implied any contradiction. The doctrine of Divine government was not based on any assumptions concerning the limitations of Divine power. Providence instructed that God, freely incited by love, had an immediate care for the welfare of each individual.

Moreover, the ways of God are mysterious. 'The divines', to whom Johnson refers throughout his review of Jenyns, typically insisted that men could not fully determine the method and rationale of Divine government. Joseph Butler, for example, described providence as 'a Scheme, System, or Constitution, whose Parts correspond to each other, and to a Whole'.[47] This might be mistaken for universal optimism, yet an entire chapter of *Analogy of Religion* is devoted to arguing that this scheme is 'quite beyond our Comprehension'.[48] By observing that providence ordinarily rewards virtue and punishes vice, we have reason to believe by analogy that the same benevolent order presides over apparent irregularities in the creation. But we have no way of knowing exactly how these irregularities are consistent with the larger scheme; as Johnson put it, we cannot explain 'the adaptation of one part to the other', even if we are convinced that this adaptation exists. Two decades after Butler's *Analogy*, Caleb Fleming charged Jenyns with venturing into 'thick clouds of inpenetrable darkness', in his attempts to explain the nature of this order.[49] The same complaint was lodged by Johnson, who castigated Jenyns for deciding 'too easily on questions out of the reach of human determination'.[50]

Nevertheless, it was not so easy to decide how much could or could not be determined about God's plan: not only the optimists, but also the divines were attacked for probing presumptuously beyond the limits of human reason. As Hume showed in 'Of a Particular Providence and of a Future State' (1748), the type of reasoning used by Butler was not wholly sound, for Butler used one part of the visible creation as an analogy for the rest. Why should the frequent 'irregularities' in God's scheme be excluded from our conception of His

[47] Butler, *Analogy*, I, vii, 122.
[48] Ibid.
[49] Caleb Fleming, *Necessity not the Origin of Evil, Religious or Moral* (London, 1757), 17-18.
[50] Review of *Free Inquiry*, in Schwartz, *Evil*, p. 99.

attributes? Since we see that the creation is not perfectly benevolent and ordered, how can we deduce that the First Cause *is* perfectly benevolent, or even capable of producing universal order? Hume's essay was the century's most powerful expression of the argument that orthodoxy had attributed many qualities to the Creator, such as benevolence and care for His creation, which had their basis in wishful thinking rather than sound reasoning. Roughly the same charge had been made by Lord Bolingbroke. Just as orthodox writers contended that the optimists were delving into knowledge beyond the limits of human reason, Bolingbroke upbraided the 'divines' for assuming that they could know anything at all about God's responsibilities to mankind. 'Infinite wisdom and infinite power have made things as they are,' wrote Bolingbroke: 'how goodness and justice required that they should be so made, is neither *coram judice*, nor to any rational purpose to enquire.'[51] It is likely that this is the sentiment which inspired Pope's famous lines: 'presume not God to scan; / The proper study of mankind is Man.'[52] How Pope and Bolingbroke could express this view, and then go on to construct a massive system of interdependencies between all beings (even on other planets), is one of the great curiosities of eighteenth-century literature.

Orthodox writers, on the other hand, agreed that our knowledge of God was very limited—this was an attitude which was increasingly prevalent following Tindal—but they also affirmed against Bolingbroke that the goodness of God was not among those attributes which were beyond human determination. In his reply to Bolingbroke, Bishop Warburton agreed that it would be presumptuous 'to *inquire*, much more to prescribe *how things should be made*', yet 'it is another thing to say (which is all the Divines had said, how differently soever his Lordship is pleased to represent the matter) that God will act equitably with his rational Creatures'.[53] Thus, the divines rejected the belief that we should *entirely* cease to scan the providence of God. In this respect, it must be admitted, Johnson's review of Jenyns actually departed from the orthodox case. Johnson began by questioning Jenyns's premise

---

[51] Bolingbroke, *Works*, iv. 362.
[52] *Essay on Man*, ii, ll. 1–2.
[53] William Warburton, *Bolingbroke's Philosophy*, p. 103.

that God is infinitely good, and even utilized an argument against belief in Divine goodness which strongly recalled Hume's 'Of a Particular Providence and of a Future State'. Johnson argued that Jenyns could not explain the existence of evil by first assuming the goodness of God, since the existence of evil, in turn, weakens the evidence for the goodness of God.[54] But this statement must be regarded as an anomaly in Johnson's writings. We have already seen that many of his religious beliefs—his defence of the miracles, his argument for a future state—are based on precisely the same supposition of Divine goodness that was made by Jenyns. Johnson's solution to the problem of suffering usually assumed that God was infinitely benevolent. As he wrote in Sermon 16 on Divine government, 'this great Being is infinitely wise, and infinitely good; so that the end which he proposes must necessarily be the final happiness of those beings that depend upon him, and the means, by which he promotes that end, must undoubtedly be the wisest and the best' (xiv. 173).

This statement reflects the most important distinction between universal optimism and Divine government. The optimists assumed that suffering was necessary in the 'present' system of the universe; the divines looked ahead to the 'final happiness' of mankind, for which present suffering was only a preparation or, as Johnson wrote, 'means'. In the present state of 'trial' or 'probation', affliction served to direct men towards the virtuous and pious practices that would qualify them for happiness in the next world. As Samuel Clarke explained in a sermon on 'The End of God's Afflicting Men', 'that mixture of *Affliction* and Disappointment in the World, which, by the wise order and appointment of Providence, puts men in mind of their Weakness and Infirmity, brings them to a right Sense of themselves and their dependence upon God'.[55] This is very much the lesson of Johnson's 'The Vanity of Human Wishes': we learn from the unhappiness of life that we must depend entirely on the aid and support of Divine benevolence. As he wrote in *Idler*, No. 89, on the quality of 'Godliness, or piety': 'None would have recourse to an invisible power, but that all other subjects have eluded their hopes. None would fix their

---

54 See Review of *Free Inquiry*, in Schwartz, *Evil*, p. 99.
55 Clarke, *Sermons*, vi. 277–8.

attention upon the future, but that they are discontented with the present' (ii. 277). Not only piety was promoted by the vanity and pain of life, but, moreover, 'almost all the moral good which is left among us, is the apparent effect of physical evil' (ii. 276). The most commonly cited example of this was the virtue of charity. As the divine and philosopher John Balguy wrote in a treatise on *Divine Rectitude* (1730), 'Opportunities of exercising the amiable Virtues of *Humanity*, and *Charity*, are chiefly owing to Adversity, as it produces and points out the most proper Objects.'[56] Johnson made the same point in *Idler*, No. 89. Charity, he wrote, 'would have no place if there were no want, for of a virtue which could not be practised, the omission could not be culpable' (ii. 277). And other virtues were similarly promoted by suffering. Men could not show patience or fortitude without adversity. Moderation was increased by the knowledge that physical ailments usually accompanied habits of intemperance.

This doctrine taught that if men responded to suffering with increased piety and goodness they would be fulfilling God's purpose in allowing affliction to exist. Most important, the individual would finally be rewarded with eternal happiness. For this reason, orthodox writers argued that providence bestowed a real comfort in affliction which, despite the claims of Pope or Jenyns, universal optimism could simply not provide. Addison, for instance, argued in *Spectator*, No. 574, that those who 'gravely tell the Man who is miserable, that it is necessary he should be so, to keep up the Harmony of the Universe . . . rather give Despair than Consolation'.[57] 'Religion', on the other hand, 'bears a more tender Regard to humane Nature. It prescribes to every miserable Man the Means of bettering his Condition . . . because it can make him happy hereafter.'[58] We see once again what a key role the future state played in much eighteenth-century thought. It was central to the Christian epicureanism of John Clarke, and it was the foundation of orthodox consolations for the afflicted.

---

[56] John Balguy, *Divine Rectitude, or a Brief Inquiry Concerning the Moral Perfections of the Deity* (London, 1730), 32.
[57] *Spectator*, iv. 565.
[58] Ibid.

As we have seen, Bolingbroke denied the existence of a future state of rewards and punishments, arguing that the divines were 'much more impious than HOBBES' when they suggested that such a state was necessary to perfect the universal system. This was one of many heterodoxies that were almost inescapable components of the case for universal optimism. There were attempts, particularly by William King, to resolve the differences between orthodoxy and optimism. For example, although King had to concede that the fall did not cause the afflictions we now endure, he rationalized that the fall deprived man of the grace which had originally raised him above his natural imperfection.[59] King also attempted to free God from the determinism imposed by universal optimism: he argued that God had not chosen the present scheme of creation because it was good, but instead had made the present scheme good by the very act of choice. 'We may conceive a Power', he argued, 'which can produce Goodness or Agreeableness in the things, by confirming itself to them, or adapting them to it: hence things please this Agent, not because they are good in themselves, but because they are chosen.'[60] It is, in fact, rather difficult to conceive such a power. Nor is it clear why a benevolent Creator, if He truly possessed free will, would have chosen such an imperfect universe. In any event, King's arguments were not generally accepted, and universal optimism continued to be regarded with considerable suspicion within the Anglican Church.

The alternative doctrine of Divine providence was, of course, highly traditional, and is by no means unique to the eighteenth century. But the explanations of affliction which we have examined are at least as typical of the age as philosophical schemes of universal optimism. The systems of Bolingbroke, Pope, or Jenyns were not only essentially heterodox, but also failed to provide the type of consolation which most Christians seemed to want. To assume that most writers of the eighteenth century relied on the great chain of being, or the theodicies constructed around this scheme, is greatly to underestimate the deeply traditional and pragmatic character of much eighteenth-century thought. Johnson's attack on Jenyns's *Free Inquiry* will

---

[59] See King, *Evil*, i. 221.   [60] Ibid. ii. 286.

remain an important critique of a philosophy which had briefly attained a fashionable popularity. By Johnson's time, however, that popularity was quickly waning. So far from being the first to attack this philosophy, he was contributing a particularly strong and penetrating defence of the doctrine of his Church.

3. *Stoicism and Christian Patience*

The nature of Johnson's attitudes towards stoicism has been the subject of a long-standing debate among scholars. This controversy has resulted from the apparent ambiguity of Johnson's writings on stoicism. The portrait of the stoic philosopher in *Rasselas*, Chapter 18, and certain periodical essays such as *Rambler*, No. 66, suggest that he was deeply scornful of the stoic claim that a wise man could maintain a state of rational indifference to all pains and afflictions. Some critics, however, have contended that works such as 'The Vanity of Human Wishes' and *Rambler*, No. 32, express a great deal of sympathy for the stoic ideal of courage and rational equanimity in affliction.[61] It was a teaching which Johnson was very often forced to practise in his own life.

It should be considered, however, that there is nothing peculiarly stoic about doctrines of endurance in affliction. In particular, this is the traditional teaching of Christianity. The cardinal virtues of patience and fortitude, while they must be carefully distinguished from stoic indifference, have tradition-ally been interpreted in a way that is hardly less rigorous than the classical doctrine. St Augustine, for example, experienced agonies of guilt when he was grieving the death of his mother:

I blamed the weakness of my feelings and refrained my flood of grief, which gave way a little unto me; but again came, as with a tide, yet not so as to burst out into tears, nor to a change of countenance; still I knew what I was keeping down in my heart. And being very much displeased, that these human things had such power over me, which in the due order and appointment of our natural condition, must

---

[61] The fullest attempt to show Johnson's sympathy with some aspects of stoicism is by C. McIntosh, 'Johnson's Debate with Stoicism', *ELH* 33 (1966), 327–36. His view was refuted by D. J. Greene in 'Johnson, Stoicism, and the Good Life', in J. J. Burke and D. Kay (edd.), *The Unknown Samuel Johnson* (Madison, Wis., 1983), 17–38. Greene argued that Johnson had no sympathy with stoicism whatsoever. I will align Johnson with an entirely distinct tradition of classical and Christian teachings on affliction.

needs come to pass, with a new grief I grieved for my grief, and was thus worn by a double sorrow.[62]

St Augustine believed that the Christian should, in principle, abandon all attachment to worldly joys and gladly accept the dispensations of providence in hopes of happiness in the next world. The prospect of eternal happiness, and the demand for ardent devotion rather than apathy, make this quite different from stoicism. But the traditional Christian teaching on affliction was perhaps little more satisfactory to Johnson than stoicism. Passages in his work which criticize stoicism also roughly apply to a Christian ideal of fortitude which demands that the individual rise completely above all temporal considerations.

For example, Johnson's portrait of the stoic philosopher in *Rasselas* examines a contradiction between principle and practice similar to that described by St Augustine. The philosopher idealizes a state of rational tranquility in which a man is 'no more the slave of fear, nor the fool of hope; is no more emaciated by envy, inflamed by anger, emasculated by tenderness, or depressed by grief'.[63] The death of the philosopher's daughter, however, throws him into the depths of grief and destroys all his pretensions to indifference. Unlike St Augustine, Johnson seems unwilling to condemn this grief as any sort of failure: Imlac's warning that moralists 'discourse like angels, but . . . live like men' suggests the inevitability of some contradiction between what a moralist teaches and what men are capable of achieving, a division which Johnson elsewhere confessed was a characteristic of his own writings.[64] In this way, Johnson showed more tolerance of human weakness than some Christians of his own age. John Tillotson, for example, denounced moralists who 'speak like Angels, and yet do like Devils'[65] as no better than wicked hypocrites.

The pragmatism and humanity of the chapter on the stoic philosopher are, nevertheless, fairly typical of developments in

---

[62] St Augustine, *The Confessions*, trans. E. Pusey (London and New York, 1909), 187.

[63] *Rasselas*, ch. 18, p. 50.

[64] Ibid. 51. See *Rambler*, No. 14, which concerns an author's inevitable failure to sustain the purity of life expounded in his moral writings.

[65] Tillotson, 'Of the Form and the Power of Godliness', in *Works*, iii. 319.

eighteenth-century thought. It is significant, for example, that the stoic philosopher numbers 'tenderness' among those passions which the wise man must eradicate. Eighteenth-century writers frequently questioned whether the passions could all be suppressed without great loss to the goodness and general happiness of mankind. In *Spectator*, No. 397, Addison complained that 'as the *Stoick* Philosophers discard all Passions in general, they will not allow a Wise Man so much as to pity the Afflictions of another'.[66] Passions which caused the painful sensations of grief and pity also unified mankind, a point made by Johnson in *Rambler*, No. 47, and probably hinted in the speech of the stoic philosopher.

Eighteenth-century Christians required a teaching on endurance which accepted that griefs and pain were to some degree natural and even useful to mankind, subject to consolation and control, but not complete elimination. *Rambler*, No. 32, on patience, which urged that 'the cure for the greatest part of human miseries is not radical, but palliative' (iii. 175) is a highly representative attempt to find such a scheme. Although this essay has been called an exposition of 'Christian Stoicism',[67] its classical origins are really quite different. Johnson is expressing a view of suffering that, in fact, is highly comparable to the teachings on affliction by the great opponent to stoicism, Epicurus. Epicurus' unwillingness to impose unrealistic demands on the suffering individual was amenable to the eighteenth-century desire for a useful and humane doctrine of patience. Once again, this traditionally vilified classical philosopher enjoyed new favour among Christian writers in certain areas of moral and religious thought. Among those who adopted Epicurus' teachings on affliction was Jeremy Collier, whose excellent essay, 'Of Pain', will demonstrate how close *Rambler*, No. 32, was to treatments of this subject by moralists and divines of the age.

Epicurus' discussion of pain is characterized by its scorn of the stoic notion that pain was beneath the consideration of true

[66] *Spectator*, iii. 486.

[67] See McIntosh, 'Johnson's Debate with Stoicism', It is likely that Johnson would have strongly objected to being called a 'Christian Stoic' as that term was sometimes applied in his own day. Augustus Toplady, who appears in the *Life* (ii. 247), proclaimed himself a 'Christian Stoic' on the grounds that he held 'the Doctrine of Absolute Predestination', which Johnson rejected. See ch. 3, sec. 2, above.

wisdom and virtue. Physical suffering, he argued, was real: it was a 'high piece of Folly, to affirm, that to be in pain, and to be free from pain, is one and the same thing'.[68] The part of a wise man was not to dispute the existence of suffering, but 'to endure that pain with Constancy and Bravery of mind, and patiently to expect either the Solution, or Relaxation of it'.[69] Epicurus advanced two major consolations for the suffering. First, the wise man should remember that physical torments are always transient and short. 'It is most evident', he wrote, 'that Great Pain cannot be Long; nor Long pain Great: and so, we may consolate our selves against the Violence of pain, by an assurance of the shortness of it.'[70] Second, weakness and complaining greatly increased suffering: 'the only way to heighten pain to the degree of intolerable, is to exasperate it by impatience, and oppress and wear out nature by effeminate Complainings.'[71] It was in the best interests of the wise man to face his pain with dignity, virtue, and magnanimity, qualities which Epicurus went on to praise with great warmth.

Jeremy Collier's essay 'Of Pain' was contained in a series of moral essays published in four parts between 1697 and 1709. Like Epicurus, Collier began with an attack on the stoic notion that '*Pain* was nothing of an *Evil*'.[72] We must recognize the reality of suffering, Collier suggested, in order to prepare ourselves for the challenge of maintaining our dignity and virtue in the midst of the greatest torments. 'We ought to suffer the utmost Extremity of Hardship', he wrote, 'rather than surrender our Innocence, desert our Station, or do any thing unbecoming the Dignity of our Nature.'[73] Collier thus maintained Epicurus' concern for dignity in affliction, but he also added stronger warnings concerning the need for virtue. Although suffering weakened our resistance to vice, we should remember that 'remorse of Conscience, and dismal Prospects, load the *Execution*, and are terrible Additions to *Pain*'.[74] It was

---

[68] Epicurus, *Morals*, trans. Walter Charleton (London, 1655; repr. London, 1926), 80.

[69] Ibid. 81.

[70] Ibid. 82.

[71] Ibid.

[72] Jeremy Collier, 'Of Pain', in *Essays upon Several Moral Subjects* (1697–1709) (4 pts.; 6th edn.; London, 1722), III. 7. Johnson's copy of Collier's *Essays* is now in the Hyde collection.

[73] Collier, *Essays*, III. 10–11.   [74] Ibid. 26.

indeed only prudent that we avoid vices which would aggravate suffering with the pains of guilt.

Neither Epicurus' nor Collier's discussion of pain is necessarily the direct source for Johnson's arguments in *Rambler*, No. 32. But these precedents do suggest that Johnson was working within a tradition on the subject of patience which was quite distinct and almost as ancient as stoicism. Like Epicurus and Collier, Johnson opened his essay by rejecting the 'wild enthusiastick virtue' of the stoics, his observation that 'the controversy about the reality of external evils is now at an end' (iii. 175) accurately reflecting the century's widespread scorn for the stoic teachings on pain. He then went on, again like the previous authors, to indicate certain boundaries of virtue and human dignity which should never be transgressed, even under the pressure of the severest torments. He expressed little doubt 'whether virtue can stand its ground as long as life, and whether a soul well principled will not be separated rather than subdued' (iii. 178). Moreover, 'there is indeed nothing more unsuitable to the nature of man in any calamity than rage and turbulence, which, without examining whether they are not sometimes impious, are at least always offensive' (iii. 176). Johnson thus retained the classical ideal of dignity in suffering and, like Collier, stressed in particular that it was prudent to avoid the additional sufferings of a guilty conscience: 'if we are conscious that we have not contributed to our own sufferings, if punishment falls upon innocence . . . our pain is then without aggravation, and we have not the bitterness of remorse to add to the asperity of misfortune' (iii. 176). *Rambler*, No. 32, draws to a conclusion with consolations, reminiscent of Epicurus, on the necessary shortness of great pain. 'If the pains of disease be, as I believe they are, sometimes greater than those of artificial torture, they are therefore in their own nature shorter' (iii. 178). Johnson thus initially rejects the stoic ideal of indifference in suffering in favour of the same practical consolations proposed by Epicurus and Collier. As with these authors, stoicism serves as a doctrine not to be revised, but contrasted: we cannot properly manage affliction until we have acknowledged its reality and seriousness.

The Christian message which concludes *Rambler*, No. 32, that we should rely on the unfailing care and justice of Divine providence, is conventional, and is meant to complement the philosophic teachings on patience which form the body of the essay. For Johnson's age, the Christian doctrine of patience did not so much replace as improve the best classical teachings. And the classical advice on affliction is not confined to stoicism. It is inaccurate to assume that every time an author of Johnson's time urged men to face their sufferings with courage, he demonstrated a sympathy for stoicism. Stoicism is an extreme doctrine which claims that men should not only endure sufferings but view them with indifference. Although Christian writers have used stoicism, or have advocated ideals which are similarly rigorous, Johnson's view was really quite different. In its classical origins, Johnson's understanding of patience owes more to Epicurus than Zeno or Seneca. In Christian thought, his links are with the pragmatic and tolerant understanding of affliction which prevailed in his own age.

5

Pride and the Pursuit of Applause

1. *Virtue as a Deceitful Contrivance of Pride*

We have seen how classical philosophy underwent a significant re-evaluation in the eighteenth century. Against Tindal and the tenets of 'true deism', divines stressed the meagreness and unclarity of classical teachings. The Christian epicureans attracted new favour for the ethical teachings of a historically vilified philosopher, and criticized ethical systems which derived from traditionally respected classical groups such as the stoics and peripatetics. Plato's influence became less visible and more ambiguous: though he was normally referred to with respect, Addison criticized the 'extravagant and chimerical' talk of his followers.[1] Johnson apparently laughed at the 'visionary' writings of Henry More, the Cambridge Platonist.[2] But this re-evaluation did not normally amount to an outright attack on classical values, except among a small group of writers. According to the French authors La Rochefoucault and Esprit, who strongly influenced Mandeville's *The Fable of the Bees* (1724), the main, socratic tradition in classical philosophy was essentially bogus: its view of man and virtue was based not on the highest efforts of reason, but on vanity and the most deluded self-aggrandizement.

The initial group of replies to Mandeville leave little doubt that, during the first part of the century, this claim was viewed with anger and disdain. There is evidence, however, that this abhorrence diminished somewhat as the century wore on. Moralists such as Archibald Campbell, Thomas Rutherforth, and Philip Skelton turned to Mandeville and the French writers who influenced him with interest and even admiration. Skelton's remarks in *Ophiomaches, or Deism Reveal'd* (1748) are worthy of particular consideration. Skelton argued that 'of all the writers on the side of infidelity, [Mandeville] had the greatest stock of wit and experience'. At the time that *Fable of*

---

[1] *Spectator*, No. 56, i. 237.
[2] Hawkins, *Life*, p. 542.

the Bees was published, Skelton noted, '*Self-sufficiency* had, in a greater or less degree, taken possession of all the writers and readers among us.'[3] By 'self-sufficiency' Skelton meant reliance on natural reason rather than Christianity, and, though his assessment is somewhat exaggerated, it is true that the 1720s had been dominated by much incautious praise of reason among respected writers. During this decade, Fiddes, Wollaston, Hutcheson, and disciples of Samuel Clarke, such as John Balguy, all published generally admired treatises on natural religion and non-Christian ethics. Amidst this Mandeville launched his attack on classical ethics, strongly anticipating certain positions adopted by orthodox writers against Tindal's *Christianity as Old as the Creation* (1730). For this reason, Skelton found reason to praise Mandeville in retrospect. Nor should we be surprised that Johnson declared that Mandeville 'opened my views into real life very much'.[4] Mandeville, Esprit, and La Rochefoucault had forced their readers to recognize the speciousness of airy system-making and the 'self-sufficiency' preached by the classical moralists. Their intolerance of 'cant' was amenable to the pragmatic spirit which reigned over so much mid-century writing as well as Johnson's own essays and conversation.

These authors, for example, had depicted the contempt of death as a pretence to disguise mankind's innate terror of extinction. In *Discourses on the Deceitfulness of Humane Virtues* (1691), Jacques Esprit took for 'an undoubted truth, (*viz.*) Death that makes Nature Tremble, and for which the Will hath Aversion and Abhorrence, can never be Condemn'd'.[5] He scoffed at the 'Imposture [of] those Philosophers and great Men, who boasted, that they were not Afraid of Death',[6] concluding that a 'Man out of a Thriftiness frequently us'd by Self-love, seeing that he cannot preserve his Life, thinks at least how to keep his Reputation, and to do nothing below a Reasonable and Well-bred Man.'[7] It is well known that Johnson was similarly sceptical of the claim that men could rise above the fear of death. As he told Boswell, 'no rational man

[3] Skelton, *Ophiomaches*, ii. 347–8.
[4] *Life*, iii. 292. See also Johnson's praise for La Rochefoucault, *Miscellanies*, i. 334.
[5] Esprit, *Deceitfulness of Humane Virtues*, pp. 302–3.
[6] Ibid. 302.
[7] Ibid. 304.

can die without uneasy apprehension'.[8] He also observed that vanity often caused men to disguise this fear. 'Scarce any man dies in publick,' he noted elsewhere in the *Life*, 'but with apparent resolution; from that desire of praise which never quits us.'[9] These remarks were, of course, drawn from Johnson's personal experience of the fear of death, not from the writings of any moralist. But they do indicate why the attack on classical virtues was finding sympathy among writers like Johnson. Like Esprit and Mandeville, Johnson was willing to reject even the noblest ideals of classical philosophy if they lacked foundation in the practical experience of real life.

A second example of the deceitfulness of classical virtue was the affected contempt for riches. According to La Rochefoucault's *Maxims* (1665),

The contempt of Riches was in the Philosophers a secret desire to revenge on Fortune the injustice she had done to their Merit, by despising the Goods which she had deny'd 'em: 'Twas an Art to secure themselves from the disgrace of Poverty; 'twas a by-way to arrive at Esteem, which they cou'd not come at, by the ordinary one of Riches.[10]

La Rochefoucault believed that a genuine hatred of riches was no more possible than a real contempt for death. The philosophers who claimed to despise riches were disguising their disappointment with their own lack of wealth. Johnson was less willing to ascribe the classical teachings against riches to mere vanity or envy. In *Rambler*, No. 58, he noted that 'no topic is more copiously treated by the ancient moralists' than the folly of accumulating riches, not because they were poor themselves, but because 'the love of money has been in all ages one of the passions that have given great disturbance to the tranquillity of the world' (iii. 309). Yet he agreed that 'every man would be rich, if a wish could obtain riches' (*Idler*, No. 73, ii. 227). And in *Rambler*, No. 58, he argued that most

---

[8] *Life*, iii. 249. Many orthodox writers, especially in the early part of the century, held that the contempt for death was possible. See, e.g., Addison, *Spectator*, Nos. 312 and 349. Johnson's view that the fear of death was indomitable also contrasts with Bacon's opinion, expressed in his essay 'Of Death'.

[9] *Life*, iii. 154.

[10] François, duc de La Rochefoucault, *Moral Reflections and Maxims* (London, 1706), Maxim liv, p. 11. See Esprit, *Deceitfulness of Humane Virtues*, p. 362.

people claimed to hate riches because they lacked the diligence necessary to earn them:

It is true, indeed, that many have neglected opportunities of raising themselves to honours and to wealth, and rejected the kindest offers of fortune: but, however their moderation may be boasted by themselves, or admired by such as only view them at a distance, it will be, perhaps, seldom found they value riches less, but that they dread labour or danger more than others (iii. 310).

Like La Rochefoucault, therefore, Johnson believed that the contempt for riches was usually deceitful. But he did not feel that men should, for that reason, give up this deceit. Johnson's essential pragmatism asserted itself at the end of *Rambler*, No. 58, when he noted that the lower orders of society could placate their envy of the rich by recalling the teachings against love of wealth. Johnson recognized that the specious virtues exposed by La Rochefoucault, Esprit, and Mandeville were, at least, often useful to happiness.

A third and more important area of attack was on the dignity of reason and human nature itself. This is where these moralists cut to the heart of ideals that dominated Christian and philosophical thought during the early decades of the eighteenth century. Classical philosophy imposed an obligation on man to suppress his natural appetites and to imitate God by always acting according to the highest principles of his nature, a duty generally harmonious with Christ's instigation, 'Be ye perfect, even as your Father which is in heaven is perfect' (Matt. 5: 48). In works of Christian humanism, such as Erasmus' *Enchiridion militis christianiti* (1504), the old classical precept was easily given a strongly Christian orientation. This marriage of classical and Christian teachings on human perfection was also made in William Law's *A Serious Call to a Devout and Holy Life* (1729), a work which Johnson is well known to have admired. The following passage from *Serious Call* was cited as an illustration for 'rational' in Johnson's *Dictionary*: 'If it is our glory and happiness to have a rational nature that is endued with wisdom and reason, that is capable of imitating the divine nature, then it must be our glory and happiness to improve our reason and wisdom, to act up to the excellency of our rational nature, and to imitate God in all our actions to the utmost of our power.'[11] William Law had been among those who had most strongly defended the dignity of human nature against Mandeville in 1724. According to Mandeville, the desire to imitate Divine nature and act up to the greatness of our nature was simply a form of pride, a drive which hypocritical moralists theoretically condemned yet freely exploited: 'sagacious moralists draw men like angels, in hope that the Pride at least of some will put 'em upon copying after the beautiful Originals which they are depicted to be.'[12] *Serious Call*, like the previous *A Treatise of Christian Perfection* (1726), was a defiant exercise in precisely that form of moral and religious exhortation.

Law clearly felt that what Mandeville called 'pride' was quite compatible with a genuine Christian humility, which was also to be 'perfected'. And according to other writers who had replied to *Fable of the Bees*, Mandeville's use of the term 'pride' was fundamentally inaccurate and misleading. This was how Mandeville was answered by Richard Fiddes, a highly respected Anglican scholar: '*Pride*, as used by [Mandeville] in this Place, is an equivocal Term. If we understand by it, a natural Consciousness of Worth in a Man, arising from a Sense of his having acted according to the Order and Perfection of his Nature, there is nothing criminal or irregular in such a Principle.'[13] Less than a decade later, however, orthodox writers would be taking quite a different view of this question. Although Christian writers upheld the dignity and strength of human reason against Mandeville, Tindal used the same ideal in 1730 to support his deistic claim that reason was sufficient without Christianity: 'as God has made us rational Creatures, and Reason tells us, that 'tis his Will, that we act up to the Dignity of our Nature; so 'tis Reason must tell when we do so.'[14]

This was basically the line of argument used throughout Law's *Serious Call* only a year before: in other words, Law

[11] William Law, *A Serious Call to a Devout and Holy Life* (1729), ed. P. G. Stanwood (London, 1978), 93.

[12] Mandeville, *Fable of the Bees*, i. 52. See Esprit, *Deceitfulness of Humane Virtues*, p. 116.

[13] Richard Fiddes, *A General Treatise of Morality form'd upon the Principles of Natural Reason Only* (London, 1724), preface, p. xxvi.

[14] Tindal, *Christianity as Old as the Creation*, p. 6.

found Christianity threatened by his own theological position. Law's response to Tindal was a stunning reversal of his previous doctrine. In *The Case of Reason* (1730) he proclaimed the utter helplessness of reason, and attacked pride in reason as diabolical. This was the beginning of Law's gradual shift away from reason and towards mysticism, which he studied throughout the 1730s. The more general shift in orthodox thought was less dramatic. Yet it is not surprising that there was a lack of praise for the dignity of reason in most of the numerous replies to *Christianity as Old as the Creation*.

Law and other orthodox writers were able to make this change because Mandeville's attack on reason, no less than the praise for human dignity, was capable of a Christian interpretation. For example, Jacques Esprit's *Deceitfulness of Humane Virtues* posed, at least, as a Christian tract maintaining the essential corruption of human nature and man's entire dependence on revelation and grace. This was close to the Augustinian teachings on human corruption, which were perhaps never very compatible with the celebration of human dignity characteristic of Christian humanism. While it would be quite inaccurate to claim that after Tindal there was a sharp turn towards Augustinianism, with its strong emphasis on original sin and grace, we might say that there was a clearer perception of an important tension in the Christian tradition which the eighteenth century had inherited. It is a tension which many eminent Christian thinkers have been able to accommodate, even celebrate. As Pascal observed of man's 'greatness and wretchedness', 'if he exalts himself, I humble him. If he humbles himself, I exalt him.'[15] Though Johnson never formulated this paradox so succinctly, his writings do embody a similar flexibility, a determination neither to exalt man too highly, nor degrade him completely.

Johnson's expressed attitudes on human dignity seem to vary according to his objective at a particular time. When necessary to dissuade men from envy and the desire for revenge, he urged them 'to maintain the dignity of a human being' (*Rambler*, No. 183, v. 200). Elsewhere he adopted the standard argument of apologetics that the recognition of

[15] Blaise Pascal, *Pensées* (1669), trans. A. J. Krailsheimer (Harmondsworth, 1962), 62.

human dignity, like the calculation of philosophical truths, was beyond the power of all but the most enlightened reasoners. For example, he approved of the use of prudent, self-interested incentives to virtue by Methodist preachers. 'To insist against drunkenness as a crime, because it debases reason, the noblest faculty of man,' Johnson observed, 'would be of no service to the common people.' It made more sense to tell common people that they might die painfully in a fit of drunkenness; such an incentive could not fail to be understood.[16]

But elsewhere Johnson expressed considerable sympathy for Mandeville's attack on human dignity. Because this attack could be justified on Christian grounds, it was upheld in Sermon 3, a treatise on sin and repentance. Just as Mandeville had claimed that virtue was 'the Political Offspring which Flattery begot upon Pride',[17] Johnson wrote:

The philosophers of the heathen world seemed to hope, that man might be flattered into virtue, and therefore told him much of his rank, and of the meanness of degeneracy; they asserted, indeed with truth, that all greatness was in the practice of virtue; but of virtue, their notions were narrow; and pride, which their doctrine made its chief support, was not of power sufficient to struggle with sense or passion (xiv. 30-1).

According to the definition of 'pride' set forth in Richard Fiddes' answer to Mandeville, Johnson misused this word in Sermon 3. There was, at least, nothing wrong with a 'pride' that strives to be great through reason and virtue. In Sermon 3, however, Johnson seemed concerned to demonstrate the superiority of Christianity to classical ethics and natural religion. 'Of that religion, which has been taught from God,' he went on, 'the basis is humility' (xiv. 31). By contrasting Christian 'humility'—the conviction in man's helplessness without God—to classical 'pride', Johnson laid down a distinction that had not always been favoured by the majority of eighteenth-century divines. Sermon 3 adopts an essentially Mandevillian argument to prove the distinctiveness of Christian virtue, an approach more favoured by divines in replies to Tindal.

---

[16] *Life*, i. 459.
[17] Mandeville, *Fable of the Bees*, i. 51.

As Philip Skelton argued in 1748, Mandeville had actually rendered a service to Christianity by ridiculing the notion that unassisted reason was 'self-sufficient'. The same year Johnson made a similar point in *Vision of Theodore*. In this allegorical tale Johnson suggested that pride, though really the only incentive to virtue available to classical and natural ethics, was insufficient to protect individuals from vicious habits. Though Pride sometimes helps the travellers to keep on the road of Reason, she 'generally betrayed her confidence, and employed all her skill to support Passion'.[18] This reflects a very common worry in Johnson's moral writings that corrupt social standards often make vice rather than virtue the object of praise. Like Sermon 3, *Vision of Theodore* indicates that pride in reason and virtue is not a proper or secure motivation for Christians. Only those on the road of Religion are protected by Conscience, which is a strong and faithful ally. Thus, Johnson deprived natural reason of a conscience, a position also taken by Skelton, yet roundly attacked as atheistical in replies to Mandeville.

We should keep in mind, however, that *Vision of Theodore* was strongly coloured by Johnson's objective to uphold the superiority of the revelation to reason. A few years later his moral essays would be back to inciting the reader to maintain the dignity of reason. And in some of his sermons we discover still another understanding of pride, one that had very little to do with the controversies with Mandeville and the deists. Sermons 6 and 8 on pride, for example, belonged to a well-established genre of homiletic writings on this subject. The conventional, down-to-earth definition of pride used in these sermons had at least one major virtue: it could convince even the most unintellectual congregation that pride blocked the way to worldly fortune, as well as the way to heaven. As we will recall, Johnson praised the use of such prudential incentives in Methodist preaching.

As a background to Sermons 6 and 8, we might consider Isaac Barrow's sermons 'Of Self-Love'; like much of this popular divine's work, these sermons seem to have strongly influenced later homiletic writings on the same subject. Barrow defined pride as a state in which 'we overvalue ourselves, our qualities and endowments, our powers and abilities, our fortune and external advantages'.[19] It is easy to see how this understanding of pride differs from the definition used by Mandeville or Johnson in Sermon 3. Barrow's definition is very like the idea of pride often used in ordinary conversation: a man is 'proud' if he thinks more highly of himself than he deserves. Pride, according to this view, is easily correctable. The proper Christian disposition of 'humility', as John Jortin would write in a later sermon, was simply when we 'entertain no better an opinion of ourselves than we deserve'.[20] A talented man who justifiably commends himself on his qualities is not, for this reason, truly guilty of 'pride' in its sinful sense.

Johnson's treatment of 'pride' in Sermon 6 is based on the same definition. 'Pride, simply considered, is an immoderate degree of self-esteem, or an over-value set upon a man by himself, and, like most other vices, is founded originally on an intellectual falsehood' (xiv. 67). This is indeed pride 'simply considered', yet Johnson found this definition satisfactory enough that he used it in his *Dictionary*: pride is defined there as 'Inordinate and unreasonable self-esteem'.[21] Such a view demanded primarily that the Christian judge himself honestly; it opposed not only unjustified self-aggrandizement, but also unnecessary self-condemnation. Moreover, writers were able to use this idea to demonstrate how 'pride', in the sense of an inaccurate self-assessment, could hinder the achievement of worldly objectives. Barrow, for example, displayed a special interest in the ways in which pride could hinder the progress of a scholar: '[Pride] is a great bar to the getting of wisedom, to the receiving instruction and right information about things; for he that taketh himself to be abundantly knowing, or incomparably wise, will not care to learn, will scorn to be taught; he thence becometh more incapable of wisedom than a mere idiot.'[22] Johnson made the identical observation in Sermon 8: 'how shall he, who is already "wise in his own conceit," submit

---

[19] Isaac Barrow, 'Of Self-Love in General', in *Works* (4 vols.; London, 1686), iii. 310.

[20] John Jortin, 'Humility', in *Sermons on Different Subjects* (7 vols.; London, 1771), iv. 21–2. Johnson admired Jortin's sermons and ranked him among his 'contemporaries of great eminence' (*Life*, iv. 161).

[21] Johnson's first definition of 'humility' was 'Freedom from pride; modesty, not arrogance'.

[22] Barrow, *Works*, iii. 320.

to . . . tedious and laborious methods of instruction? Why should he toil for that, which, in his own opinion, he possesses; and drudge for the supply of wants, which he does not feel?' (xiv. 90). Thus, pride in learning was not simply condemned as sinful or, as in the writings of Mandeville or Swift, absurd: pride was shown to be harmful to the self-interest of the scholar and teacher. Both Barrow and Johnson reminded men of the weakness of all human wisdom, the greatness of our ignorance concerning ourselves and the universe.[23] But this reminder was intended not to humiliate man, but to stimulate his renewed efforts to extend knowledge beyond its present boundaries.

The idea of 'pride' as 'inordinate self-esteem' is distinctly untheological, and assumes nothing about the reasons for our fall from Eden or the effects of original sin. Sermons 6 and 8 implied that 'pride' understood in its more rigorous theological sense (as it was used in Sermon 3) was actually quite useful; we should all strive to merit the praise we might tend to heap on ourselves unjustly. Because of the legalism of much Anglican theology and its weakened emphasis on faith, orthodox writers were generally willing to accept worldly motives so long as they efficiently produced outward virtue. Modern critics have noted the same tendency in Johnson's writings. Yet, as we shall see, he was actually less willing than many of his contemporaries to give full and unrestrained liberty to the powerful and potentially dangerous forces of human ambition.

2. *The Regulation of the Love of Fame and Applause*

'Upon an attentive and impartial review of the argument,' wrote Johnson in *Rambler*, No. 49, 'it will appear that the love of fame is to be regulated, rather than extinguished' (iii. 266). For W. J. Bate, this and other statements exemplifies Johnson's effort to provide a healthy and creative outlet for human hopes and ambitions, his 'more generalized and sensitive understanding of the need to exploit and re-direct human energies'.[24] Indeed *Rambler*, No. 49, is in important respects an

---

[23] See Sermon 6, xiv. 71; Barrow, *Works*, iii. 318–19. In *The Improvement of the Mind*, Isaac Watts gives similar advice that pride in human learning can hinder the individual's progress in knowledge. See Isaac Watts, *The Improvement of the Mind, or a Supplement to the Art of Logic* (1741) (London, 1784), ch. 1, pp. 6–29.

[24] W. J. Bate, *The Achievement of Samuel Johnson* (New York, 1955), 95.

unusual and original examination of human desires. It is significant, for example, that Johnson ranks the love of fame, and all of man's competitive urges, among the artificial or 'adscititious' desires. These are desires which have no foundation in nature, but are instead produced and given value by social custom and by the mind's restless search for new occupations. The mind, as Johnson indicated elsewhere, is a 'vacuum' which must always fill itself with new information, and will turn to any activity rather than remain entirely idle.[25] Pursuing fame is one such activity valuable primarily because it satisfies the human need for novelty and constant employment. While this understanding of desire has a lengthy history, especially in the peripatetic tradition of Aristotle, Aquinas, and Hooker, it was unusual in the eighteenth century. The majority of Johnson's contemporaries followed what might roughly be called the 'Hobbesian' belief that man is innately competitive, and has a natural desire to raise himself over his peers. *Rambler*, No. 49, indicates that Johnson disagreed. The love of fame is created by social custom.

This is what we might regard as unusual about *Rambler*, No. 49; what is *not* particularly unusual about this essay is Johnson's suggestion that the love of fame and other competitive urges can be directed towards virtuous or socially beneficial ends. Although some scholars have apparently assumed that Johnson was departing from the prevailing view on this subject,[26] he himself never pretended to have any original insights into the usefulness of pride and the desire for fame. *Rambler*, No. 49, is claiming only to review an 'argument' which, as the essay makes clear, was characterized by the clash of opinions both strongly against and strongly for the exploitation of these drives. On one side, there were writers who condemned the desire for applause; but on the other side were writers who wished to give this drive full and uncontrolled liberty. What Johnson really does in *Rambler*, No. 49, and elsewhere in his work is to define a sensible mean between positions that were too restrictive or too permissive.

---

[25] See *Rambler*, No. 85, iv. 86.
[26] See e.g., K. C. Balderston, 'Dr. Johnson and William Law', *PMLA* 75 (1960), 382–94; Alkon, *Moral Discipline*, p. 175; Gray, *Johnson's Sermons*, p. 65.

There continued to be writers in the eighteenth century who were more-or-less insensitive to the need to redirect human energies. As Johnson remarked, some considered the love of fame 'as nothing better than splendid madness, as a flame kindled by pride, and fanned by folly', for 'to what end shall we be the darlings of mankind, when we can no longer receive any benefits from their favour?' (iii. 265). This was a question asked not only by some traditionally minded Christians, but also by some secular writers who ridiculed the notion that we can receive any benefit from praise after our death. William Wollaston, for example, was among those who observed, 'Men please themselves with notions of *immortality*, and fancy a perpetuity of fame secured to themselves by books and testimonies of historians: but, alas! it is a stupid delusion, when they imagin themselves *present*, and *injoying* that fame at the reading of their story after their death'.[27] Against this position, Johnson went on, were 'the advocates for the love of fame' who 'allege in its vindication, that it is a passion natural and universal; a flame lighted by heaven, and always burning with greatest vigour in the most enlarged and elevated minds' (iii. 266). As A. O. Lovejoy indicated in a series of lectures on this subject, the advocates for fame generally predominated in the eighteenth century. This was the position, for example, of Addison and Hume.[28] The following passage from Archibald Campbell's *An Enquiry into the Original of Moral Virtue* (1733) suggests how, as Johnson observed in *Rambler*, No. 49, the love of fame was often imputed to true greatness of character: 'The Desire of true Fame and Glory, which is nothing else but *universal unlimited Esteem*, with which all men ought to be inspired, can be found only in great and elevated Minds, that are open, generous, and aspiring according to the original Frame of human nature.'[29]

Campbell is among a number of eighteenth-century moralists who concluded that the love of fame was not only

[27] Wollaston, *The Religion of Nature Delineated*, p. 117.

[28] See A. O. Lovejoy, *Reflections on Human Nature* (Baltimore, 1961), 152–98. Addison connected the desire for fame with greatness of spirit in *Spectator*, No. 255, where he cites Cicero, *De officiis*, I, viii, as his source for this view. See also Hume, *An Enquiry Concerning the Principles of Morals* (1751), in *Philosophical Works*, iv. 243.

[29] Archibald Campbell, *An Enquiry into the Original of Moral Virtue* (Edinburgh, 1733), 75–6.

useful to virtue, but was in fact the very foundation of our moral distinctions. According to these moralists, the ideas of esteem and virtue are inseparable, for virtue is, by definition, a mode of conduct which we have agreed to praise. A great deal of mid-century ethical philosophy was preoccupied with the question of why we praise virtue, the most famous discussion of this question being Hume's *An Enquiry Concerning the Principles of Morals* (1751).

Like Campbell, Hume was interested primarily in the praiseworthiness of virtue. His objective was to determine why certain actions are praised as virtues, while others are condemned as vices. His conclusion was that our admiration for benevolence and social virtues is at least partly based on our perception of their utility: 'Upon the whole, then, it seems undeniable, *that* nothing can bestow more merit on any human creature than the sentiment of benevolence in an eminent degree; and *that*, a *part*, at least, of its merit arises from its tendency to promote the interests of our species, and bestow happiness on human society'.[30] Hume's qualification that our admiration for the benevolent man was perhaps only *partly* based on utility reflects his awareness of the previous discussion of this question. In *An Inquiry into the Original of Our Ideas of Beauty and Virtue* (1725), Francis Hutcheson had argued very similarly that we can determine the virtue of an act by weighing its utility. Nevertheless, Hutcheson claimed that this calculation of the 'greatest good' would be of no significance to us unless we possessed an instinctive and disinterested propensity to love and admire beneficial acts, what Hutcheson termed 'the moral sense'. This opinion, we should note, cannot be attributed solely to a gushing sentimentalism; Hutcheson was trying to discriminate between the mere recognition of moral truth and our desire to praise and imitate goodness. Hume agreed with Hutcheson that our esteem for virtue must be partly based on 'sentiment', and in this way he avoided the more sceptical and provocative alternative that we admire beneficent acts solely as the result of self-interest, or the perceived utility of an action to us personally. This had been Archibald Campbell's conclusion. 'In my Opinion,' wrote Campbell, 'we love and

[30] Hume, *Principles of Morals*, in *Philosophical Works*, iv. 179.

esteem the Temperate, the Brave and Generous, the Prudent, the Just, the Bountiful and Beneficent, only from *Self-interest*, or because they minister to our *Pleasure.*'[31] This position—which, in British philosophy, goes back at least as far as Hobbes—was strongly favoured by Christian epicurean moralists such as Thomas Rutherforth.[32]

As we shall see more clearly in the next section, Johnson was less convinced than Hume and the others that there really was such a consistent correspondence between virtue and the prevailing standards of praise and blame. Nevertheless, he did not dispute that usefulness has always been a major subject of applause. All mankind, he wrote in Sermon 4, have 'agreed to assign the first rank of excellence to him, who most contributes to improve the happiness, and to soften the miseries of life' (xiv. 40). Even if, according to Johnson, the truth was not quite so simple, it was at least useful for people to believe that by being beneficent they would be allotted the 'first rank of excellence.' As might be expected of a moralist who generally favoured the Christian epicurean position on the self-interested basis of virtue, Johnson also indicated that our esteem for a benevolent man was founded largely on the desire for personal benefit rather than an instinctive attraction towards goodness. In *Rambler*, No. 104, for example, he contended that, at the first establishment of society, 'every man was then loved in proportion as he could contribute by his strength, or his skill, to the supply of natural wants' (iv. 190). As riches became concentrated in the hands of a few, men learned to flatter in order to gain some share in this wealth. This cynically suggested that our praise for beneficence is not only *unconsciously* self-interested, as Campbell argued, but is often feigned and deliberately self-seeking. *Rambler*, No. 104, expounded the theory of self-interest in its most extreme and provocative form. Later in his career, however, Johnson took a rather more charitable view on this issue. In 'The Life of Halifax' he admitted that the admiration of dependants for their patrons was very often genuine. 'We admire in a friend that understanding that selected us for confidence; we admire more in a patron that judgement which, instead of scattering bounty

---

[31] Campbell, *Original of Moral Virtue*, p. 361.
[32] See Rutherforth, *Nature and Obligations of Virtue*, pp. 100–1.

indiscriminately, directs it to us.'[33] According to this assessment, men flattered their benefactors because they were flattered themselves to be chosen for favour; the strictly mercenary desire for continued benefits was, at best, a subordinate motive to praise. 'To these prejudices, hardly culpable, interest adds a power always operating, though not always, because not willingly, perceived.'[34]

Johnson agreed that there was a broad if inconsistent connection between virtue and esteem; for this reason, the love of fame could conceivably benefit society if it were carefully regulated. Yet there were important theoretical objections to making ambition the primary incentive to moral conduct. In ethical philosophy, the objection was that the desire for fame necessarily lessened the moral worth of an action in the opinion of its observers. This was the argument of Francis Hutcheson, who argued that the moral value of an act was proportionate to the selflessness of its motives. 'If we knew an *Agent* had no other Motive of Action, than *Ambition*,' Hutcheson observed, 'we should apprehend no Virtue even in the most useful Actions, since they flow'd not from any *Love* to others, or *Desire* of their Happiness.'[35] It is important to keep in mind that Hutcheson was not, strictly speaking, prescribing to the reader that he *should* judge actions in this way: his argument was that we *do* make the lack of personal ambition a criterion in our judgements of what qualifies as a virtuous act. For this reason, writers such as Hume could complain that it was very unreasonable for the world to use this standard, but could not deny its influence on moral judgements.[36] In a discussion of Mrs Elizabeth Montagu's beneficence in the *Life*, Johnson also urged that we should not concern ourselves with the motives to charity:

A literary lady of large fortune was mentioned, as one who did good to many, but by no means 'by stealth,' and instead of 'blushing to find it fame,' acted evidently from vanity. JOHNSON. 'I have seen no beings who do as much good from benevolence, as she does, from

33 *Lives of the Poets*, ii. 47.
34 Ibid. For a similar analysis of gratitude, see Smith, *Moral Sentiments*, p. 214.
35 Hutcheson, *Beauty and Virtue*, p. 225.
36 See Hume, 'Of the Dignity or Meanness of Human Nature' (1741), in *Philosophical Works*, iii. 155–6.

whatever motive . . . No, Sir; to act from pure benevolence is not
possible for finite beings. Human benevolence is mingled with vanity,
interest, or some other motive.'[37]

Johnson's views are, as usual, characterized by a preoccupation with the actual benefits of greater virtue, rather than
with purely theoretical questions such as the relative value of
the motives underlying virtue. It cannot be said, however, that
he has really answered Hutcheson's position that our ideal of a
beneficent action is inseparably connected with some regard to
its motives. Johnson ratified a similar criterion when he told
Boswell that 'if I fling half a crown to a beggar with intention to
break his head . . . the physical effect is good; but, with respect
to me, the action is very wrong'.[38]

   Johnson's point in that episode was not that we should give
alms unselfishly: such a principle would contradict his position
that only self-interest can impose an obligation to act virtuously.
But he often did insist that our motives must be religious.
A good Christian could not entirely ignore Christ's injunction in
the Sermon on the Mount, 'take heed that ye do not your alms
before men, to be seen of them' (Matt. 6: 1). Some eighteenth-
century divines interpreted this text as a clear condemnation of
praise as a motive to beneficence. The High-Churchman
Francis Atterbury, for example, retained the traditional notion
that 'as far as the Nature of [charity] will admit of *Privacy*, our
Saviour hath enjoin'd it, and in Terms of a particular
Significancy and Force'.[39] Nevertheless, because there was a
great deal of sympathy with Johnson's argument that the
actual performance of charity was more important than any
question of its motives, there was some effort to reinterpret
Christ's command in a way that gave greater leeway to the
motive of ambition. The Archbishop of Canterbury, Thomas
Secker, urged his congregation to 'give Demonstration to the
World, how far the true Charity of a good Christian goes
beyond the boasted Benevolence of Unbelievers',[40] and he
elsewhere promised that 'the Givers of memorable single

---

[37] *Life*, iii. 48.

[38] Ibid. i. 397–8.

[39] Francis Atterbury, 'A Spittal-Sermon, Easter, 7 April 1707', in *Sermons and
Discourses on Several Subjects and Occasions* (2 vols.; London, 1726), ii. 156.

[40] Secker, 'Preached before the Right Honourable the Lord Mayor, on Monday in
Easter Week, 1738', in *Sermons*, p. 89.

Benefactions indeed will be longest and most extensively respected: but such as join with others, will also have Praise for it, equal to their Modest Desires'.[41]

This is where Johnson drew the line in his advocacy of ambition; he was not so willing to give Christians full latitude in their desire for praise. In his discussion of Matthew 6: 1 in Sermon 19 he attempted to define a mean between the intolerance of ambition, as exemplified by Atterbury, and Secker's unabashed encouragement of this drive:

We are commanded by Jesus Christ, when we give our alms, to divest ourselves of pride, vain-glory, and desire of applause; we are forbidden to give, that we may be seen of men, and instructed so to conduct our charity, that it may be known to our Father which seeth in secret. By this precept it is not to be understood, that we are forbidden to give alms in publick, or where we may be seen of men; for our Saviour has also commanded, that our 'light should so shine before men, that they may see our good works, and glorify our Father which is in heaven.' The meaning, therefore, of this text is not that we should forbear to give alms in the sight of men, but that we should not suffer the presence of men to act as the motive to our charity, nor regard their praise as any object to our wishes (xiv. 210).

According to this view, men should not hesitate to demonstrate the greatness of charity in public, but neither should they make the desire for glory a motive to charity. This opinion was by no means restricted to Johnson's religious writings. When we return to *Rambler*, No. 49, we find that Johnson adopts roughly the same position as in Sermon 19. 'It must be strongly impressed upon our minds', he concludes, 'that virtue is not to be pursued as one of the means to fame, but fame accepted as the only recompense which mortals can bestow on virtue' (iii. 267).

Despite his defence of Mrs Montagu's charity, therefore, Johnson did have important theoretical objections to making the love of fame a basis for our virtuous acts. Even in his secular writings he reminded his readers that ambition was not the proper Christian motive to goodness. Moreover, he also saw, with great clarity, that there were numerous practical objections to the encouragement of ambition. Quite apart from

---

[41] Secker, 'Preached before the Governors of the London Hospital, February 20, 1754', in Ibid. 275–6.

the theoretical question of the legitimacy of such motives, he recognized that the desire for fame could, if not carefully regulated, justify the most vicious acts.

Most eighteenth-century writers acknowledged that the desire for fame could never be extinguished, but many also saw that this drive had often entirely overwhelmed individuals at the expense of all honour and virtue. As Jacques Esprit wrote, 'let [a man] be of never so mild a Disposition, as soon as he desires to Immortalize himself, he will not stick to destroy all with Fire and Sword, and exterminate whole Nations, if he hath no other means to perpetuate his Fame'.[42] It was the possibility of such consequences which led a large number of moderate Christian authors such as Richard Fiddes, John Mason, and John Brown to confine the love of fame and applause to a subordinate role. John Brown, for example, contended that,

this Love of *Fame* and Fear of *Disgrace*, though as a secondary Motive to Action, it be often of the highest Consequence to Life . . . yet as a *principal* Motive, there cannot be a more *pernicious* Foundation of Virtue. For the *Effects* of this Principle will always depend on the *Opinions* of others. . . . Thus 'tis a Matter of mere *Accident*, whether its Consequences be *good* or *bad*, *wholesome* or *pernicious*.[43]

This is essentially the doctrine taught in *Rambler*, No. 49. Like Brown, Johnson argued that the effects of ambition were uncertain and accidental, and could tend either to the benefit or destruction of mankind: 'History will inform us, that this blind and undistinguished appetite for renown has always been uncertain in its effects, and directed by accident or opportunity, indifferently to the benefit or devastation of the world' (iii. 267). For this reason, again like Brown, he advised that, if 'the love of fame is so indulged by the mind as to become independent and predominant, it is dangerous and irregular; but it may be usefully employed as an inferior and secondary motive, and will serve sometimes to revive our activity, when we begin to languish' (iii. 267).

[42] Esprit, *Deceitfulness of Humane Virtues*, pp. 91–2.
[43] Brown, *Essays on the Characteristics*, pp. 202–3. See also Fiddes, *Treatise of Morality*, pp. 156–61; John Mason, *Self-knowledge* (London, 1745), 98–9; Jortin, 'Prayer', in *Sermons*, i. 347.

When considering Johnson's statement that 'the love of fame is to be regulated, rather than extinguished', we should keep in mind his injunction for *regulation*. While, like most eighteenth-century writers, he acknowledged the potential benefit of the desire for praise, he also knew that this powerful instinct had been the source of enormous villainy. This danger was sometimes forgotten by his contemporaries. It was Johnson's conviction in the need to keep ambition subordinate to the dictates of reason and virtue, rather than any particular sensitivity to the need to exploit and redirect human energies, which really distinguished his views. His attitude on this, as on so many issues, was moderate, conservative, and fundamentally Christian. He represented a group of writers who were unsatisfied with any easy or simple advice on the use of fame, who balanced their acceptance of irrational drives in human nature with the awareness that only reason and religion provided stable rules of conduct.

Yet the problem was even more complicated than this balanced and moderate conclusion would suggest. As Johnson realized, men would continue to sacrifice virtue for the sake of applause no matter how eloquently the moralist instructed them to do otherwise. He accepted as an unchangeable fact of life that the thirst for fame exercised a powerful influence even on the motives of good men, and was the overriding incentive for the great majority of mankind. And because, in Johnson's view, the standards of praise and blame did not always correspond with the standards of Christian virtue, immoral actions were often the object of applause. Thus, the great challenge before the moralist was to help correct the discrepancy between moral truth and the vague, fluctuating standards of applause. This was a task upon which the welfare of society depended, yet it could not be achieved by any single moralist. It was ultimately the responsibility of all men to ensure that only the virtuous received the rewards of fame.

3. *Social Custom and Immutable Truth*

Locke's attack on innate ideas perhaps did most to alert the century's writers to the great discrepancy between what different nations esteemed as virtue and condemned as vice.

This discrepancy was used by Locke as evidence that man possessed no natural conceptions of right and wrong: we learn to call some actions vicious and other virtuous through experience and through familiarity with the standards held by society at large. But the standards of moral conduct could be divided into three categories—the Divine law, the civil law, and the law of opinion or reputation. While 'Divine law' signified an ultimate, immutable standard of goodness, what was usually called 'virtue' or 'vice' derived from a particular society's law of opinion or reputation:

Virtue and *Vice* are names pretended and supposed every where to stand for actions in their own nature right and wrong: And so far as they are really applied, they so far are co-incident with the *divine law* above mentioned. But yet, whatever is pretended, this is visible: that those Names Virtue and Vice, in the particular instances of their application, through the several Nations and Societies of Men in the world, are consistently attributed to such actions as in each country and society are in reputation or discredit.[44]

Although what 'passes for *Vice* in one country . . . is counted a *Virtue*, or at least not *Vice*, in another',[45] these vicissitudes represented divergencies from the higher and stable Divine law.

This, at least, was Locke's opinion. But Locke's observations on the discrepancy in moral standards among nations were also used, most notably by Bernard Mandeville, to demonstrate that custom or 'fashion' was the *only* distinction between virtue and vice. In *Fable of the Bees* Mandeville remarked on the great difference between the social habits of various nations, concluding that, 'in Morals there is no greater certainty. Plurality of Wives is odious among Christians, and all the Wit and Learning of a Great Genius in defence of it has been rejected with contempt: But Polygamy is not so shocking to a Mahometan.'[46] While Locke's remarks on the vicissitudes of social custom were widely accepted, *Fable of the Bees* incited popular outrage against, as Chesterfield declared to his son, 'wretches in the world profligate enough to explode all notions of moral good and evil; to maintain that they are merely local

---

[44] Locke, *Human Understanding*, II, 353.
[45] Ibid. 354.
[46] Mandeville, *Fable of the Bees*, i. 330.

and depend entirely upon the customs and fashions of different countries'.[47] The source of this antagonism was Mandeville's failure to supply a higher, controlling standard of moral goodness. Those who replied to *Fable of the Bees*, therefore, returned to Locke's division between the Divine law and the changeable law of opinion or reputation.[48]

Another major contributor to this debate was David Hume. Hume began his *Enquiry Concerning the Principles of Morals* by proposing to examine only those qualities which make up our customary perception of 'personal merit'; like Mandeville, he cast doubt on the notion that moral distinctions have any basis in the 'nature' of the universe. Unlike Mandeville, however, Hume believed that morals *do* have a basis in 'the nature of the mind'.[49] Although, as he argued, some moral sentiments are 'created' by custom, the love of beneficence or justice is founded in the constitution of human nature, and is antecedent to all custom and education.

It is interesting to compare Hume's opinion on the basis of moral distinctions with Johnson's, for Johnson almost certainly disagreed with the very methodology of *An Enquiry Concerning the Principles of Morals*. Hume relied heavily on the customary notion of what constitutes 'personal merit', yet such a broad concept must include an extensive range of varying and even contradictory passions and responses. As Johnson commented in *Rambler*, No. 56, we often 'love' those we do not 'esteem', and we often 'esteem' those we do not 'love':

Every one must, in the walks of life, have met with men of whom all speak with censure, though they are not chargeable with any crime, and whom none can be perswaded to love, though a reason can scarcely be assigned why they should be hated; and who, if their good qualities and actions sometimes force a commendation, have their panegyrick always concluded with confessions of disgust; 'he is a good man, but I cannot like him' (iii. 301).

Thus, a virtuous man might be despised for his bad manners, while a morally worthless individual might gain our affection because of his witty conversation. Although Hume wished to

[47] Philip Dormer Stanhope, Lord Chesterfield, *Letters to His Son*, ed. E. Strachey (2 vols.; London, 1901), ii. 14.
[48] See, e.g., Fiddes, *Treatise of Morality*, preface, pp. lii–liii.
[49] See Hume, *Principles of Morals*, in *Philosophical Works*, iv. 203.

base his system on 'fact and experience', it would be extremely difficult to reduce such complications to regular theory. This, at least, was almost certainly Johnson's opinion. He frequently insisted that men were praised for qualities that had little to do with what, in the common parlance used by Hume, we call 'virtue'.

Johnson was convinced that the standard of opinion or reputation was so inconsistent that even the most criminal behaviour was admired among certain groups.[50] But we have already considered his belief that the distinction between good and evil was not accidental or temporary, but represented an immutable standard of moral order, 'everlasting and invariable principles of moral and religious truth, from which no change of external circumstances can justify any deviation' (*Adventurer*, No. 74, ii. 396). In *Rambler*, No. 201, he indicated that most societies endorsed, through the law of opinion or reputation, only certain facets of the ultimate moral standard; the individual must judge where a society deviated and where it conformed to real virtue:

So much are the modes of excellence settled by time and place, that men may be heard boasting in one street of that which they would anxiously conceal in another. The grounds of scorn and esteem, the topicks of praise and satire are varied according to the several virtues and vices which the course of life has disposed men to admire and abhor; but he who is solicitous for his own improvement, must not be limited by local reputation, but select from every tribe of mortals their characteristical virtues, and constellate in himself the scattered graces which shine single in other men (v. 283).

The problem which presented itself was how the individual could determine the ultimate, unchangeable standard of moral truth: according to Locke, man possessed no innate faculty to provide this criterion. Scripture was certainly agreed to represent a reliable guide to right and wrong, but most writers argued that men could also rely on the judgements of 'conscience', which was usually thought to have some basis in human nature.[51] As the result of Locke, writers stopped

---

[50] See *Adventurer*, No. 50, ii. 362, and compare to Mandeville, *Fable of the Bees*, i. 275.

[51] See, e.g., *Spectator*, No. 224 (of uncertain authorship); Fiddes, *Treatise of Morality*, pp. 394-7; Isaac Watts, 'Christian Morality; viz. Courage and Honour; or, Virtue and Praise', in *Works* (6 vols.; London, 1753), i. 326.

alluding to 'innate ideas', but they continued to theorize on moral 'instincts' and mankind's intuitive grasp of moral distinctions. Even Johnson, though he seemed sceptical of conscience in *Vision of Theodore*, argued in *Rambler*, No. 185, that 'the approbation of men' was 'of no weight till it has received the ratification of our own conscience' (v. 210).

The ideal was a man who uniformly consulted the dictates of conscience. On the other hand, it could not be denied that the 'approbation of men' exercised a powerful influence on the mind. No matter how strongly the moralist or divine protested, Locke remarked, he would find that the majority of men 'govern themselves chiefly, if not solely by the Law of Fashion'.[52] Johnson's moral writings are similarly directed to readers whom, he is aware, rely heavily on what they find others approve or disapprove. 'Most minds', he observed in *Rambler*, No. 70, 'are the slaves of external circumstances, and conform to any hand that undertakes to mould them' (iv. 6). This conviction inspired his deep sense of the responsibility which all authors shared in the shaping of moral attitudes, a responsibility which Mandeville and Fielding had, in his opinion, betrayed. But his belief in the influence of custom produced another effect which is characteristic of his moral outlook—an unusual sympathy with men who had been misled by corrupt standards of reputation.

Duelling, for example, was strongly sanctioned by the law of reputation yet condemned by the law of God. Intended to protect a widely accepted code of 'honour', duelling flourished in the eighteenth century—especially in the aristocracy and the military.[53] Moralists and divines almost all condemned duelling, yet it was often acknowledged that even a virtuous individual was under a great deal of pressure to respect a code upon which his reputation and even his livelihood depended. Robert South, for example, accepted that the individual who was challenged to a duel had, at least, a much better excuse to obey this custom than the man who offered the challenge:

it is confessed that the case of the challenger, and of him that is challenged, is very different. As for the former, there are few that

[52] Locke, *Human Understanding*, II, xxviii, 356–7.

[53] For some account of duelling in the eighteenth century, see J. G. Millingen, *The History of Duelling* (2 vols.; London, 1841); Ben C. Truman, *The Field of Honor* (New York, 1884).

patronize him or absolve him, under what pretence soever, he may absolve himself. But for the latter, many fair allegations may be made: as, that he loses his reputation upon refusal of the combat; and that, as to the real concernments of life, and the advantage of his fortunes, he is thought unfit for any public command or preferment which requires a person of courage; he is despised, scorned, and trampled upon, by which the contents and comforts of life, dearer than life itself, are torn from him.[54]

South showed a great deal of sympathy for the dilemma of the virtuous man challenged to a duel, but he finally made clear that, in the eyes of God, there could be no excuse for murder. 'Will you lose your soul, or your reputation,' he asked, 'the favour of God, or the opinion of men?'[55] We were to obey the Divine law, regardless of how it breached the law of opinion or reputation. This stringent Christian response to duelling was not often obeyed, but it was very often preached. In Fielding's *Amelia*, for instance, Dr Harrison similarly condemns Booth's acceptance of a challenge, despite even Amelia's concern for her husband's honour.[56] Richardson's Sir Charles Grandison exemplified a new code of honour by refusing to accept a challenge from Sir Hargrave Pollexfen. 'Where is the magnaminity', asks Sir Charles, 'of the man that cannot get above the vulgar breath?'[57]

As an essayist, Johnson wished to defend only the best standards of conduct: it was the responsibility of moral writers to vindicate ultimate moral truths. Probably for this reason, he adopted the ideal Christian response to duelling in *Rambler*, No. 185, an essay on revenge. In this essay he advocated 'an habitual appeal to everlasting justice', condemning the man who 'has nothing nobler in view than the approbation of men, of beings whose superiority we are under no obligation to acknowledge' (v. 209–10). Like Richardson, he wished to establish a new opinion of what was 'noble' or 'honourable'. In private conversation, however, Johnson was far more sympathetic to the excuses for duelling. Like the advocates for

---

54 South, Sermon VII (Rom. 12: 18), in *Sermons*, x. 224.
55 Ibid. 225.
56 See Henry Fielding, *Amelia* (1751), ed. M. C. Battestin (Oxford, 1983), XII, iii. 503–4.
57 Samuel Richardson, *Sir Charles Grandison* (1754), ed. Jocelyn Harris (3 vol.; London, 1972), Letter xxxix, i. 206.

duelling mentioned by South, Johnson suggested that this custom, though regrettable, was the only way an individual could protect his reputation and livelihood: 'He . . . who fights a duel, does not fight from passion against his antagonist, but out of self-defence; to avert the stigma of the world, and to prevent himself from being driven out of society. I could wish there was not that superfluity of resentment; but while such notions prevail, no doubt a man may lawfully fight a duel.'[58] Boswell, who seemed anxious to vindicate such a controversial opinion on duelling, explained that Johnson's argument was 'applicable only to the person who *receives* an affront. All mankind must condemn the aggressor.'[59] This apology is not very accurate or convincing because Johnson was not saying that either combatant should be 'condemned' for duelling. And by defending not only those who accept, but also those who *offer* a challenge, he showed himself far more tolerant to duelling than even the open-minded Robert South.

Johnson may have felt that, ideally, an individual should rise above the vagaries of social custom, but this was not an objective he expected most men to achieve. The onus was therefore placed on society to change the law of reputation so that it conformed with higher moral truths. But how was this change to be executed? Unlike some moralists, Johnson did not seem to think that legislation (Locke's category of the 'civil law') could have much effect on social attitudes.[60] He turned to less direct and formal means of rectifying custom. Besides his insistence on the responsibility of authors to advocate only the best standards of conduct, Johnson also focused on the importance of complete honesty in our praise or dispraise of others. This rule applied especially to the praise of great men who, because of their power and prestige, exercised enormous influence on the fashions of conduct.

The standards of reputation were especially corrupted by the dishonest praise of great men by their dependants. Although flattery had always been a topic for ridicule among moralists, no essayist of the eighteenth century so frequently warned that

[58] *Life*, ii. 180.

[59] ii. Ibid.

[60] As recommended by, e.g., George Blewitt, *An Enquiry whether a General Practice of Virtue tends to the Wealth or Poverty, Benefit or Disadvantage of a People* (London, 1725), 74; Addison, *Spectator*, No. 99, i. 419.

this practice was not only degrading, but extremely harmful to the moral welfare of society. As he wrote in *Rambler*, No. 136:

To scatter praise or blame without regard to justice, is to destroy the distinction of good and evil. Many have no other test of actions than general opinion; and all are so far influenced by a sense of reputation, that they are often restrained by fear of reproach, and excited by hope of honour, when other principles have lost their power; nor can any species of prostitution promote general depravity more than that which destroys the force of praise, by shewing that it may be acquired without deserving it, and which, by setting free the active and ambitious from the dread of infamy, lets loose the rapacity of power, and weakens the only authority by which greatness is controlled (iv. 355).

Johnson recognized that the law of opinion and reputation, despite its fluctuations, was controlled by certain stable qualities—wealth, rank, and power.[61] The danger was that these attributes were very often combined with the most pernicious vices. Great men were not necessarily more wicked than other men, but their imperfections became an example to all society, especially when they were glossed over by indiscriminate flattery. The great problem, as he explained elsewhere, was that the wealthy and powerful were the most common models for moral conduct.

All men wish to be like those they admire. 'The greater part of humankind', Johnson wrote in *Rambler*, No. 164, 'speak and act wholly by imitation' (v. 107). But imitation was frequently as indiscriminate as flattery. Unable to achieve wealth, rank, or power, men attempted to share in the greatness of their heroes by imitating all their actions and habits, both good and bad. As Johnson went on to warn in *Rambler*, No. 164:

There is scarce any failing of mind or body, any error of opinion, or depravity of practice, which, instead of producing shame and discontent, its natural effects, has not at one time or other gladdened vanity with the hopes of praise, and been displayed with ostentatious industry by those who sought kindred minds among the wits or heroes, and could prove their relation only by similitude of deformity (v. 108).

---

[61] A truth also noted by Addison, *Spectator*, No. 219, ii. 352; La Rochefoucault, *Maxims*, Maxim ccxii, p. 87; Jean de la Bruyère, *Characters, or Manners of the Present Age* (1688), in *Works* (2 vols.; London, 1713), ii. 173.

This was not to argue that imitation was itself an undesirable habit. Indeed, this incentive could produce very positive effects if it were properly directed. Most eighteenth-century moralists agreed with Johnson that 'emulation' could benefit both society and the individual on the condition that 'the original is well-chosen and judiciously copied' (v. 107).[62] 'Judiciously copied' meant that the imitator should carefully choose between what was worthy and unworthy to be emulated in the great man's character, a distinction greatly confused by dishonest flattery.

In their praise of a great man, therefore, encomiasts should laud all that was worthy in his character, but also condemn all that was vicious. By this means, the allure of greatness would be associated only with what was truly admirable. Moreover, great men must accept their considerable responsibility in regulating the standards of praise and censure. As Johnson wrote in Sermon 17, 'superiority of riches, or hereditary honour, is frequently made use of to corrupt and deprave the world', but the same prestige 'might be employed, if it were to be obtained only by desert, to the noblest purposes. It might discountenance vanity and folly; it might make the fashion cooperate with the laws, and reform those upon whom reason and conviction have no force' (xiv. 189–90). Johnson would never seriously suggest that moral character could, or even should, be made the only means to obtain rank or riches, but he did believe that the reformation of society must begin with the effort of its great men to set a standard of real goodness. In this way, qualities such as rank and wealth which determined the laws of reputation would cast their lustre on goodness. Common men who, as Locke observed, regulated their conduct almost entirely by opinion, would seek to be like men as remarkable for their goodness as for their riches and prestige. And the great problem of harmonizing reputation and immutable truth would be resolved by making 'fashion cooperate with the laws'.

4. *Johnson's New Standard of Human Greatness*

Johnson's efforts to unite virtue with fashion illustrate the pragmatism which is one of the most characteristic features of

---

[62] See, e.g., Fiddes, *Treatise of Morality*, pp. 257–8; Mason, *Self-knowledge*, 46 and 97–8; La Rochefoucault, *Maxims*, Maxim ccxxx, p. 96.

his moral writing. His attitude towards those 'upon whom reason and conviction have no force', was not without a certain disdain, yet it was an unchangeable truth of society that a great many individuals—including the majority of his readership—found wealth and prestige far more alluring than virtue. It would be very wrong to assume, however, that Johnson lacked his own ideal of true greatness, or believed that the prevailing standards of reputation were without their disadvantages, even when redirected towards beneficial ends. While Johnson recognized the potential benefits of wealth and prestige to society, he also saw that, as the result of the prevailing standard of reputation, the virtues and talents of those in the lower ranks of society were usually ignored. The same majority which idolized and emulated the rich man, unjustly scorned the true greatness of those who toiled in poverty and obscurity.

There was little novel about this observation in itself. As Johnson admitted in *Rambler*, No. 166, 'No complaint has been more frequently repeated in all ages than that of the neglect of merit associated with poverty, and the difficulty with which valuable or pleasing qualities force themselves into view, when they are obscured by indigence' (v. 116). Indeed, the ignominy of poverty had long been a topic for moralists. Richard Steele had dedicated a whole section of *The Christian Hero* (1701) to this problem: 'It is in every Body's Observation, with what disadvantage a Poor man Enters upon the most ordinary Affairs. . . . For as certainly as Wealth gives Acceptance and Grace to all that it's [*sic*] possessor says and does, so Poverty creates disesteem, scorn, and prejudice to all the Undertakings of the Indigent.'[63] It is significant, however, that Johnson would later censure Steele for his unjust treatment of the impoverished Richard Savage;[64] and even in *The Christian Hero* Steele does not finally launch the defence of the poor which the reader probably expects. Before Johnson the indignity of poverty was often treated as an unfortunate reality that perhaps only the Last Judgement would rectify. Very few anticipated Johnson's appeal in *Adventurer*, No. 67, to look beyond the superficial disgrace of poverty, and to allot our own

[63] Richard Steele, *The Christian Hero: An Argument Proving that No Principles but those of Religion are Sufficient to make a Great Man* (London, 1701), 51.
[64] See *Lives of the Poets*, ii. 331–2.

praise and blame according to a higher standard of greatness:

he whose comprehension can take in the whole subordination of mankind, and whose perspicacity can pierce to the real state of things through the thin veils of fortune or of fashion, will discover meanness in the highest stations, and dignity in the meanest; and find that no man can become venerable but by virtue, or contemptible but by wickedness (ii. 386).

One group that did strongly defend the dignity of the poor was the Methodists, whom Johnson frequently complimented for spreading religion among the common people.[65] In this way he differed from the great majority of the Anglican clergy who, like Joseph Trapp in his 1739 attack on the Methodists, condemned those 'ignorant, illiterate people' who 'presume to *expound the Scriptures*'.[66] This does not mean that Johnson was entirely without a strong personal sense that poverty was disgraceful, even in virtuous men. In 1765, for example, he invited a poor, meanly dressed man home to dinner—'a kind of Methodist'. But he finally let the man leave without dinner, later admonishing himself in his diaries, 'let me not be prejudiced hereafter against the appearance of piety in mean persons' (i. 94). To judge men solely by their virtue and piety was an ideal which Johnson himself had to struggle to achieve.

Johnson's effort to see through the trappings of fashion was exemplified not only by his defence of impoverished merit, but also by his interest in the virtues or defects of individuals in the unadorned simplicity of domestic life. It had often been noted that an intimate familiarity with even the most prestigious men usually deprived them of the admiration allotted by public opinion. As Addison remarked in *Spectator*, No. 256, 'we may generally observe, that our Admiration of a famous Man lessens upon our nearer Acquaintance with him'.[67] Eighteenth-century writers evidently attached great importance to this tendency: even Robert Nelson's popular book of devotion, *A Companion for the Festivals and Fasts of the Church of England* (1705), touched on it. Moreover, it was agreed by Addison and Nelson that the lessening of esteem through intimacy was the result of

[65] See *Life*, ii. 123.
[66] Joseph Trapp, *The Nature, Folly, Sin and Danger of Being Righteous Over-much* (London, 1739), 12.
[67] *Spectator*, ii. 495.

hidden vices in the character of famous men, 'those Frailties and Imperfections which are sometimes mixt with great Virtues, and which are only discovered by a great Intimacy with them'.[68] Familiarity weakened esteem because it gradually exposed the great man's imperfections.

It was this assumption which Johnson believed was inaccurate. *Idler*, No. 51, is devoted to the same precept, 'that eminent men are least eminent at home, that bright characters lose much of their splendor at a nearer view' (ii. 158). He went on to note that 'This disparity of general and familiar esteem is . . . imputed to hidden vices, and to practices indulged in secret, but carefully covered from the publick eye' (ii. 158). Yet such a conclusion, Johnson contended, was exceedingly unjust. In reality, it would be found that the 'awe which great actions or abilities impress will be inevitably diminished by acquaintance, tho' nothing either mean or criminal should be found' (ii. 159). Our admiration for a great man was originally founded only on a superficial knowledge which refused to acknowledge the existence of a plain, domestic existence behind the ornaments of fame; it was the exposure of an ordinary man, not hidden vices, which really lessened our esteem. For Johnson, however, it was the challenge of every individual to rise above these prejudices, to appreciate the simple merits of common life. As he wrote in *Rambler*, No. 68, 'it is, indeed, at home that every man must be known by those who would make a just estimate either of his virtue or felicity' (iii. 360).

As Isobel Grundy remarked in *Samuel Johnson and the Scale of Greatness*, Johnson wished 'to readjust the human scale without reference to anything more than human, to inculcate measurement by a scale more humane than those customarily used by literature or morality'.[69] Indeed, he departed from the majority of his contemporaries by attempting to see beyond the trappings of public eminence, and to demonstrate the value of life in its humblest circumstances, in poverty and in the uneventful rounds of domestic privacy. The distinctiveness of this feature of Johnson's thought might be made clearer by comparing an essay on greatness by Addison with one on the same theme by Johnson. In *Spectator*, No. 317, Addison cited

[68] Nelson, *Festivals and Fasts*, p. 497. See *Spectator*, No. 256, ii. 495.
[69] I. Grundy, *Samuel Johnson and the Scale of Greatness* (Leicester, 1986), 77–8.

an anecdote from Suetonius' *Lives of the Caesars*. Suetonius had recalled that 'Augustus, a few Moments before his death, asked his Friends who stood about him, if they thought he had acted his Part well; and upon receiving such an Answer as was due to his extraordinary Merit, *Let me then*, says he, *go off the stage with your Applause*.'[70] For Addison, this story contained a lesson for all individuals. He wished that 'Men, while they are in Health, wou'd consider well the Nature of the Part they are engaged in, and what Figure it will make in the Minds of those they leave behind them.'[71] Instead of this, he complained: 'if we look into the Bulk of our Species, they are such as are not likely to be remember'd a Moment after their Disappearance. . . . Their Actions are of no Significancy to Mankind, and might have been performed by Creatures of much less Dignity, than those who are distinguished by the Faculty of Reason.'[72] Although Addison undoubtedly accepted that most men would never achieve the greatness of Augustus, he felt that the failure of ordinary people to desire anything more than obscurity was unworthy of the dignity of human reason. Despite the popular topics often treated in the *Spectator*, Addison was not always patient with those satisfied with the mediocrity of domestic happiness and minor virtues.

In *Idler*, No. 88, Johnson suggested that the view expressed by Addison represented a 'mistaken notion of human greatness' (ii. 274). He offered this consolation for those 'much irritated or pained by the consciousness of their meanness': 'a little more than nothing is as much as can be expected from a being who with respect to the multitudes about him is himself little more than nothing' (ii. 274–5). Citing the same anecdote on the death of Augustus, Johnson proposed what might be called his new standard of human greatness:

He that has improved the virtue or advanced the happiness of one fellow-creature, he that has ascertained a single moral proposition, or added one useful experiment to natural knowledge, may be contented with his own performance, and with respect to mortals like himself, may demand, like Augustus, to be dismissed at his departure with applause (ii. 275).

[70] *Spectator*, iii. 152.
[71] Ibid.
[72] Ibid. 152–3.

This passage does not embody the whole truth about Johnson's understanding of greatness. As W. J. Bate pointed out, Johnson also reminded us (as in *Rambler*, No. 4) that 'few enterprises that involve labour or risk would ever be undertaken to begin with if we did not magnify the importance of what we are doing'.[73] Yet he also knew that this delusion would inevitably be shattered, and with it the desire to struggle on. 'He who has pleased himself with anticipated praises', he wrote in *Rambler*, No. 126, '. . . will soon remit his vigour, when he finds that from those who desire to be considered as his admirers nothing can be hoped but cold civility' (iv. 314). For the sake of our continued endeavours, and for the sake of our happiness, it was finally necessary to face our obscurity and relative smallness with honesty and submission. It was then that Johnson's more moderate and realistic standard of greatness would become mankind's major solace in this world.

Like very few others, Johnson endeavoured to give a new dignity to the virtues and struggles of those who were not, nor ever could be, the object of public applause. This was a concern which inspired much of his best work—*The Life of Savage* (1744); 'The Death of Dr. Robert Levet' (1783). Moreover, his new standard of human greatness reflects some of the most distinctive features of his moral writing. First, he was convinced that the happiness and virtue of individuals relied not so much on great acts, but on the goodness of daily life amidst our small and, in comparison to the multitudes of humanity, obscure circle of friends and dependants. Second, Johnson's moral writing is characterized by an enormous compassion which, even in an age which prided itself for beneficence, was in fact quite rare. Johnson was deeply sceptical of what was usually accounted greatness or fame; he passionately admired those who did their best without recognition. And in both his scepticism and idealism, rather than in any new realization of how the pursuit of applause could be redirected, he excelled his age.

[73] Bate, *Achievement*, p. 137.

6

Christian Charity in Theory and Practice

1. *The Christian Theory of Charity*

Eighteenth-century attitudes on charity and the poor are filled
with conflict and indecision. The same eighteenth-century
writer can, at different times, impress the modern reader with
the extraordinary exuberance of his generosity or with his cold
lack of sympathy for the poor. For example, few authors have
defended the poor so eloquently as Henry Fielding the novelist,
yet the same author, in his capacity as justice of the peace,
enjoined the most stringent legal measures to keep the lower
classes docile and subservient to the wealthy.[1] In this respect,
Fielding was highly representative of an age torn between its
lofty and often sentimentalized ideals of beneficence, and the
practical realities of a society—especially in London—afflicted
with an increasingly brutal, drunken, and crime-ridden low
life. On the one hand, the century celebrated the ready
beneficence of the Christian hero; on the other, it discouraged
charity as harmful to social order and created a penal code of
alarming violence and inflexibility.

With Johnson, we have quite a different approach to the
theory and practice of charity. His ideals of charity are not
nearly so lofty or exacting as those of writers such as Fielding.
Although there is no doubt that Johnson thought a great deal
about the nature of the charitable duties commanded by Scripture, his conclusions leave the individual with considerable
freedom concerning the choice and extent of his beneficence
and good will. In practice, however, Johnson's charity was so
frequent and extensive that it prompted not only admiration,
but also discomfort and criticism among some of his compan-
ions.[2] And nowhere is the efficiency of Johnson's charity better

[1] Fielding's plans for reducing the growing blight of urban crime and poverty are
outlined in two pamphlets, *An Inquiry into the Late Increase of Robbers* (1751) and *A
Proposal for the Effectual Provision of the Poor* (1752). As M. R. Zirker shows in *Fielding's
Social Pamphlets* (Berkeley and Los Angeles, 1966), Fielding's harsh opinions on
poverty were very conventional.

[2] Sir John Hawkins, for instance, wondered how Johnson 'could bear to be
surrounded by such necessitous and undeserving people as he had about him'. See
Hawkins, *Life*, p. 306.

exemplified than in his principles of social reform, principles so liberal and humane that they would remain at the liberal fringe of political thought until at least the nineteenth century.

First, however, we must examine the Christian theory of charity which was a primary basis and incentive of Johnson's altruism. We have already seen that, according to eighteenth-century divines, Christian charity was distinguished from all previous forms of beneficence by its insistence that 'universal Love' was a 'necessary and essential Duty'.[3] But quite apart from their controversy with the deists, Christian writers staged their own debates on the precise nature of this universal love, and the extent to which this duty was truly necessary and absolute. This debate ranged through a series of key Scriptural texts which, interpreted in varying ways, imposed very different standards of charity on the individual.

The first issue concerned the definition of charity. 'Charity' has traditionally meant far more than the distribution of alms to the poor: in scholastic literature, Christian charity included both alms or 'corporeal' charity, and 'spiritual' charity—ways of caring for others which do not concern their physical welfare. Edward Stillingfleet noted in a charity sermon that 'The Schoolmen reckon up seven sorts of Corporeal Alms, and as many of Spiritual.' The seven forms of spiritual alms were, '*to teach the ignorant, to advise the doubtful, to comfort the sorrowful, to correct the wicked, to forgive the injurious, to bear the troublesome, to pray for all*'.[4] Johnson's five definitions of 'charity' in the *Dictionary* are, like many of his definitions of moral and religious terms, wide enough to encompass almost any understanding of this virtue. In his sermons, however, his definition of charity is very precise. In Sermon 4 Johnson was willing to extend the definition of charity beyond the distribution of alms, but it will be noted that he added only the duties of instruction and correction from the schoolmen's seven forms of spiritual alms:

every degree of assistance given to another, upon the proper motives, is an act of charity; and there is scarcely any man, in such a state of imbecillity, as that he may not, on some occasions, benefit his

---

[3] See ch. 2, sec. 3, above.

[4] Edward Stillingfleet, 'Of Protestant Charity', in *Works* (6 vols.; London, 1710), i. 313. Eighteenth-century divines often cited the scholastic definition of charity. See also Samuel Clarke, 'Of the Duty of Charity', in *Sermons*, vi. 418.

neighbour. He that cannot relieve the poor, may *instruct the ignorant*; and he that cannot attend the sick, may *reclaim the vicious*. He that can give little assistance himself, may yet perform the duty of charity, by inflaming the ardour of others, and recommending the petitions, which he cannot grant, to those who have more to bestow (xiv. 45 [my italics]).

The other major forms of spiritual alms—commiseration, tolerance, forgiveness—were included in Sermon 11 on what Johnson called 'the system of domestic virtues' (xiv. 118 and 126), a subject sometimes treated separately by the divines, but usually introduced randomly into general discussions of charity. Unlike many contemporaries, then, Johnson tended to use the word 'charity' to signify substantial, practical forms of support (alms, instruction, correction), rather than the various manifestations of a charitable temperament. This is a preliminary indication of his strongly pragmatic understanding of this virtue. In addition, his more restrictive use of the term 'charity' will strike us as typical of a lexicographer, yet it is in his essays and sermons, not in his *Dictionary*, that he defines 'charity' and similar terms most rigorously.

Eighteenth-century writers liked the scholastic definition of charity partly because it gave the individual such latitude in his choice of beneficent acts. In their own discussions of charity, independent of the debate with the deists, divines and moralists usually argued that charity should *not* be a 'necessary and essential duty', but should be left open, unsystematized and regulated by a man's particular circumstances and opportunities. They generally rejected the notion that the Christian was absolutely required to give alms. As the clergyman David Fordyce wrote in *The Elements of Moral Philosophy* (1754), charity should be 'left to the Candour, Humanity, and Gratitude of Individuals',[5] and not enforced by any binding law, secular or divine. Johnson advocated the same idea of charity in *Rambler*, No. 81:

[5] David Fordyce, *The Elements of Moral Philosophy* (London, 1754), 178–9. The same unwillingness to make charity an absolute duty is expressed by Stillingfleet, 'Of Protestant Charity', in *Works*, i. 313; William Sherlock, 'The Nature and Measure of Charity', in *Sermons Preach'd upon Several Occasions* (2nd edn.; London, 1702), 248; Sir Matthew Hale, 'Of doing as we would be done unto', in *The Works, Moral and Religious* (2 vols.; London, 1805), i. 399.

We may certainly, without injury to our fellow-beings, allow in the distribution of kindness something to our affections, and change the measure of our liberality according to our opinions and prospects, our hopes and fears . . . liberality and kindness, absolutely determined, would lose their nature; for how could we be called tender, or charitable, for giving that which we are positively forbidden to withhold? (iv. 63).

Johnson and other writers took this position as the result of a basic principle of ethical philosophy: freedom of choice is essential to the definition of a virtuous act. It should be noted, however, that the principle of freedom hindered progress during the eighteenth century towards efficient systems of relief for the poor. Even the parish relief law that ensured the survival of a large proportion of England's rural poor, the 43rd Elizabeth, was attacked on precisely the grounds described by Johnson in *Rambler*, No. 81—that charity should be left entirely voluntary.[6]

Moreover, eighteenth-century divines had to explain their understanding of certain texts of Scripture which seem to require charity as an absolute duty. Chief among these texts was Matthew 19: 21, where Christ instructs a rich young man, 'go and sell that thou hast and give to the poor'. For a fundamentalist like William Law, at least, Christ's instruction applied literally to all Christians; men must dedicate their estates to the needy through the practice of habitual almsgiving, if not in one great act of beneficence.[7] But Law was a rare dedicated theorist in an age which favoured a more pragmatic scheme of social duties. Most writers on charity did their best to show that Matthew 19: 21 did not actually instruct Christians to open all their possessions to the poor. Joseph Trapp's attack on Law's theology, *The Nature, Folly, Sin and Danger of Being Righteous Over-much* (1739), included angry remarks on the impracticality of Law's interpretation of this text, arguing that Matthew 19: 21 was applicable only to rich men in Christ's time.[8] Other divines reduced Christ's words to a metaphorical injunction against a worldly spirit.[9] In Sermon

[6] See Thomas Alcock, *Observations on the Defects of the Poor Laws* (London, 1752), 11.

[7] See William Law, *A Practical Treatise on Christian Perfection* (1726) in *Works* (9 vols.; London, 1762, repr. Setley, Hants., 1862–3), iii. 47–57.

[8] See Trapp, *Righteous Over-much*, pp. 19–20.

[9] See, e.g., South, 'The Recompense of the Reward', in *Sermons*, iv. 187–8.

27 Johnson argued that they referred only to those who made the priesthood their vocation.[10] Little wonder Matthew Tindal complained that orthodox writers were simply avoiding an acknowledgement that Matthew 19: 21 was essentially less reasonable than the dictates of common sense.[11]

It was because eighteenth-century Christians wanted charity to be regulated by common sense that praise for Matthew 7: 12, 'all things whatsoever ye would that men should do to you, do ye even so to them', became such an obsessive topic of charity sermons. Again and again 'the Universal Rule of Equity' was lauded for its simplicity, comprehensiveness, and, above all, its appeal to the individual's private judgement rather than to some absolute rule for giving. As the seventeenth-century judge, Matthew Hale, wrote in an essay on Matthew 7: 12:

As it is a compendious and comprehensive, so it is a plain and perspicacious, and self-evident rule; it sends not a man to consult with this or that philosopher, schoolman or casuist, to be resolved touching the thing to be forborn or done, but sends a man to himself; namely, what he would wish to be done to himself in the like condition; which, if a man will be but so honest to himself as he may, he can easily determine and judge.[12]

Johnson's *Rambler*, No. 81, is largely derived from the very large group of eighteenth-century sermons and essays on Matthew 7: 12. His initial praise for this text uses precisely the same reasoning found in Hale's essay:

The measure of justice prescribed to us, in our transactions with others, is remarkably clear and comprehensive: 'Whatsoever ye would that men do unto you, even so do unto them.' A law by which every claim of right may be immediately adjusted, so far as the private conscience requires to be informed; a law, of which every man may find the exposition in his own breast, and which may always be observed without any other qualifications than honesty of intention, and purity of will (iv. 61).

---

[10] Sermon 27, xiv. 291.

[11] See Tindal, *Christianity as Old as the Creation*, p. 339.

[12] Hale, 'Of doing as we are done unto', in *Works*, i. 380. Matthew 7: 12 is praised in almost exactly the same words by Isaac Watts, 'The Universal Rule of Equity', in *Works*, i. 359; Atterbury, 'The Rule of doing as we would be done unto', in *Sermons*, i. 313.

The Golden Rule left individuals with the freedom of judgement that eighteenth-century writers desired in their rule of charity. Yet, despite the supposed clarity and simplicity of Matthew 7: 12, even this text became the topic of debate regarding its precise meaning.

The controversy stemmed from the study of problematic issues of conscience undertaken by the 'casuists' of the Roman Catholic Church, a group energetically assailed by many eighteenth-century Englishmen.[13] The casuists had raised two problems concerning Matthew 7: 12 that, according to the English divines, dangerously perplexed the Rule of Equity. First, the casuists noted that this test of charity might justify supporting the vicious desires of another person, since in the same circumstances we would like our own vices supported. Divines such as Francis Atterbury responded that the Rule of Equity was 'to be understood not of vicious and excessive Desires, but of such only as are fit and reasonable'.[14] In *Rambler*, No. 81, Johnson also discussed the problem raised by the 'sons of sophistry', similarly admonishing that 'surely there needed no long deliberation to conclude, that the desires, which are to be considered by us as the measure of right, must be such as we approve' (iv. 61–2). A second problem raised by the casuists concerned the duty of a magistrate, who might believe that he was required to pardon every criminal. After all, in the same circumstances he would also want a pardon. Atterbury and Isaac Watts discussed this problem at some length in their sermons on Matthew 7: 12, and seemed to experience some difficulty in finding a really satisfying resolution.[15] Johnson was more curt in his discussion of this problem in *Rambler*, No. 81, generally elaborating on Sir Matthew Hale's dictum, cited in *Rambler*, No. 60, 'Let me remember . . . when I find myself inclined to pity a criminal, that there is likewise a pity due to the country' (iii. 323): the judge should identify his wishes with those of the whole nation, not just the criminal. Nevertheless, *Rambler*, No. 81, leaves the reader with the distinct impression that Matthew 7: 12 was not

---

[13] Even Lord Chesterfield warned against the 'refinements of Casuists' in *Letters to His Son*, i. 271.

[14] Atterbury, *Sermons*, i. 313.

[15] See ibid. 314; Watts, *Works*, i. 357.

nearly so clear, simple, and comprehensive as had been claimed. Like other writers who had praised this text, Johnson was forced to buttress the Golden Rule with various other criteria and measures of right and wrong.

The controversies surrounding Matthew 7: 12 and 19: 21 reflect a general uncertainty about how laymen should be instructed on the virtue of charity, an uncertainty created by the unwillingness to set down any hard rules. But these controversies were minor compared with the disagreement aroused by a feature of Christian charity that, against the deists, had been praised as perhaps revelation's major contribution to ethics—the law of universal love. This idea derives from more than one text of Scripture, including Galatians 5: 14 ('Thou shalt love thy neighbour as thyself') and Matthew 5: 44 ('Love your enemies'). Its theoretical demand on the individual is considerable, yet many divines, including Samuel Clarke and William Law, insisted that we must take the law of universal love literally: we must love all men equally, even those who do us wrong.[16] But this interpretation was not likely to find general sympathy among most orthodox Christians. Although universal love continued to be a mainstay of the case against the deists, pragmatic divines such as Daniel Waterland insisted that this rule should not be interpreted so strictly that it imposed unreasonable demands on human nature. 'Such an *equal* degree of love is neither practicable nor reasonable,' wrote Waterland; 'it is not *possible* to love Friends and Enemies, Allies and Aliens, Worthy and Unworthy, All in the same *Degree*: or if it were possible, yet both *Scripture* and *Reason* direct us to love with *Distinction*, and to give the Preference where it is found due.'[17]

The same pragmatism generally characterized Johnson's treatment of universal love. 'To love all equally is impossible', he wrote in *Rambler*, No. 99; 'at least impossible without the extinction of those passions which now produce all our pains and all our pleasures' (iv. 166). Like Waterland, Johnson believed not only that universal love was an unattainable

---

[16] See Samuel Clarke, *Natural Religion*, pp. 95–6; Law, *Serious Call*, ch. 20, pp. 297–8.

[17] Daniel Waterland, 'The Duty of Loving Our Neighbour as Ourselves', in *Sermons on Several Important Subjects of Religion and Morality* (2 vols.; London, 1742), i. 48.

standard, but also that its theoretical attainment would not be in the best interests of mankind. 'The necessities of our condition require a thousand offices of tenderness, which mere regard for the species will never dictate. . . . The great community of mankind is therefore, necessarily broken into smaller independent societies' (iv. 166). This idea of 'smaller independent societies'—by which Johnson meant professions, clubs, friendships, and so forth—is curiously reminiscent of those forms of limited benevolence on which Christianity was supposed to have improved.[18] Nevertheless, Johnson did not entirely abandon the Christian ideal of a more comprehensive concern for mankind. *Rambler*, No. 99, proposes a more practical and certainly less idealistic alternative to the literal interpretation of universal love, what Johnson described as 'a general habit of benevolence' (iv. 166).

This general habit of benevolence was largely intended to overcome the possible dangers of the 'independent societies'. While it is inevitable and even beneficial that we feel greater affection for our associates and friends than for mankind in general, this preference should not harden into spite for others not in our group, 'the rage of party' by which, as Johnson warned in Sermon 27, 'the ardour of charity is overborn and destroyed' (xiv. 295–6). Both the Civil War and the flourishing of political factions in contemporary society contributed to the eighteenth century's deep concern to control (though not eliminate) party spirit: Johnson's injunction for at least a peaceable benevolence towards those in other parties was conventional.[19] Yet there is a further and more difficult question. How far should this general habit of benevolence extend? Should we, for instance, live in peace and charity with atheists, heretics, or dissenting Christians who advocated erroneous doctrines?

The answer for many Whig and Low-Church divines was a qualified 'yes'. John Jortin urged that all Christians should be 'united in charity, though not in opinion', and advised that we 'not pass a rash and a hard sentence on those errors, which

---

[18] See ch. 2, sec. 3, above.

[19] See, e.g., Swift's comparable attack on party spirit in his sermon 'Of Brotherly Love', in *Irish Tracts 1720–23 and Sermons*, ed. H. Davis and L. Landau (Oxford, 1963).

have not a manifest connection with immorality'.[20] There were
even a few idealists, such as Samuel Lobb, who applied the
dictum 'Love your enemies' quite literally, 'without excepting
either God's enemies or our own cursers, haters of their
fellow-creatures, malicious persons, and persecutors'.[21] But for
divines who spent their careers amidst the turbulent pamphlet
wars of the eighteenth century, who condemned deists, and, if
they were High-Churchmen, opposed toleration for dissenters,
such an extension of Christian benevolence was neither
practical nor consistent with their own conduct. Daniel
Waterland, for example, justified his belief that Christians
were not prohibited from breaking the peace on important
religious questions by appealing to Christ's own 'Contests and
warm Disputes with the Scribes and Pharisees. . . . It is
manifest therefore that we ought not, and in Reason cannot
seek Peace any otherwise, than in regard and in subordination
to . . . the Glory of God.'[22]

An unwavering and vehement opponent to full rights for
dissenters, Johnson's understanding of universal love was
predictably restricted in the same way: like Waterland, he felt
that the Christian was under no obligation to live peaceably
with those whose religious opinions threatened the maintenance of truth or civil order. His sermon on the general
habit of benevolence, Sermon 11, focuses on the need for peace
and charity among those who disagree on purely political or
philosophical issues, but it also alludes to the struggles against
heathenism in the primitive Church.[23] The sermon makes no
effort to justify benevolence towards dissenters, and places a
high importance on the need to correct religious errors.

Johnson's notion of universal love or even the 'general habit
of benevolence' can therefore be whittled down to a fairly
narrow range of duties. He was far less idealistic in his conception of Christian love than even many orthodox writers in
his own day. And his fullest explanation of universal love in
Sermon 11 particularly emphasizes that our expression of love
towards non-Christians, and perhaps even fellow-Christians

[20] Jortin, 'The Difference of Duties', in *Sermons*, iii. 59.

[21] Samuel Lobb, *The Benevolence Incumbent on us, as Men and Christians, Considered*
(London, 1746), 7.

[22] Waterland, 'The Nature of Peaceableness', in *Sermons*, i. 13–14.

[23] See *Yale Edition*, xiv. 118.

who advocate erroneous doctrines, should take the form of instruction, rather than simply peaceableness and alms-giving:

Charity, or universal love, is named by Saint Paul as the greatest and most illustrious of Christian virtues; and our Saviour himself has told us, that by this it shall be known that we are his disciples, if we love one another. Every affection of the soul exerts itself most strongly at the approach of its proper object. Christians particularly love one another, because they can confer and receive spiritual benefits. They are indeed to love all men, and how much the primitive preachers of the gospel loved those that differed from them, they sufficiently shewed, when they incurred death by their endeavours to make them Christians. This is the extent of evangelical love, to bring into the light of truth those who are in darkness, and to keep those from falling back into darkness to whom the light has been shewn (xiv. 123).

Johnson's argument that Christians will naturally love each other 'because they can confer and receive spiritual benefits' relates to an essentially selfish basis for affection: our greatest love is for those who are able to benefit us the most. This idea of love is consistent with Johnson's advocacy of the epicurean tradition in ethics, but its appearance in a sermon on Christian altruism is perhaps a bit surprising. Surely Christians should love each other for a more idealistic reason than that they can confer benefits on each other. Yet Johnson's idea of universal love resists placing any obligation on Christians that is inconsistent with what he believed to be the true nature of men, or with the interests of a society that relies on the imposition of religious order through the established Church.

The lack of lofty or challenging ideals in Johnson's theory of altruism clearly did not diminish the energy and extensiveness of his personal alms-giving. Nor is this really surprising. Whatever else we say about Johnson's theory of charity, it is intended above all to be workable. He asks for nothing that human beings cannot be expected to perform. He accepted the inequality of love between men, and incorporated the right to dispute and to defend one's convictions on serious religious issues. His idea of charity is also strongly evangelical, recognizing Christians as worthy of greater love, and recommending instruction as a suitable expression of love for the unconverted. Far more than idealized celebrations of a universal love felt equally towards all men, both friends and enemies, this more qualified standard of benevolence attests to a sincere desire to define a range of practical acts from which no Christian can be justly excused.

2. *The Importance of Charity to Salvation*

A historian of the eighteenth century might easily forget that there had ever been any question that men 'merit' salvation through good works. Hostility towards the doctrine of meritorious works had in fact been one of the founding tenets of Protestantism, and continued to be the official position of the Anglican Church as set down in its articles. But Article XI, which condemns justification by works, was one of the many official doctrines which eighteenth-century orthodoxy conveniently ignored. There was little doubt not only that men would finally be judged by their works, but that charity was exalted above all other virtues as the chief condition of salvation. Francis Atterbury made this point in a passage which used the commonplace, but significant image of Judgement Day as a great courtroom where deeds rather than faith would be scrutinized:

> we are apt, extremely apt . . . to persuade our selves, that, if we do but observe the Rules of Moral Honesty in all our Transactions; if we wrong no Man, or make Restitution to those we have wrong'd; such a Righteousness and Faultless Conduct will secure our Title to Happiness . . . yet the Rule of Proceeding shall be very different . . . we shall be Try'd at that Bar, not merely by our Righteousness, but moreover and chiefly by our *Charity* . . . it will not avail us then to say, We have done no Evil, if we have done no Good.[24]

Atterbury was a highly controversial figure—a Jacobite High-Churchman whose doctrinal positions frequently inclined towards Anglo-Catholicism. Yet even those at the opposite political and theological extreme of the Church, the latitudinarians, agreed that charity was 'the *Principal Part* and *Great Design* of Religion'.[25] Johnson also affirmed that on the Judgement Day, 'the practice or neglect of charity [will] be chiefly noted' (Sermon 27, xiv. 292). The neglect of charity

---

[24] Atterbury, 'A Spittal-Sermon, Easter, 7 April 1707', in *Sermons*, ii. 170–1.
[25] Samuel Clarke, 'Of the Virtue of Charity', in *Sermons*, iii. 296.

was Johnson's major criticism of the monastic life, for 'surely it cannot be said that they have reached the perfection of a religious life . . . or that he fills his place laudably, who does no ill, *only* because he does *nothing*' (xiv. 33). This is a criticism of a traditional ideal of Christian perfection described by, for example, William Law in *A Serious Call to a Devout and Holy Life* (1729). Law had borrowed the distinction made by the ecclesiastical historian, Eusebius, between the 'lower' state of perfection achievable by men engaged in secular life, and the state of religious retirement which 'Christianity receives . . . as the perfect manner of life'.[26] Like most writers in the eighteenth century, Johnson rejected this idea of perfection because it neglected Christianity's function not only as a route for personal salvation, but also as a source of social improvement. No ideal so characterized the century's Christianity as its conviction in the importance of religion to social happiness and order, and it was partly this ideal which prompted the century's special concern for the virtue of charity.

But it was possible, at least from Johnson's point of view, to attribute excessive importance to the virtue of charity. His condemnation of Fielding's *Tom Jones* (1749), for example, was likely incited by the novelist's tendency to denigrate the virtues of temperance, chastity, and justice in favour of mere altruism. Moreover, the excessive admiration for charity was associated with Roman Catholicism. Among the Catholic articles originally rejected by Protestantism was the belief in the atoning power of charity, a doctrine based largely on 1 Peter 4: 8 ('charity shall cover a multitude of sins'). Francis Atterbury's strong support for the doctrine of atoning charity marked the point at which his teachings on charity crossed the line into a distinctively 'Papist' theology. 'The Virtue of *Charity*', wrote Atterbury, 'is of so great a price in the Sight of God, that Those Persons, who possess and exercise it in any Eminent manner, are peculiarly Entitled to the Divine Favour and Pardon, with regard to numberless Slips and Failings in their Duty, which they may be Otherwise guilty of.'[27] This was a bold assertion, for even the nonjuring William Sherlock had condemned the doctrine of atoning charity as 'Popish Superstition'. Sherlock

---

[26] See Law, *Serious Call*, ch. 9, p. 130.

[27] Atterbury, 'The Power of Charity to Cover Sin', in *Sermons*, i. 40.

adopted a more traditionally Protestant line in contending that 'we understand better than to think of meriting any thing of God, much less of purchasing a liberty of sinning, by Acts of Charity'.[28]

This issue is of interest to the study of Johnson's charity because it has been claimed, both in the eighteenth century and in recent criticism, that Johnson held the doctrine of atoning charity.[29] Such a position would be significant; although Anglicans had weakened the traditional Protestant emphasis on faith over works, atoning charity continued to be widely condemned as Papist. But the evidence for Johnson's sympathy with this doctrine is slight, and Sermon 2 contains a conventional rejection of atoning charity, though Johnson did not mention the Catholics by name:

There is indeed a partial restitution, with which many have attempted to quiet their consciences, and have betrayed their own souls. When they are sufficiently enriched by wicked practices, and leave off to rob from satiety of wealth . . . they then become desirous to be at peace with God, and hope to obtain, by refunding part of their acquisitions, a permission to enjoy the rest. In pursuance of this view churches are built, schools endowed, the poor cloathed, and the ignorant educated. Works indeed highly pleasing to God, when performed in concurrence with the other duties of religion, but which will never atone for the violation of justice. . . Ye ought doubtless to be charitable, but ye ought first to be just (xiv. 23–4).

This passage puts Johnson's praise for charity into its true perspective. Although Johnson did, like most orthodox writers, consider charity to be the most important Christian virtue, he was always careful not to lose sight of the need for a fully purified life. Whereas Atterbury, in the first passage we considered, was concerned to correct the delusion that men could be saved only through justice and temperance, Sermon 2 corrected the fallacy that men could be saved only through charity. Similarly, his moral essays turn far more often to the challenge of attaining moral purity than to the duties of

---

[28] Sherlock, 'The Nature and Measure of Charity', in *Sermons*, p. 266. See also William Warburton, 'A Charity Sermon', in *Works* (12 vols.; London, 1811), x. 265.

[29] See Quinlan, *A Layman's Religion*, p. 79. Quinlan cites Laetitia Hawkins's view in *Memoires, Anecdotes, Facts and Opinions* (1822) that Johnson held the doctrine of atoning charity.

charity. His major writings on charity are four sermons on this subject, and even there he indicated that charity had been sufficiently, even excessively praised. Once again we see that it was, paradoxically, moderation rather than exuberance which characterized the ideals of one of the century's most charitable men.

3. *Eighteenth-century Arguments against Charity*

By Johnson's time, writers of sermons and tracts on charity were faced with a difficult rhetorical problem. So much had been written on this duty that it was nearly impossible to praise charity with any originality and effectiveness. As John Conybeare wrote in a 1738 charity sermon, it was a 'Beaten Subject' and 'such as hath been treated to the best Advantage by Others'.[30] Johnson was also aware of this problem, and prefaced Sermon 19 with a similar admission: 'very few of those, who frequent the publick worship . . . can receive much information, with regard to the excellence and importance of this virtue' (xiv. 203). For this reason, sermons on charity increasingly focused on the problem of why Christians understood the duty of charity, yet failed to practise it. The answer, they concluded, was that Christians habitually justified their inactivity through an elaborate series of excuses. This related to a more general preoccupation in homiletic writing with the dangers of self-delusion. As Robert South admonished, most men 'miss of their way to heaven, not because they do not *know it*, but because they know it, and will not choose it'.[31] In *Rambler*, No. 175, Johnson cited the same precept with an important revision: 'We fall frequently into error and folly, not because the principles of action are not known, but because, for a time, they are not remembered' (v. 160). South placed this failure in a mere lack of volition— rather like Law's insistence in *Serious Call* that men are impious simply because they do not 'intend' to be pious.[32] Johnson's view that men do not always heed known duties because 'they

---

[30] John Conybeare, *A Sermon Preach'd in the Parish-church of Christ-Church, London* (London, 1738), 8. See the same type of apology, Atterbury, *Sermons*, i. 37–8.
[31] South, 'The Folly of Trusting to Our Own Hearts', in *Sermons*, vi. 417.
[32] See Law, *Serious Call*, ch. 1.

are not remembered' reflects his preoccupation with the difficulty of keeping religious motives uppermost in the mind, and strong enough to overbalance the more numerous and forcible temptations to sensual indulgence. The failure of men to obey their duties was not the result of choice or intention, but of numerous ideas and impressions constantly impinging on the consciousness of the individual and drawing his mind away from the consideration of his religious beliefs.

This was how Johnson could justify another sermon on the 'Beaten Subject' of charity. While Conybeare rather weakly promised to give the old lessons a new turn, Johnson launched into a lengthy explanation of the need for 'frequent repetitions of the instructions, which, if not recollected, must quickly lose their effect' (xiv. 203). This principle was frequently mentioned in Johnson's moral writings, and no doubt had some connection in his mind with the consciousness that he often was recapitulating the instructions of previous writers. His charity sermons are a good example of this. These sermons elaborate on the conventional Anglican teaching that men contrive specious arguments to excuse themselves from their known duty to give alms: 'we are ready to plea every avocation, however trifling, as an exemption from the necessity of holy practices' (Sermon 19, xiv. 204). In a 1709 charity sermon Francis Atterbury had also focused on the 'false *Pleas* and *Pretences*'[33] which men use to justify a neglect of charity, describing the same set of excuses later rehearsed by Johnson and numerous other writers. For example, Atterbury noted that men plead that 'their Circumstances will not permit them to become Benefactors', but still find the money for sumptuous entertainments, houses, and gardens, 'unnecessary Expences . . . such as are unsuitable to our Circumstances, and the Duties of our Rank and Station'.[34] In Sermon 19 Johnson remarked that 'One of the pleas, which is alleged in justification of the neglect of charity is inability to practice it.' This pretended incapacity, he argued, results only 'because they will not diminish any particle of their splendour, nor reduce the pomp of their equipage' (xiv. 205). Atterbury went on to censure 'those that

---

[33] Atterbury, 'A Sermon Preach'd before the Right Honourable the Lord-Mayor, Easter-week, April 26 1709', in *Sermons*, ii. 216.
[34] Ibid.

plead *Unsettled Times*, and an *Ill Prospect of Affairs*', arguing that 'no Man, not even the most Wealthy, and Great, and Powerful among the Sons of Men, is exempt from the Chances of Human Life'.[35] In Sermon 27 Johnson also noted that some 'of a timorous and melancholy temper, are hindered from the practice of charity, by an unreasonable fear of future want', answering like Atterbury 'that the uncertainty of life allows no distant prospects, or dilatory measures' (xiv. 295).

Even Johnson's phrasing was rather like Atterbury's, a measure of how deeply conventional the eighteenth-century charity sermon had become. Yet Johnson departed from the conventionalities of the charity sermon in his treatment of one standard excuse for withholding alms. As Atterbury and others had noted, men often pleaded that charity encouraged vice and idleness and threatened to disrupt social order. So far from condemning this excuse, however, most divines acknowledged that it was justified and responsible. Atterbury recommended that for this reason men should give their alms to institutions rather than individuals.[36] Edward Stillingfleet, who also rehearsed the standard pleas against charity, more harshly affirmed that idle beggars 'deserve the hand of Justice to punish them, [rather] than that of Charity to relieve them'.[37] It was at this point that the eighteenth-century's lofty ideals of benevolence collided with what was perhaps an even stronger tendency in its thought: an overriding concern for the general welfare of society, a pragmatism that was willing to sacrifice the individual in order to preserve the social order. The century's social pamphlets on the poor make clear that, according to the great majority of writers, it was the civic duty of the individual to withhold his charity from the idle or vicious beggar. This stipulation would not have been such a hindrance to altruism except that it was usually argued that *most* beggars were idle and vicious. Theoretically, eighteenth-century writers were as convinced as Johnson that charity must be an active and habitual practice of the good Christian, yet a practical concern

[35] Ibid. 222-4.

[36] See ibid. 231-2.

[37] Stillingfleet, 'Of Protestant Charity', in *Works*, i. 309; see also Conybeare, *Sermon*, p. 26.

for social order helped to block the age from the exuberance of altruism celebrated in its literature.[38]

Johnson's sermons deliberate on this argument against charity with considerable hesitation and uncertainty. He was too great a pragmatist simply to dismiss the concern for social order, or suddenly strike out in an unwonted mood of idealism to recommend charity to all, regardless of the poor man's moral character. In both Sermons 19 and 27 he agreed that 'we ought not to suffer our beneficence to be made instrumental to the encouragement of vice, or the support of idleness' (xiv. 211). But he also suggested that this excuse was made use of too frequently. Like few other authors of charity sermons, he urged that 'In the choice of objects . . . we are not to be too scrupulous, and he may justly suspect himself to want charity, who finds objections too frequently against its expediency' (xiv. 297). This departure from the conventional treatment of this excuse resulted not only from, as might be inferred, an unusually warm heart, but also from Johnson's ability to see the relationship between poverty and vice in an unusual way. Most writers assumed that vice and poverty were seen together because the individual's corruption and idleness had depleted his means of support: he would remain poor so long as his vices were encouraged by charity. But Johnson saw that the cause-and-effect relationship was often just the opposite—that vice and idleness were created and increased by the enormous temptations which filled a life of poverty. As he wrote in Sermon 4, 'Let any man reflect upon the snares to which poverty exposes virtue . . . and he will discover the necessity of charity, to preserve a great part of mankind from the most atrocious wickedness' (xiv. 47). According to this reasoning, charity to idle or vicious beggars might not increase, but actually decrease the prevalence of these social evils.

This type of reasoning had been the foundation for one of the century's really notable achievements in combating the ills of poverty—the charity-school movement. As historians of this

[38] An important exception to the eighteenth century's harsh attitudes on the poor was John Wesley. It is significant that Wesley's efforts to organize relief for common beggars received little praise from the establishment, and he was publicly suspected of profiting from his charitable projects. See R. F. Wearmouth, *Methodism and the Common People of the Eighteenth Century* (London, 1945), 203–4.

movement have shown, the original intention or justification of
charity schools was that they would lessen vice and crime.[39] As
Thomas Yalden wrote in a 1728 sermon on charity schools, the
education of poor children benefited the public by 'restraining
[them] from falling into the common and ensnaring Paths of
Wickedness and Vice; from the Contagion of evil company and
pernicious Examples; and by generously rescuing them from
the many Temptations to Ruin, that Poverty and Idleness
would otherwise expose them to'.[40] Predictably, Johnson
strongly supported the idea of charity schools, but his full
reasoning on this subject is worth considering: it makes clearer
the really unusual liberalism of his attitudes on poverty and
related social problems.

The rationale that educating poor children would help cure
many social evils was challenged in Mandeville's famous
'Essay on Charity and Charity Schools', published in 1724
along with the complete *The Fable of the Bees*. Mandeville argued
that educating the poor would break down social and economic
order by promoting a pride in learning unsuitable to the poor's
station as the labourers of society. Although Mandeville's
pragmatism was only slightly more brutal than that of many of
his contemporaries, his essay on charity schools was widely
attacked in the group of replies to *The Fable of the Bees*. These
replies generally accused Mandeville of misrepresenting the
education received at the charity schools. There was little
dispute that a full education would, as Mandeville had maintained, promote pride and insubordination in the lower
classes.[41] But the charity schools offered only a little writing
and reading plus, most important, the type of religious
education that would make the students humble, pious, and
respectful to their superiors. The poor might inherit the earth

---

[39] See, e.g., M. G. Jones, *The Charity-school Movement: A Study of Eighteenth-century Puritanism in Action* (Cambridge, 1938), 36–8.

[40] Thomas Yalden, 'The Education of Poor Children, the Most Excellent Kind of Charity', in *Twenty-five Sermons*, p. 568.

[41] There had never been much disagreement that a formal education would disrupt public order by raising pride and ambition in the lower classes. For example, in a 1706 sermon entitled 'The Charity of Schools for the Poor Children', White Kennet anticipated the arguments of Mandeville. The charity schools of the Reformation, Kennet complained, 'gave [the children] such an imperfect Taste of Learning, as . . . did but fill their Heads with Noise, and help to make them more vain and conceited' (repr. in *Twenty-five Sermons*, p. 64).

in the next world, but not in this. This was how the critic John Dennis answered Mandeville:

But to come to the particular Knowledge which the Children of the Poor are taught in Charity-Schools. The chief Knowledge which they acquire there, is the Knowledge of the Principles and Doctrines of the Christian Religion. Now this Knowledge is so far from having a Tendency to the enlarging and multiplying their Desires, etc. that nothing is so capable of weaning them from the World as that, or of teaching them, in what State soever they are, therewith to be contented.[42]

The advocates of the charity-school movement agreed with Mandeville that the poor must be kept subordinate. This was an important justification of the religious instruction given in these schools. One of Johnson's favourite religious lessons, that all worldly wishes are vain, was very useful in 'weaning' the poor from disruptive ambition.

Johnson himself recognized that the vanity of human wishes could serve a useful social purpose. Yet he did not seem comfortable with this application of the Scriptural teachings against worldliness. In *A Free Inquiry into the Nature and Origin of Evil* (1757), Soame Jenyns had quoted Pope's famous line, 'A little knowledge is a dangerous thing', and then gone on to praise Divine beneficence for wisely keeping the poor ignorant. Johnson's initial response to this view was very like Dennis's conventional answer to Mandeville. A little knowledge of Christianity, Johnson pointed out, would help allay vanity and inculcate submission to one's allotted station in society:

There is undoubtedly a degree of knowledge which will direct a man to refer all to providence, and to acquiesce in the condition with which omniscient goodness has determined to allot him; to consider this world as a phantom that must soon glide from before his eyes, and the distresses and vexations that encompass him, as dust scattered in his path, as a blast that chills him for a moment and passes off for ever.[43]

But Johnson immediately undercut this conventional defence of education for the poor with highly unconventional criticisms

---

[42] John Dennis, *Vice and Luxury Public Mischiefs* (London, 1724), preface, pp. xxxiii–iv.

[43] Review of *Free Inquiry*, in Schwartz, *Evil*, p. 102.

of the very principle of a rigidly enforced social order. 'To entail irreversible poverty upon generation after generation,' he complained, 'only because the ancestor happened to be poor, is in itself cruel, if not unjust.'[44] Moreover, he advanced a significant practical objection to subordination, which 'is wholly contrary to the maxims of a commercial nation, which always suppose and promote a rotation of property, and offer every individual a chance of mending his condition by his diligence'.[45]

This response was not entirely unprecedented. In one of the more enlightened replies to Mandeville, George Blewitt argued more boldly that upward movement from the lower classes was good for society, and that the division of labour would take care of itself.[46] Economists might discern a significant irony in this debate. Mandeville has been praised for anticipating the principles of free-market economies ('Private Vices, Public Benefits'), yet Blewitt and Johnson attacked his views on charity schools for reasons closely associated with those very principles—that a rigidly maintained hierarchy was detrimental to economic prosperity. For literary scholars, this debate is interesting because it shows Johnson questioning rather than supporting the need for rigidly maintained subordination. Largely as the result of Boswell's *Life*, his name has become closely associated with the principle of subordination, yet he seemed willing enough in his review of Jenyns to admit the potential cruelty and theoretical weakness of this system.

Like other orthodox writers, therefore, Johnson supported the idea of education for the poor, but his reasoning for this support was peculiarly liberal. As in his comments on the dangers of charity to vicious and idle beggars, he seemed grudgingly to concede that the conventional arguments were not without merit. It is important to keep this in mind: Johnson was not a revolutionary idealist who abandoned the orthodox opinions of his age without hesitation. But finally he disagreed with the century's conventional response to poverty; he disagreed not only because he had had personal experience

[44] Ibid. 103.
[45] Ibid.
[46] See Blewitt, *General Practice of Virtue*, pp. 180–96. Johnson's liberal views were also anticipated by Isaac Watts, *An Essay towards the Encouragement of Charity Schools* (London, 1728).

with poverty, but also because he did not believe on practical grounds that the relief of poverty, either through alms or education, would upset social order. He was not entirely alone in these ideas. But Johnson's views on the poor do reflect the most liberal extremes of eighteenth-century social thought.

4. *Johnson and Legal Reform: Debtors and Capital Punishment*

Johnson's support for two important legal causes, the campaigns to abolish debtors' prisons and the death penalty for theft, demonstrates how he gave his charitable principles a strong practical orientation. Again, the age of benevolence was remarkably lacking in warm-heartedness and clemency when it came to correcting its social ills. It was Johnson, an anti-sentimentalist without high ideals of benevolence, who led the way in advocating reforms that would not be made law until well into the nineteenth century.

Eighteenth-century law allowed creditors to imprison debtors indefinitely until even petty debts were paid. The pamphlet campaign against this regulation went on throughout the century without success, largely because of the backwardness of the eighteenth century's legislative machinery: the penniless could have very little influence on governments dependent for their survival on the favour of the landed or monied classes, groups with a natural interest on the side of the creditors. But there was so little written *against* the repeal of the debtors' law that a 1724 pamphleteer could truly claim that 'almost every one either wishes Success to so good a Design, or is ashamed to oppose it'.[47] Johnson joined the campaign with two essays, *Idler*, Nos. 22 and 38, which indicate that he had followed the pamphlet war against the debtors' law with great interest and attention. *Idler*, No. 22, for example, begins, 'As I was passing lately under one of the gates of this city, I was struck with horror by a rueful cry, which summoned me "to remember the poor debtors" ' (ii. 69). This would appear to be an allusion to the frontispiece of a 1691 defence of the debtors, Moses Pitt's *The Cry of the Oppressed* (see plate). The frontispiece depicts a man collecting alms beneath a gateway, on either side of which are jail-cells crowded with debtors. One prisoner calls

---

[47] Anon., *The Case of Insolvent Debtors Considered* (London, 1724), 1.

The frontispiece of Moses Pitt's *The Cry of the Oppressed*

from behind the bars, 'Pray Remember y^e poor Debtors'. Pitt's book is comprised mostly of letters from debtors describing the noisome conditions of the jails, the barbarity of the keepers, and the misery incurred by the debtors' wives and children. In Johnson's two essays on the debtors he touched on all these circumstances, more formally describing them as the 'multiplication of misery' (ii. 118), and concluding *Idler*, No. 38, with the assertion, 'If there are any made so obdurate by avarice and cruelty, as to resolve these consequences without dread or pity, I must leave him to be awakened by some other power, for I write only to human beings' (ii. 121). This is an interesting instance of Johnson appealing to the innate kindness of his readers, very much as Fielding did in *Tom Jones*.[48] Again, Johnson was not so hostile to the doctrine of natural benevolence that he was unwilling to use it when it suited his purpose.

Many pamphlets, however, urged reform on practical, rather than purely emotive grounds. Perhaps the most common argument was that the debtors' laws condemned active and talented men, often in the prime of their lives, to idleness and waste. This argument was used by Johnson in both his essays.[49] Samuel Byrom, writing in 1729, introduced an economic theory prevalent at least until Malthus: that the prosperity of a nation was proportionate to the number of its inhabitants. It was believed that the number of people shut up in the monasteries of Catholic nations was, for this reason, a severe drain on their economies; the same could be said of the many condemned to the debtors' prisons:

it [is] a received Maxim, that nothing makes a Country flourish more, than by the Increase of People: Now if these Countries suffer so much by the Cloysters and Convents, and the vast numbers that are shut up in them, it is too obvious to be denied, that the many

---

[48] See, e.g., Fielding's rhetorical challenge to the reader in his introductory chapter to Book VI, 'Of Love'. Fielding remarked that, if the reader was unmoved by the sentiments of the novel, 'you have already read more than you have understood. . . . To treat of the effects of Love to you, must be as absurd as to discourse on Colours to a Man born blind.' (*The History of Tom Jones, a Foundling* (1749), ed. M. C. Battestin and F. Bowers (2 vols.; Oxford, 1974), i. 271).

[49] *Idler*, No. 22, ii. 69; *Idler*, No. 38, ii. 119. See William Cole, *Legal and Other Reasons . . . why the Subjects of England should not be Imprisoned for Debt or Damages* (London, 1675), 10.

Prisons in *England*, where so many Thousands of both sexes are detained, is [*sic*] a greater Loss and Injury to the King and Country, than if they were detained in Cloysters and Convents. . . When People are kept in Convents and Cloysters, it is for the most part their own Choice, and there is decent Provision made for them.[50]

Johnson borrowed this argument in both his essays on debtors. In *Idler*, No. 22, he remarked that 'The prosperity of a people is proportionate to the number of hands and minds usefully employed' (ii. 69), and, working from the same premise in *Idler*, No. 38, he cited the analogy of cloisters and convents in Catholic nations. Like Byrom, he noted that people at least entered cloisters by free choice and were not subjected to the miseries of a prison:

The monastick institutions have been often blamed, as tending to retard the increase of mankind. . . . But whatever be the evil or folly of these retreats, those have no right to censure them whose prisons contain greater numbers than the monasteries of other countries. It is, surely, less foolish and less criminal to permit inaction than compel it; to comply with doubtful opinions of happiness, than condemn to certain and apparent misery; to indulge the extravagancies of erroneous piety, than to multiply and enforce temptations to wickedness (ii. 119–20).

This type of argument was, as Byrom and Johnson realized, particularly useful because it combined an appeal to economic concerns, the primary obstacle to parliamentary action on the debtors' law, with that great mover of legislation, anti-Catholic propaganda. It cannot be said that Johnson added many new arguments against the debtors' law, but the pamphleteers, ordinary men with an often feeble grasp of written language, did gain an advocate who could express their case with unusual eloquence.

Johnson's attack on the death penalty for theft was, on the other hand, an unprecedented reappraisal of eighteenth-century theories on how to deter serious crime. His essay on this subject, *Rambler*, No. 114, was widely cited in the 1760s and the 1770s when the campaign against the death penalty first became a flourishing and active movement. He was useful

50 Samuel Byrom, *An Irrefragable Argument fully Proving, that to discharge Great Debts is less Injury, and more Reasonable, than to discharge Small Debts* (London, 1729), 24–5. See also *Case of Insolvent Debtors*, p. 6.

to the cause not only because of his fame as a moralist, but because his case was based on strong reasoning and empirical evidence, rather than, like most previous writings against capital punishment, an emotional condemnation of the self-evident injustice of this penalty.

The attack on capital punishment in More's *Utopia* (1516), for example, was based primarily on the principle that punishments must be proportioned to crimes. 'Surely everyone knows', urges Hythloday, 'how absurd and even dangerous it is that a thief and a murderer should receive the same punishment.'[51] This was also the main argument against capital punishment in Montesquieu's *The Spirit of the Laws* (1748) and in the most famous treatise against the death penalty, Cesare Beccaria's *On Crimes and Punishments* (1764). Yet, as Johnson realized, this argument was not convincing to many eighteenth-century proponents of capital punishment. That was because the disproportionate severity of hanging as a punishment for theft was generally acknowledged, but considered an insufficient reason to change the law. The prevailing eighteenth-century philosophy of legal punishment might be roughly termed 'utilitarian': the effectiveness of a punishment to deter crime was, in the minds of most writers, a criterion that outweighed all other considerations and principles. As Henry Fielding argued in *An Inquiry into the Late Increase of Robbers* (1751), it was only the need to deter theft that justified the otherwise absurdly disproportioned punishment of death:

No man indeed of common humanity or common sense can think the life of a man and a few shillings of an equal consideration, or that the law in punishing theft with death proceeds (as perhaps a private person sometimes may) with any view to vengeance. The terror of the example is the only thing proposed, and one man is sacrificed to the preservation of thousands.[52]

Fielding's implication that deterrence should be the overriding criterion in the institution of punishments was supported not

[51] See Sir Thomas More, *Utopia* (1516), ed. E. Surtz and J. H. Hexter (New Haven and London, 1965), 73–7.

[52] Henry Fielding, *An Inquiry into the Late Increase of Robbers* (1751), in *Complete Works*, ed. W. E. Henley (16 vols.; London, 1903), xiii. 120–1. Fielding's view was anticipated by many works, including anon., *Hanging not Punishment Enough for Murtherers, High-way Men, and House-breakers* (London, 1701), 2.

only in legal and social literature, but also in theological discussions of the rewards and punishments exacted by God. In their efforts to make the mysteries of Christianity seem reasonable, Restoration divines had been faced with the problem of explaining how a just God could condemn a man to an eternity in Hell for a few minor sins. In order to remove this appearance of injustice, John Tillotson wrote a defence 'Of the Eternity of Hell-Torments' which advanced a principle of justice very like Fielding's: 'the measure of Penalties, is not to be taken from any strict proportion betwixt Crime and Punishment; but from one great end and design of Government, which is to secure the observation of wholesome and necessary Laws; and consequently whatever Penalties are proper and necessary to this end are not unjust.'[53] Thus, the example of God seemed to uphold the principle that the justice of a penalty should be evaluated solely by its effectiveness as a deterrent. This left the advocates and opponents of capital punishment debating at cross purposes, for they disagreed on the fundamental principle and justification of punishments. There could be no reform in the law until the majority of legislators and judges were persuaded that the principle of justly proportioned crimes and punishments outweighed the principle of deterrence.

A more effective way to change the law, then, might be to convince the legislators that capital punishment was in fact not an effective deterrent against theft. There was, indeed, considerable evidence to support this claim: by general acknowledgement, theft was continuing to increase at an alarming rate despite the threat of death. For a great number of eighteenth-century writers, however, this indicated only that the punishment for theft should be made even *more* severe than mere hanging. A group of astonishing pamphlets proposed that 'an Execution that is attended with more lasting Torment, may strike a far greater Awe, to lessen, if not put a stop to, their shameless Crimes'.[54] This is what Leon Radzinowicz has called

[53] Tillotson, *Works*, iii. 412.

[54] George Ollyffe, *An Essay Humbly Offer'd for an Act of Parliament to prevent Capital Crimes, and the Loss of many Lives* (London, 1731); see also *Hanging not Punishment Enough*, pp. 3–5; Charles Jones, *Some Methods Proposed towards Putting a Stop to the Flagrant Crimes of Murder, Robbery, and Perjury* (London, 1752), 15.

'the Doctrine of Maximum Severity':[55] it is among the most vivid examples of eighteenth-century practicality over-running all sentiments of humanity or speculative ideals of justice.

Against this 'Doctrine of Maximum Severity', *Rambler*, No. 114, proposed Johnson's 'scheme of invigorating the laws by relaxation' (iv. 247). Johnson was, in part, concerned to establish the basic principle of justly proportioned crimes and punishments:

A slight perusal of the laws by which the measures of vindictive and coercive justice are established, will discover so many disproportions between crimes and punishments, such capricious distinctions of guilt, and such confusion of remissness and severity, as can scarcely be believed to have been produced by publick wisdom, sincerely and calmly studious of publick happiness (iv. 242).

But the primary thrust of his argument was to show that 'The frequency of capital punishments rarely hinders the commission of a crime . . . and is, if we proceed only upon prudential principles, chiefly for that reason to be avoided' (iv. 245). His purpose was not simply to prove that capital punishment for theft was unjust, but rather that this punishment did not work. Like no other major writer, he met the advocates for capital punishment on their own ground by breaking down the assumed relationship between the severity of a punishment and its effectiveness as a deterrent.

Instead of simply denouncing the absurdity of such a disproportioned punishment, he explained how this imbalance could disrupt a special ethical association that, as we have already discussed in detail, was a central concern in his moral outlook. This was the association between ultimate truth and the law of opinion or 'fashion'—the code which, in a particular society and at a certain time, represented the popularly accepted distinction between right and wrong. Despite the unreliability of this code, the majority of men possessed no other clear understanding of moral truth. Hence, 'To equal robbery with murder', by subjecting both crimes to the same punishment, 'is to reduce murder to robbery, to confound in

[55] See L. Radzinowicz, *A History of English Criminal Law* (3 vols.; London, 1948), i. 231–69.

common minds the gradations of iniquity' (iv. 244). Since the civil law strongly influenced the public perception of virtue and vice, it was essential to social order that it accurately reflect the 'Divine law', the real nature of moral truth.

By punishing both murder and theft with the same penalty, the law also failed to deter the thief from killing his victim in order to eliminate the main witness of his crime, a problem briefly noted in previous works against the death penalty, but seldom elaborated upon so thoroughly as in *Rambler*, No. 114.[56] Johnson also focused on a problem more often treated by the advocates for capital punishment than its opponents—the frequency of pardons for convicted thieves. Legal pamphlets such as Fielding's *Late Increase of Robbers* urged the king to resist the temptation to pardon thieves condemned to the gallows: the punishment for theft was severe, but had to be consistently enforced to curb the prevalence of this crime.[57] Yet, as Johnson pointed out, it was the inordinate severity of the punishment for theft that caused the high number of pardons: 'From this conviction of the inequality of the punishment to the offence proceeds the frequent solicitations of pardons . . . severity defeats itself by exciting pity' (iv. 245).

Johnson's case against capital punishment was, in this way, unusually practical and well reasoned. It was designed to change the minds of those who made social order the sole objective of punitive justice, and who had dismissed all humanitarian concerns in the name of this objective. His argument challenged the assumption that there was any exact proportion between the severity of a punishment and its effectiveness as a deterrent. This does not mean, however, that Johnson himself would have endorsed 'the Doctrine of Maximum Severity' even if he had been convinced of its usefulness to control crime. The inspiration for *Rambler*, No. 114, and its underlying spirit, was an impassioned intolerance of cruelty and injustice. 'The heart of a good man', he exhorted, 'cannot but recoil at the thought of punishing a slight

[56] See Sollom Elmyn, Preface to *A Complete Collection of State Trials* (2nd edn; London, 1730), p. ix; C. de Secondat, Baron de Montesquieu, *The Spirit of the Laws* (1748), trans. Thomas Nugent (2 vols.; London, 1823), XII, iv. 88.

[57] See Fielding, *Late Increase of Robbers, in Works*, xiii. 118–21.

injury with death' (iv. 246). Although his writings often maintained that 'the general good' was the most reliable measure of right and wrong, he was seldom willing to promote this end in opposition to deeper feelings of compassion.

7

Doctrinal Controversy

1. *The Idea of Christian Perfection*

As we discussed in the last chapter, Johnson differed from many eighteenth-century writers and theologians by refusing to place such a high value on charity that its practice excused moral impurity. Moreover, the rule of charity which he described in his essays and sermons was practicable rather than unrealistically exalted; he did not encourage literal interpretations of texts such as Matthew 19: 21 which seemed to impose an absolute duty to give all one could spare to the needy. Yet the Scriptural law of moral purity, no less than Christ's directions on charity, is extremely demanding: 'Be ye . . . perfect,' said Christ in the Sermon on the Mount, 'even as your Father in heaven is perfect' (Matt. 5: 48). Could Johnson expect Christians to achieve this perfection, any more than he could expect them to give all they had to the poor? Among Johnson's modern commentators, discussion of this question has repeatedly focused on a single book—William Law's *A Serious Call to a Devout and Holy Life* (1729). It is well known that Johnson was deeply impressed by *Serious Call* when he read it as a student at Oxford. According to several modern studies, Law was partly responsible for Johnson's religious melancholy by exhorting him to struggle towards an ideal of perfection which he tried but could not reach.[1] In the first major study of Law's influence on Johnson, Katherine C. Balderston argued that Johnson finally repudiated Law's perfectionism as the result of this failure:

In Law . . . Johnson saw the moralist he must not be. . . . Law's dogmatic 'either–or' alternatives, his rigid perfectionism, and his limited and theoretical view of the real nature of man, were the earliest, and the strongest, external factors which forced Johnson's

---

[1] See Quinlan, *Layman's Religion*, p. 73; Gray, *Johnson's Sermons*, pp. 50–6; Pierce, *Religious Life*, pp. 29–31. P. K. Alkon has expressed some reservations concerning the importance of Law's influence on Johnson: see 'William Law, Robert South and Samuel Johnson', *SEL*, 6 (1966), 499–528.

mind towards the need for realism, balance, and human insight in judging the complexities of human nature. [2]

Admittedly, it is far more intriguing to see an author's religion as the product of a single, overwhelming encounter with an unusually inspiring book than to place his views within a wide background of theological writing and controversy. None the less, a broad view of Restoration and eighteenth-century divinity reveals that he did not have to go to Law to learn perfectionism. Of special interest is a 1739 controversy on perfectionism with which Johnson had some incidental connection. It was Law's doctrine that came under attack in this debate, yet the Church of England was also forced to give official notice that perfection, understood in a particular way, must be the objective of all good Christians. Public reaction to the controversy gave ample demonstration that 'the real nature of man' could never be proposed as an adequate standard of Christian virtue without seriously embarrassing the Church.

'Perfectionism' became a major issue with the rise of Methodism in the late 1730s. As John Wesley admitted in *A Plain Account of Christian Perfection* (1770), he had been strongly influenced by Law's perfectionism early in his career; later, having combined Law's teachings with his own distinctive theology of grace, he preached that 'perfection' was actually achievable in the Christian life. This immediately raised an outcry: 'after a time, a cry arose, and, what a little further surprised me, among religious men, who affirmed, not that I had stated perfection wrong, but that "there is no Perfection on earth"; nay, and fell vehemently on my brother and me for affirming the contrary.' [3] As Wesley went on to complain, this attack was grounded in an important misconception that by 'perfection' he meant 'sinless perfection'. Tracts written against him, such as William Fleetwood's *The Perfectionists Examin'd* (1741), assumed that Wesley had denied original sin and the inherent weakness and corruption of human nature. We will go on to discuss why 'perfection' does not mean 'sinlessness'. At this point, however, we might cite a revealing anecdote. As the result of his avowed perfectionism, Wesley was called before the ever-watchful Bishop of London, Edmund

[2] Balderston, 'William Law', p. 394.

[3] John Wesley, *A Plain Account of Christian Perfection* (1770), in *Works* (1830), xi. 374.

Gibson. When Wesley explained to the Bishop what he really meant by 'perfection', Gibson answered, 'Mr. Wesley, if this be all you mean, publish it to all the world.'[4]

Amidst this controversy, there appeared a pamphlet which caused a special furore. This was Joseph Trapp's *The Nature, Folly, Sin and Danger of Being Righteous Over-much* (1739), a compilation of four sermons on Ecclesiastes 7: 16. Trapp's pamphlet differed from most others because he attacked not only the Methodists themselves, but in particular William Law, whom he rightly assumed had strongly influenced both Whitefield and the Wesley brothers. Moreover, Trapp argued quite explicitly not just that man's fallen nature was incapable of absolute perfection, but that Christians should not attempt to achieve anything more than a mediocre standard of virtue and piety. He borrowed the classical ideal of the Golden Mean to argue that virtue itself must be kept within bounds of moderation: 'Whenever any Virtue rises beyond its due Bounds, and runs into an Extreme; it loses its Nature, and degenerates into Vice.'[5] Too rigorous a standard of piety, he argued, would unjustly cause good Christians to feel that they would certainly be damned; a man who spent all his time going to church and praying would neglect his responsibilities as a good citizen; in brief, that a pragmatic concern for the real nature of man must regulate even our desire for salvation in the hereafter.

What may seem an extraordinary claim from a minister of the established Church—that we must be careful not to be overly virtuous—had in fact been preached by previous divines.[6] Those divines had generally been ignored, but Trapp had made the mistake of attacking one of the most active and skilled controversists in England. Law's reply to Trapp was predictably masterful. Adopting a tone of patient remonstrance, he protested that Trapp had uselessly preached the virtues of mediocrity to a society that already aspired to nothing better. Law conceded that sinless perfection was unachievable in this life, but argued that the majority of Christians would remain in

---

[4] Ibid. For a full account of Wesley's complex idea of Christian perfection, see L. G. Cox, *John Wesley's Concept of Perfection* (Kansas City, Mo., 1964).

[5] Trapp, *Righteous Over-Much*, p. 6.

[6] See Francis Ayscough, *A Sermon Preach'd before the Honourable the House of Commons, January the 30th, 1735/6* (London, 1736). Ayscough claimed that most divines agreed upon the need to moderate piety, but were afraid to acknowledge this openly.

a state of lethargy and self-satisfaction unless the doctrine of perfection was upheld by every minister of the Church.[7] Deserted by his fellow Anglicans, ignominiously derided by a series of obscure Methodists, Trapp was forced to defend himself, claiming rather desperately that he had been misunderstood and that he believed in Christian perfection as much as Law did.[8] He also threatened legal action against the *Gentleman's Magazine* for printing an abridged version of *Rightous Over-much* in instalments. This is what brought Johnson into the controversy. Edward Cave asked Johnson to write a defence of the publisher's right to abridge, and Johnson produced 'Considerations on the Case of Dr. T.'s Sermons, Abridged by Mr Cave, 1739', withheld from publication when Cave decided to discontinue the instalments of Trapp's work, but finally printed by the *Gentleman's Magazine* after Johnson's death. Johnson's article reveals little about his personal reaction to Trapp's case against perfection, but it does contain strong hints concerning the general mood prompted by *Righteous Over-much*: Trapp rightly believed that his pamphlet was ruining his reputation as a divine.[9]

Prominent historians of eighteenth-century thought, such as J. H. Overton, have portrayed Trapp's pamphlet as highly typical of the laxity and mediocrity of contemporary Anglicanism.[10] The reaction to Trapp's pamphlet suggests, on the other hand, that the Anglican establishment was not prepared to accept religious standards based on human limitation and social convenience rather than on a reasonably literal reading of Scriptural law. Although there was, we might justly assume, a strong underlying sympathy for Trapp's pragmatism, the Church's high value for orthodoxy, its belief that social order

---

[7] See William Law, *An Earnest and Serious Answer to Dr. Trapp's Sermon* (1740), in *Works*, vi.

[8] See Joseph Trapp, *A Reply to Mr. Law's Earnest and Serious Answer (as it is called) to Dr. Trapp's Discourse* (London, 1741). Trapp acknowledged here that he had been attacked in seven pamphlets, and defended only in one.

[9] See Samuel Johnson, 'Considerations on the Case of Dr. T.'s Sermons, Abridged by Mr. Cave, 1739', *The Gentleman's Magazine*, 62 (1789), 555–7. Johnson reminded Trapp that 'my reputation as an author is at the mercy of the reader, who lies under no other obligation to do me justice than those of religion and morality' (p. 556). The notes to this essay contain information concerning the circumstances of its composition.

[10] See J. H. Overton, *William Law: Non-juror and Mystic* (London, 1881), 297–300.

relied on the unquestioned moral authority of the Church, generally kept its theoretical standards of virtue high and inflexible. In an effort to elucidate the Church's official position, Bishop Gibson wrote [A] Pastoral Letter . . . against Lukewarmness on One Hand, and Enthusiasm on the Other (1739), a pamphlet which carefully balanced a condemnation of Methodist fanaticism (as it was seen) with exhortations for Christian perfection not entirely dissimilar to Law's teachings in *Serious Call*. Gibson began with a definition of 'lukewarmness': 'By *Lukewarmness* I mean an Opinion and Perswasion, that if Men go to Church as others do, and give the common Attention to the Business of their Stations, and keep themselves from Sins of a gross and notorious Nature, and are in no way hurtful or injurious to their Neighbours; they are as good Christians as they need to be.'[11] This is basically the lukewarmness attacked in *Serious Call*, where Law sets out to condemn not 'professed rakes' but Christians with generally 'sober lives', the individual who has 'religion enough according to the way of the world to be reckoned a pious Christian'.[12] Johnson's sermons also castigate those who 'please themselves with a constant regularity of life, and decency of behaviour' (xiv. 144), but lack a full commitment to Christian devotion. This does not show, however, that either Gibson or Johnson meant to ratify the theology of William Law. The common denominator between Gibson, Johnson, and, in certain respects, William Law was an idea of Christian perfection that had been strongly upheld by most of the major Anglican divines since the Restoration.

The doctrine of Christian perfection has a long history in patristic literature, yet, as R. Newton Flew showed in *The Idea of Perfection in Christian Theology*, 'perfectionism' became a term of contempt among early reformers such as Luther and Calvin.[13] Law and Wesley frequently credited Jeremy Taylor with reviving the doctrine of perfection among seventeenth-century divines, though there was a drift towards perfectionism

[11] Edmund Gibson, *The Bishop of London's Pastoral Letter to the People of His Diocese, by Way of Caution against Lukewarmness on One Hand, and Enthusiasm on the Other* (London, 1739), 4.

[12] Law, *Serious Call*, ch. 1, p. 53.

[13] See R. Newton Flew, *The Idea of Perfection in Christian Theology* (London, 1934), 244–51.

in much Arminian divinity. Moreover, one cannot read Erasmus' *Enchiridion militis christiani* (1503) without sensing an important connection between the doctrine of perfection and Christian humanism. With the decline of Calvinism in the Anglican Church after the Restoration, perfectionism virtually gained the status of an established doctrine among divines such as South, Tillotson, William Sherlock, Barrow, and Clarke. In the writings of these divines perfection represents a peculiar doctrine of the Anglican Church distinguished from Roman Catholicism on the one hand and, as it was perceived, Puritan antinomianism on the other.

Against Roman Catholicism, Anglican divines denied the doctrine of supererogation and the distinction between mortal and venial sins. The doctrine of supererogation—the belief in meritorious works over and above the regular call of religious duty—is rejected in Article XIV of the Anglican Church. As Clarke and South made clear, it followed from this rejection that there could be no sufficient standard of virtue when there was the possibility of doing more: it was always the Christian's duty to perform all possible acts of virtue and piety.[14] In opposition to the Catholic distinction between mortal and venial sins, Restoration divines contended that all sins were of equal seriousness. 'There are no such *little* commands (as they call them),' wrote South, 'but . . . the very least of them obliges so indispensably, that the violation and neglect of it will, without repentance, exclude from heaven and bind over to damnation.'[15] Other divines, such as Tillotson, cited James 2: 10—'whosoever shall keep the whole law, and yet offend in one point, he is guilty of all'—to substantiate their insistence that no sin was venial or worthy of anything less than damnation.[16]

A second influence on the creation of an Anglican idea of perfection was the desire to confute supposedly antinomian doctrines of justification by faith. Justification by faith is, of course, not equivalent to antinomianism, a heresy with a limited and often uncertain history among the early Anti-baptists

[14] See, e.g., Samuel Clarke, 'Christians ought to endeavour to achieve Perfection', in *Sermons*, ix. 112-13; South, 'Sermon on 1 Titus 18', in *Sermons*, vii. 113-14.

[15] South, *Sermons*, vii. 111.

[16] Tillotson, 'The Distinguishing Character of a Good and a Bad Man', in *Works*, i. 128.

and certain Commonwealth sects such as the Ranters. Most Protestant groups have regarded outward obedience to the law as a manifestation or sign of inward regeneration or election.[17] None the less, Anglican divines of the Restoration insisted on equating justification by faith with antinomianism, a habit which Wesley would struggle hard to discredit. In a 1722 treatise against Puritanism, Henry Stebbing argued that justification by faith contradicted the principle that full obedience to the law was an essential element of conversion: 'I will now leave it to any Reasonable Man to determine, whether that Doctrine which supposeth *wilful Sin* to be consistent with a *Regenerate State*, doth not contradict . . . all those Places of Scripture, which speak of *Regeneration* as that which *qualifies* us for the *Kingdom of Heaven*.'[18] The key idea here is the escape from 'wilful sin'. Most divines of the Restoration and eighteenth century consistently instructed that an individual who had been truly converted to the Christian faith would be free from the practice of all deliberate sins. This included habitual sins that had, over the course of time, become more-or-less natural rather than voluntary. 'All true Christians', wrote Samuel Clarke, 'are free from all Habits of Sin.'[19]

Freedom from wilful or habitual sin does not, however, mean freedom from all 'sin'. Anglican divines acknowledged that there are 'sins of infirmity' which arise involuntarily from our fallen nature and which can never be fully overcome. According to Daniel Waterland, the sins of infirmity were those 'owing either to *Inadvertancy, Forgetfulness, Surprize*, Strength of *Passion*, or to the *Suddeness* and *Violence* of an unlooked for *Temptation*'.[20] It would be wrong to consider this a generous moderation of the idea of perfection. As R. Newton

[17] John Bunyan provides a good example of justification by faith in a form which placed a high importance on the outward manifestation of good works. In *Grace Abounding to the Chief of Sinners* (1666), ed. R. Sharrock (London, 1966), Bunyan lists 'a learning to the Works of the Law' among the seven 'abominations in my heart' (p. 105). Yet he also attacks the antinomianism of the Ranters (see pp. 18–19).

[18] Henry Stebbing, *Discourses upon Several Subjects* (London, 1722), 50. Like *A Treatise Concerning the Operations of the Holy Spirit* (1719), this is an abridgement, with Stebbing's additions, of a work by William Clagett.

[19] See Samuel Clarke, 'That True Christians are Free from all Habits of Sin', in *Sermons*, ix. 311.

[20] Waterland, 'The Nature and Kinds of Sins of Infirmity', in *Sermons*, i. 214.

Flew explains in his history of this idea, Christian perfection is properly understood as 'relative perfection'—not absolute sinlessness, but a condition in which there is room for continued progress and for failure, at least of the involuntary sort. Even the most rigorous perfectionists of the eighteenth century, such as Law and Wesley, accepted roughly the same range of insurmountable infirmities as Waterland. And it was when Wesley assured Gibson that such sins could not be overcome that the Bishop gave him leave to publish his doctrine 'to all the world'.

There can be little doubt, I think, that Johnson finally acknowledged that this idea of perfection must be the objective of every Christian, including himself. Nevertheless, we should first consider those parts of his work that express doubts and hesitations with the perfectionism conventionally upheld in eighteenth-century theology. For example, Johnson expressed scepticism with the tendency of Protestant divines to refute the Catholic doctrine of venial sins by making all sins of equal seriousness. In Sermon 13 he cited James 2: 10, which he interpreted fairly strictly as a 'condemnation of those who presume to hope, that the performance of one duty will obtain excuse for the violation of others' (xiv. 144). But Johnson also insisted that St James's 'meaning is not, that all crimes are equal, or that in any one crime all others are involved' (xiv. 144–5), a predictable qualification by a man whose campaign against capital punishment was based on the varying seriousness of crimes such as murder and theft. Elsewhere, he complained about the tendency of eighteenth-century writers to treat the achievement of perfection as merely a question of adopting the correct side in a doctrinal controversy. This is one of the most notable features of *Serious Call*, which appears to claim that Christians lack perfection because they have failed to recognize the irrefutable logic of Law's position. Many eighteenth-century divines based their exhortations to perfection on the same assumption. In a sermon 'Religion a Consistent and Uniform Character', for example, James Foster proved by pure, abstracted deduction that the man who deliberately committed just one sin implicitly denied his obligation to obey any moral law: 'If when the reason is the *same*, it does not oblige in *all* cases, it can justly oblige in *no* case at all; if it be not, in itself, *always* a sufficient motive, it can *never* be a sufficient motive.'[21] It was this kind of reasoning, divorced from the experience of real life, that Johnson attacked in *Rambler*, No. 70:

> it is very easy to the solitary reasoner to prove that the same arguments by which the mind is fortified against one crime are of equal force against all, and the consequence very naturally follows, that he whom they fail to move on any occasion, has either never considered them, or has by some fallacy taught himself to evade their validity; and that, therefore, when a man is known to be guilty of one crime, no farther evidence is needful of his depravity and corruption (iv. 5).

This passage expresses Johnson's strongest objection to Christian perfection as it was conventionally explained by eighteenth-century divines. Partly because perfectionism had emerged in Anglican theology through a process of doctrinal controversy, its achievement continued to be seen as a matter of accepting certain arguments. Johnson retorted that the failure to achieve perfection resulted from frailty, not illogic. He urged that we must not judge sinners too harshly, or assume that 'all goodness is lost, though it may for a time be clouded and overwhelmed' (iv. 6).

Nevertheless, it is important to recognize the difference between this argument in *Rambler*, No. 70, and Trapp's tract against perfectionism. Trapp openly questioned whether perfection should be the goal of a Christian, but *Rambler*, No. 70, certainly did not. *Rambler*, No. 70, defends men from the charge that they are irredeemable because they have failed to overcome all sins, but Johnson does not question that perfection (understood in its 'relative' sense) must be the goal even of those who are presently unreformed. Although Johnson points out that even 'the wisest and best men deviate from known and acknowledged duties, by inadvertancy or surprise' (iv. 4), these were among the 'sins of infirmity' which, according to even the most rigorous perfectionists, are insurmountable. Johnson described the same 'sins of infirmity' elsewhere in his essays.[22] In Sermon 2, for example, he affirmed that 'our

---

[21] Foster, *Sermons*, iv. 297.
[22] See, e.g., *Rambler*, No. 77, iv. 43.

errours, if involuntary will not be imputed to us' (xiv. 19). But nowhere does Johnson argue that *wilful* sin will be forgiven. He himself wrote a disquisition against the sin of wavering between loyalty to God and a few deliberate sins—his Latin poem 'Christianus perfectus'. In this poem he exhorted that the Christian 'should neither vacillate, choosing now this side and now that, nor hesitate about whom he should call his master, but entirely in unity he should devote himself in loyalty to Christ, despising the transient things of this life'. [23]

'Christianus perfectus' is directed against a sin which homiletic literature usually called 'double-mindedness'. Law's *Serious Call* was a particularly compelling condemnation of this sin, though there were many others. George Smalridge's sermons on 'The Sinfulness of Double-mindedness', for example, are an especially good example of this homiletic genre by a divine whom Johnson praised. [24] These Anglican sermons and tracts (rather than just *Serious Call*) may well have been the source of Johnson's religious anxieties, for they generally condemned as sinful and unregenerate precisely the type of failings which seem to have characterized his religious life. William Sherlock's enormously popular treatise, *A Practical Discourse Concerning Death* (1689), portrayed the unregenerate 'double-minded' Christian in this way: 'This is the case of those Men, who after all their good resolutions, are ever and anon conquered by temptation; who as soon as their tears are dried up for the last fall, fall again, and then lament their sins, and resolve again.' [25] Johnson's diaries provide ample evidence of his guilt over his repeated failures to fulfil his resolutions. 'I have resolved, I hope not presumptuously,' he wrote in 1761, 'till I am afraid to resolve again' (i. 73). On his birthday in 1764 he remarked again, 'I have now spent fifty years in

[23] 'Christianus perfectus', ll. 16–18, translated privately by Dr Sheelagh Grier, formerly of Christ Church College, from *Yale Edition*, vi.

[24] Johnson listed Smalridge among his favourite divines in *Life*, iii. 248. In one of his sermons on 'The Sinfulness of Double-mindedness', Smalridge divided mankind into three categories—perfect Christians, abandoned profligates, and the 'double-minded'. See Smalridge, *Sixty Sermons Preached on Several Occasions* (Oxford, 1724), 394. Precisely the same division is used at the beginning of Rambler, No. 70, iv. 3–4. Though Johnson does not use the term 'double-minded', *Rambler*, No. 70, is partly an exercise in this homiletic genre. See also Thomas Wilson, 'The Perplexity and Danger of the Double-minded', in *Works* (2 vols.; London, 1781), ii.

[25] See William Sherlock, *A Practical Discourse Concerning Death* (London, 1689), 347.

resolving, having from the earliest time that I can remember been forming schemes for a better life. I have done nothing; the need of doing therefore is pressing, since the time of doing is short' (i. 81).

Johnson was, in effect, a classic example of the 'double-minded' Christian—not the abandoned profligate, but the Christian who had tried but consistently failed to overcome all his deliberate sins. There is some indication, however, that Johnson felt that he had finally achieved this goal near the end of his life. We might reconsider Johnson's famous 'late conversion' in the light of the background that I have drawn. In the prayer which Johnson composed for his final communion on 5 December 1784, he asked God to 'accept my late conversion', a plea that has caused much discussion among Johnson's modern critics since, surely, Johnson had been a serious Christian at least since his days at Oxford.[26] We will recall, however, that the idea of conversion advocated by Stebbing, Clarke, and others required the Christian to be free from all traces of wilful or habitual sin. Johnson apparently felt near the end of his life that 'I have now corrected all bad and vicious habits.'[27] Such an accomplishment would have fulfilled the idea of regeneration described by the major Anglican divines of the Restoration and early eighteenth century.

What is most distinctive about this idea of perfection described by Clarke, Tillotson, or Sherlock was that it imposed few demands on the Christian besides the achievement of moral purity. These divines rarely encouraged the love and worship of God for its own sake, preferring to regard a moral life as the surest evidence of 'piety'. Particularly as the century wore on, however, this preoccupation with Christianity's ethical role dismayed many leading theologians, who felt that the neglect of Christianity's ritual and purely spiritual role had paved the way for deism—a largely ethical and philosophical creed masquerading as 'religion'. Thus, William Warburton attacked what he called 'the new-fangled modern Christianity' which asserted that 'the man who observes the *moral* Law, shall

[26] See M. Quinlan, 'The Rumour of Dr. Johnson's Conversion', *Review of Religion*, 12 (1948), 243–61; D. J. Greene, 'Dr. Johnson's "Late Conversion": A Reconsideration', in M. Wahba (ed.), *Johnsonian Studies* (Cairo, 1962), 61–92; Pierce, *Religious Life*, pp. 162–4.

[27] *Miscellanies*, i. 156.

without any more aids, be entitled to the favour of his Maker, and consequently to all the benefits of Christ's Gospel'.[28] This objection was also made in Edward Young's *Night Thoughts* (1742-5):

> Talk they of *Morals*? O thou bleeding Love!
> Thou Maker of *new* Morals to Mankind!
> The grand Morality is Love of Thee.[29]

The Anglican writer who had led this revival of concern for Christian love was Daniel Waterland, whose 1730 attack on Samuel Clarke's legalism prompted a lively exchange of pamphlets on the eve of Tindal's *Christianity as Old as the Creation* (1730). Waterland's position was essentially the same as that later adopted by Warburton and Young: '*Piety* is not *instrumental* to social virtue, but is the *source* and *fountain*;' virtue was not truly Christian unless it proceeded from 'the *love of God*'.[30] Waterland was a High-Churchman, yet his attack on the legalistic tendencies of much latitudinarian theology gained support across a wide range of groups in the Anglican Church. Most notably, John Wesley made 'the love of God' the very heart of Christian perfection as he conceived it.[31]

Johnson was not without sympathy for this trend in English theology, yet neither was he without doubts and hesitations. In 1778 he criticized Hugh Blair for asserting in a sermon on devotion that 'he who does not feel joy in religion is far from the kingdom of heaven'.[32] 'There are many good men', he objected, 'whose fear of GOD predominates over their love.'[33] Johnson seems to have regarded Blair's exhortation for passionate love as a potential source for unreasonable scruples. Divines of the Restoration and early eighteenth century had been sceptical of the importance of love in the Christian life partly for this reason: the failure to experience love of God in devotion might cause religious melancholy, detracting from the more important moral objectives of Christianity. In a sermon

---

28 William Warburton, 'Salvation by Faith Alone', in *Works*, x. 103.
29 Edward Young, *The Complaint, or Night Thoughts on Life, Death and Immortality* (London, 1750), Night the Fourth, p. 98.
30 Waterland, *Christian Sacraments*, p. 41.
31 See Wesley, *Christian Perfection*, in *Works* (1830), ix. 371-3.
32 *Life*, iii. 339.
33 iii. Ibid.

'Of Religious Melancholy', Samuel Clarke had this consolation for those who 'cannot find in themselves such a *fervent Zeal and Love* towards God, as they think is necessary to denominate them good Christians':

if by Want of *Love* towards God he mean only, that, notwithstanding his best endeavours in the course of a virtuous Life, yet he cannot find in himself that *Passionate Love* of the Supreme God, which he finds some Writers have described in a sublime, poetical, and perhaps unintelligible manner; This is no just Ground for Uneasiness at all. For he may be directed to consider, that the Scripture speaks otherwise concerning the matter; telling us plainly and intelligibly, that *the Love of God is This, that we keep his Commandments*.[34]

This passage brings into sharp relief the predominantly moral understanding of Christianity which, as set forth by Clarke and other divines of that time, finally prompted the strictures of Waterland and Warburton. Broadly speaking, Johnson followed the tradition represented by Clarke. This does not mean, however, that he discouraged all passion in religion, even if he refused to make it an essential attribute of the perfect Christian. In Sermon 13, for example, he described the usefulness of religious exercises 'to inflame our gratitude by acts of thanksgiving, to strengthen our faith, and exalt our hope,' the objective being to 'love God with the whole heart' (xiv. 145). Never was Johnson closer to William Law than here, for *Serious Call*, properly understood, aims primarily not to make the Christian 'virtuous', but to 'train and exercise your heart into a true sense and feeling of devotion', to 'change your passions into divine love'.[35] Law was extremely hostile to the view that Christianity is 'a *School*, for the teaching of moral Virtue'.[36]

Unlike Law, however, Johnson did like restraint over the passions. He said that Blair's idea of devotion 'is the best limited, the best expressed: there is the most warmth without fanaticism, the most rational transport'.[37] Similarly, 'The Vanity of Human Wishes' calls for 'fervours' that create 'obedient passions' (ll. 360–1) and a worship that 'calms' (l. 367) rather than excites the mind. This suggests that

[34] Samuel Clarke, *Sermons*, x, 323.
[35] Law, *Serious Call*, ch. 16, p. 227.
[36] Law, *A Practical Treatise on Christian Perfection*, in *Works*, iii. 23.
[37] *Life*, iii. 339.

Johnson's commitment to the ideal of religious passion was far
weaker than, for instance, Young's: 'O ye cold-hearted, frozen
Formalists! | On such a Theme, 'tis impious to be calm.'[38] In
contrast to Young, Johnson's conception of the Christian state
of mind seems to have been dominated by the ideal of tranquillity, the 'perfect peace' which is 'the great, the necessary, the
inevitable business of human life' (Sermon 14, xiv. 154). And,
as Johnson argued at length in Sermon 14, it was only through
good morals that we could hope to achieve that peace. Thus, at
a time when many orthodox theologians were trying to reintro-
duce real passion into Christianity, Johnson was still cautious
and concerned to place limitations on this notion of piety. His
idea of the Christian life continued to be strongly influenced by
the erudite and rational theology of the early century. Divines
such as Clarke, Tillotson, and William Sherlock saw
Christianity not as a joyful celebration of God's love for
mankind, but above all as a particularly impressive ethical
code. We will see that it was this moralism which shaped
Johnson's treatment of most of the major issues in Christian
theology.

2. *The Doctrines of Original Sin, Grace, and Repentance*

Johnson's overriding concern with Christianity's ethical role is
strongly evident in his treatment of original sin, grace, and
repentance. Theoretical questions concerning man's inward
nature, the role of God and Christ in his regeneration, and the
motives to repentance were of importance to Johnson primarily
as they either promoted or hindered the individual's feeling of
responsibility for his own salvation through a moral life. With
not too much qualification, we can say that Johnson believed in
justification by works, the doctrine excoriated by early
Protestants as Pelagianism and Popery. The rise of this
doctrine in Restoration England was due very much to the
enormous influence of latitudinarian divines such as Barrow,
Tillotson, and, a little later, Samuel Clarke. The 'latitude' of
these writers consisted of a willingness to relax the restrictions
of traditional Protestant doctrine to the point where their own
positions verged dangerously on heresies such as Pelagianism,

---

[38] Young, *Night Thoughts*, Night the Fourth, p. 93.

Socinianism, and Arianism. For this reason, 'latitudin-arianism' was originally used in a strongly pejorative sense. Though the term began to lose its pejorative connotations as the century wore on, Richard Bentley grouped latitud-inarians with other heterodox groups such as the deists and free-thinkers in his 1713 reply to Collins. Whether these divines really were guilty of the charges of heresy which were constantly levelled against them is a more difficult question. Even Johnson seemed to accept that Samuel Clarke, for example, was an Arian, though Clarke publicly denied this.

The doctrine of original sin has an extremely complex history, and some modern historians might justly complain that the eighteenth-century description of this doctrine was over-simplified and over-generalized. In *The Body of Divinity* (1718), a textbook for Anglican divines sometimes consulted by Johnson, Richard Fiddes resolved the controversy surrounding original sin into a straightforward dichotomy. On the one hand, he wrote, there was the 'calvinistical' view of original sin as 'the actual corruption of man's nature, formally consider'd as sin'.[39] On the other hand, there was the position supported by Fiddes which described original sin as man's 'natural propension to sin, arising from the irregular state of his body since the fall, and what the scriptures express by the name of concupiscence'.[40] The Calvinist doctrine teaches that mankind's fallen nature is itself abhorrent to God and worthy of damnation even at birth. According to Fiddes, the propensity to sin—concupiscence—was not itself sinful; 'sin' properly signified only the actual breach of Divine law. We have previously cited his strong objection to the belief that 'a creature should be treated as criminal upon the charge of a crime, which it has not, in fact, committed'.[41] For this reason, Fiddes criticized as 'very strong' Article IX of the Church of England, which upholds the Calvinist teaching on original sin. Like so many Anglicans who found themselves at odds with the articles of their own Church, he attributed this Calvinistic leaning to 'the controversies which were manag'd with such

---

[39] Fiddes, *Body of Divinity*, I. 228.
[40] Ibid. 227.
[41] Ibid.

heat at the time of their being compiled'.[42] Johnson used the same observation to explain why the Article XVII upholds predestination.[43] It is worth noting that, according to recent historical research, this opinion was not strictly accurate. In 1571, when the Thirty-nine Articles were approved, Calvinism so prevailed in the English Church that the only disagreement concerned how strongly its tenets should be expressed.[44]

Johnson's comments on original sin are rare and rather cursory. They generally ratify Fiddes's view that original sin represented a propensity to evil, rather than inherited guilt. In 1773 he told Boswell that 'original sin was the propensity to evil, which no doubt was occasioned by the fall'.[45] There was, however, a theoretical problem with this treatment of the doctrine which led some writers to question the existence of any connection between the fall and concupiscence, and even of original sin itself. In *The Scripture Doctrine of Original Sin* (1741), a nonconformist minister named John Taylor pointed out that it was contradictory to claim that the fall caused our present propensity to sin, since the fall itself must have been caused by such a propensity:

For *Eve* saw that the forbidden Fruit was pleasant to the Eye, and to be desired to make one wise; and, accordingly, she indulged those irregular Desires, and did eat. What was the Cause of *her* Lust, *her* irregular Desire, or Inclination? Shall we feign an *Original Sin*, a previous Corruption of Nature for her, as we have done for ourselves?[46]

Taylor's conclusion was that Scripture provided no foundation for believing in the existence of original sin, an opinion which John Wesley feared was becoming widespread by the 1750s. In his *Doctrine of Original Sin* (1757) he called Taylor's view a

---

[42] Ibid. 152. The same defence of the Articles was later made by John Tottie, *A Charge Relative to the Articles of the Church of England* (Oxford, 1772), 5. The lack of full consensus among Anglicans on the Articles had fomented a petition, initiated by Archdeacon Francis Blackburne's *The Confessional* (1766), to eliminate subscription to the Articles by clergymen and university students. The petition was rejected by parliament in 1772, but the reasoning for this rejection was that an orderly institution must maintain some official principles. Very few Anglicans could say that they wholeheartedly agreed with all the Thirty-nine Articles.

[43] See *Life*, ii. 104.

[44] See D. D. Wallace, *Puritans and Predestination* (Chapel Hill, 1982), 29–42.

[45] *Life*, v. 88.

[46] John Taylor, *The Scripture Doctrine of Original Sin* (London, 1741), 127.

'deadly poison which has been diffusing itself for several years through our nation, our church, and even our Universities'.[47]

Wesley's defence of original sin will help bring Johnson's views into sharper focus, and demonstrate that Johnson's understanding of original sin was not only quite distant from the Calvinist doctrine, but also the Arminian doctrine which Wesley set out to uphold. Like Fiddes and Johnson, Wesley placed original sin in concupiscence. Against the Calvinists, he also insisted that all men possess free will to obtain grace to overcome original sin. None the less, Wesley made clear that the propensity to sin was itself sinful, even if it did not result in outward or what he called 'actual' sin. He argued against Taylor that 'to say "Eve had irregular desires before she sinned" is a contradiction; since all irregular desire is sin'.[48] This is where Johnson and Wesley disagreed, for Johnson did not regard the desire to commit sin to be itself sinful. In *Rambler*, No. 8, for example, he offered this consolation to Christians afflicted with irregular desires: 'I cannot forbear, under this head, to caution pious and tender minds, that are disturbed by the irruptions of wicked imaginations, against too great dejection, and too anxious alarms; for thoughts are only criminal, when first chosen, and then voluntarily continued' (iii. 45). Samuel Clarke had offered precisely the same consolation in his sermon 'Of Religious Melancholy'.[49] By placing guilt entirely in acts of volition, Clarke and Johnson implied that man's original perfection was achievable solely by resisting the propensity to sin. This implication was clearly stated in Johnson's review of *A Free Inquiry into the Nature and Origin of Evil* (1757). In the very same year as Wesley's vindication of original sin, Jenyns denied that there was perfection in the Garden of Eden for reasons similar to those of Taylor: mankind's 'rendering himself wicked and miserable is the highest imperfection imaginable'.[50] Johnson responded by asserting that perfection is entirely a condition of outward conduct; we achieve an Edenic condition simply by resisting temptation. 'All the duties to God or man that are neglected,' he

---

[47] John Wesley, *The Doctrine of Original Sin* (1757), in *Works* (1830), ix. 193.
[48] Ibid. 274.
[49] Clarke, *Sermons*, x. 332–3.
[50] Review of *Free Inquiry*, in Schwartz, *Evil*, p. 111.

wrote, 'we may fancy performed; all the crimes that are committed we may conceive foreborne. Man will then be restored to his moral perfection.'[51]

This is original sin in its most diluted form, because it makes men responsible only for their 'actual' sins, and in no way responsible for the sin of Adam. With no conception of inherited guilt, of what benefit was Christ's atonement? On this subject, latitudinarian divines usually explained that God was necessitated, as the consequence of His attribute of perfect justice, to punish all sinners, even those guilty of the inevitable 'involuntary' sins which spring up from our enfeebled will. As Johnson argued in discussions of the atonement in 1773 and 1781, God was freed to forgive sinners only as the result of Christ's sacrifice.[52] We should note that this interpretation was not entirely consistent with his argument, expressed in *Rambler*, No. 110, that men had always known that God was merciful and would forgive repentant sinners. Moreover, Johnson, Tillotson, Clarke, and others usually allotted the 'satisfaction' element of the sacrifice a rather lowly, subordinate status. They feared that too heavy an emphasis on the satisfaction would delude men into believing that continued obedience to the moral law had been rendered unnecessary by the crucifixion. For this reason, Isaac Barrow portrayed the atonement as a grand demonstration of God's 'love of goodness, and dislike of wickedness', so that 'every creature in heaven and earth should be solemnly admonished of its duty'.[53] Johnson seems to have upheld the same 'Government' or 'Rectoral' idea of the atonement in both his conversations with Boswell on this subject.[54]

By including a weakened conception of the satisfaction, the Anglican divines who advocated the Rectoral atonement narrowly avoided Socinianism. The Socinians denied any form of original sin, and portrayed the sacrifice as merely a demonstration of heroic virtue. Even if the divines had avoided Socinianism, however, many leading Anglicans strongly

[51] Ibid. 112.

[52] See *Life*, iv. 124; v. 88.

[53] Isaac Barrow, 'The Doctrine of Universal Redemption Asserted and Explained', in *Works*, iii. 455–6.

[54] For a fuller discussion of Johnson's view of the atonement and its background, see my 'Johnson, Socinianism and the Meaning of Christ's Sacrifice'.

disagreed with the Rectoral idea of the atonement, especially those who felt that latitudinarianism had drained all the spirituality out of religion. Edmund Gibson found this doctrine so objectionable that in 1735 he issued another of his numerous directives, this time in defence of a more integral place for propitiation in the Anglican idea of the atonement.[55]

But the great majority of Anglicans could at least agree on this: the atonement had benefited all mankind; its effects were universal and perhaps even extended to good men who died before the crucifixion. A century before this had been one of the most controversial tenets of Arminian divinity, because it contradicted the Calvinist doctrine of a 'limited' atonement— the belief that Christ died not for all mankind, but solely for the benefit of the elect. Closely connected with the limited atonement was the doctrine of predestination, which was traditionally inseparable from a theology of grace. Primarily to uphold and celebrate the greatness of God's gift of salvation, Calvin instructed that God bestows saving grace on some (election) and denies it to others (reprobation) through an act of free will in no way deserved by the sinner. With the decline of Calvinism in the Anglican Church after the Restoration, most divines upheld the Arminian objection that this doctrine made man not a 'Voluntary, but a necessary Agent'.[56] In an age so preoccupied with the task of maintaining public conviction in moral responsibility, it probably seemed needless to make any further objection, yet even latitudinarians could not dismiss the issues raised by Calvinism so easily. The articles of the Church obliged orthodox divines to maintain some notion of the individual's reliance on grace, if only in combination with limited free will. Pelagianism is denounced in Articles XI and XV; Article X states categorically that 'we have no power to do good works' without grace. These articles could not be contradicted without attacking something quite fundamental to the official beliefs of the Church.

These articles could, however, be ignored, and the lack of frequent or detailed discussions of grace in Anglican homiletics of the period (including Johnson's sermons) makes it very difficult to generalize confidently on the prevailing doctrine.

---

[55] See Edmund Gibson, *The Great Work of Our Redemption by Christ* (London, 1735).
[56] Edward Bird, *Fate and Destiny Inconsistent with Christianity* (London, 1726), 12.

None the less we might again consider Henry Stebbing's *A Treatise Concerning the Operations of the Holy Spirit* (1719), since this tract was so often cited and seems generally consistent with Johnson's various statements on grace. Stebbing was a vehement opponent to Calvinism, yet he admitted that mankind was entirely reliant on grace: 'our Savior [has] told us, that *without him we can do nothing* . . . if the Assistance of the Spirit be necessary (as it has been shewn to be) to the first Beginnings of a good Mind, and the lowest Degrees of Holiness, it must be much more necessary to the constant Continuance in well doing, and to all those higher Steps which lead to Perfection.'[57] Johnson's private writings also attest to a conviction in the Christian's dependence on grace. 'All the purposes of man are vain without the help of God' (i. 125), he wrote in his prayers, and he seems to have admired Christians like Herman Boerhaave who 'attributed every good thought, and every laudable action to the Father of Godliness'.[58] Moreover, we have already seen that he and most divines made the assistance of the Holy Spirit necessary to form a conviction in the truth of Christianity.[59]

Yet Stebbing and Johnson also wanted to maintain belief in moral responsibility. This led to the problem of how to reconcile human freedom with an orthodox conviction in man's dependence on grace. For Stebbing, the solution was to insist on the distinction between 'ordinary' and 'special' grace. 'Ordinary' grace signifies the gifts of the Holy Spirit granted to all men without exception through the merits of Christ; we are absolutely dependent on this form of grace, without which we cannot even start our efforts to achieve virtue. To proceed to higher stages of virtue and piety, however, we require 'special' grace—additional gifts of the Spirit gained only by special means. For eighteenth-century Anglicans, these means were usually prayer and, even more important, the exertion of the will to achieve greater virtue. As Stebbing went on to explain, 'the Spirit's Operations . . . do not make our own Care and Diligence after Virtue and Godliness unnecessary, but . . . on

---

[57] Stebbing, *Holy Spirit*, pp. 23–4.
[58] Samuel Johnson, 'The Life of Dr. Boerhaave', *The Gentleman's Magazine*, 9 (1739), 175.
[59] See ch. 1, sec. 2, above.

the other hand, the Operations of the Spirit will do us no good if our Endeavours be wanting'.[60] According to the idea of grace outlined by Stebbing, special grace was earned through hard struggle, and acted only as 'Helps and Assistances' to the individual's effort, even if those assistances were indispensable. This notion of a co-operation between grace and the individual will (sometimes known as 'synergism') frequently appears in Johnson's religious writings and private devotions. Throughout his prayers he asks for 'the assistance of the Holy Spirit' and reminds himself that 'God . . . hast ordained that whatever is to be desired, should be sought by labour'. 'By thy Blessing,' he went on, '[thou] bringest honest labour to good effect' (i. 260). In Sermon 9 on the Lord's supper he admonished the congregation, 'we must use our own endeavours, and exert our utmost natural powers, for God only co-operates with the diligent and the watchful' (xiv. 101).

Stebbing and Johnson were thus able to strike a compromise between Calvinism and Pelagianism, between an idea of grace that made the Christian a passive instrument of Divine will and a doctrine that denied mankind's reliance on the power of God to achieve salvation. The need for compromise also shaped their treatment of the belief in sensible grace—the claim of, for example, the Methodists that the Holy Spirit imparted an overwhelming 'assurance' of one's blessedness or salvation. Johnson's caution that 'Favourable impressions at particular moments, as to the state of our soul may be deceitful and dangerous',[61] reflected a widespread distrust of the imagination and, just as important, an indignation with the belief that an individual could achieve faith and understanding without the authoritative direction of the established Church. Moreover, Johnson and many divines objected that the 'inward light' (which Johnson wrongly attributed to the Methodists rather than the Quakers and mystics) was 'a principle utterly incompatible with social or civil security', because this private communication with God might direct the individual to act in contradiction to written law.[62] But orthodox divines were not able fully to deny the possibility of

---

[60] Stebbing, *Holy Spirit*, p. 123.
[61] *Life*, iv. 122.
[62] Ibid. ii. 126.

direct, sensible inspiration from God: this became evident during the controversy which followed Trapp's attack on Methodist perfectionism.

In his 1739 *Pastoral Letter against Lukewarmness*, Edmund Gibson condemned the 'enthusiasm' of the Methodists, which he defined as 'a strong Perswasion of the Mind, that they are guided in an *extraordinary* Manner, by the immediate *Impulses* and *Impressions* of the Spirit of God'.[63] As Whitefield pointed out in his answer to Gibson, however, the Bishop of London also admitted that 'There is no doubt, but God, when he pleases, *can* work upon the Minds of Men by extraordinary influences.'[64] This admission was necessary in order to uphold the omnipotence of God (He could not be omnipotent without the power of inspiration), and to protect belief in the inspiration of St Paul, a circumstance mentioned by Johnson in a discussion of sensible grace with Boswell.[65] Thus, Whitefield was able to correct Gibson's definition of 'enthusiasm' by using the Bishop's own acknowledgement that direct inspiration was possible: 'Had your Lordship said, a strong but *Groundless* Persuasion, that they are guided in an extraordinary Manner, it could have been to your Lordship's purpose.'[66]

In the light of this controversy, it is interesting that in his *Dictionary* Johnson defined 'enthusiasm' as not merely belief in direct inspiration from God, but a '*vain* belief of private revelation, a *vain* confidence of divine favour' (my italics). For all his distrust of the claim of supernatural communication with God, he was bound by orthodoxy to admit that it was possible, a concession that greatly weakened the Anglican case against the Methodists, the Quakers, and other sects who made this claim. In addition, even theologians who were highly sceptical of mystical impressions did accept a distinctive variation on the doctrine of sensible grace. Stebbing argued that Christians are in frequent communication with God, but these communications are blended so subtly into our thoughts and desires that we rarely or never realize their supernatural origin.[67] In

---

[63] Gibson, Pastoral Letter against *Lukewarmness*, p. 11.

[64] Ibid. 54.

[65] See *Life*, iv. 122.

[66] George Whitefield, *An Answer to the Bishop of London's Last Pastoral Letter* (London, 1739), 10.

[67] See Stebbing, *Holy Spirit*, p. 125.

particular, the desire for repentance was considered by many orthodox divines to be a direct 'call' from God.[68] In his prayers Johnson thanked God that He 'hast permitted me still to enjoy the means of Grace, and vouchsafed to call me yet again to Repentance' (i. 40). To ignore the desire for repentance was to turn one's back on the voice of God, a sin that could eventually lead to the most serious danger in the Christian life: the calls to repentance might finally cease, a sign that the individual had been denied grace and was consequently doomed to perdition.

The doctrine of repentance is much more difficult and complex than is usually realized. Maurice Quinlan's chapter on repentance in *Samuel Johnson: A Layman's Religion* rose to the level of that complexity, and showed that Johnson himself was deeply sensitive to the various controversies that have surrounded the idea of repentance. Nevertheless, I disagree with Quinlan's conclusion that 'Johnson went beyond the Church of England's teachings on contrition' by advocating certain Roman Catholic ideas on repentance.[69] Johnson's understanding of repentance in fact strongly reflects certain changes in Anglican doctrine that are worth studying because they embody characteristic movements in eighteenth-century thought as a whole.

Quinlan's assessment was based on the distinction between 'contrition' and 'attrition'. He indicated that the Protestant divines whom Johnson admired 'were strongly opposed to the Catholic doctrine of attrition', that is, the belief that fear of damnation was a sufficient motive to repentance. 'Contrition' was traditionally the Protestant doctrine of repentance: it required that the sinner repent not simply because he was afraid of being damned, but because he genuinely came to hate sin, and was sincerely grieved that he had offended God. This, we might add, was closely connected with the Protestant doctrine of justification by faith, for a life which conformed outwardly to moral law was valuable only so far as it manifested inward regeneration. According to Quinlan, Johnson recognized the efficacy of both attrition and contrition, and in this respect was closer to the Roman Catholic idea of repentance than most of his Anglican contemporaries.

[68] See, e.g., South, 'Sermon on Genesis 6: 8', in *Sermons*, xi. 232–3.
[69] See Quinlan, *Layman's Religion*, pp. 66–70.

Yet Johnson did, in fact, sometimes insist on the need for a genuine hatred of sin rather than just fear of damnation. In his 1777 sermon for Dr William Dodd, a clergyman sentenced to death for forgery, Dodd's fellow convicts are warned that 'the shortness of time, which is before us, gives little power, even to ourselves, of distinguishing the effects of terrour from those of conviction, of deciding, whether our present sorrow for sin proceeds from abhorrence of guilt, or dread of punishment' (xiv. 307). This is a fairly strong affirmation of the superiority of contrition to attrition. Nevertheless, Quinlan is correct to point out that in Sermon 2 Johnson shows little concern for the motives to repentance:

An amendment of life is the chief and essential part of repentance. He that has performed that great work, needs not disturb his conscience with subtle scruples, or nice distinctions. He needs not recollect, whether he was awakened from the lethargy of sin, by the love of God, or the fear of punishment. The Scripture applies to all our passions; and eternal punishments had been threatened to no purpose, if these menaces were not intended to promote virtue (xiv. 24).

It is probably true, then, that Johnson accepted the efficacy of both attrition and contrition. Nevertheless, this latitude does not necessarily indicate any sympathies with Roman Catholicism: Restoration divines such as Tillotson generally agreed that fear of punishment and love of God were both valid motives to repentance.[70] This was clearly not the result of any Catholic sympathies on Tillotson's part, but because latitudinarian divines placed far greater importance on the need for outward reform than on the need for any particular motive to reform. This relative disinterest in the motives to repentance was later shared by the Christian epicureans, moralists deeply scornful of any attempt to deny the fundamental self-interest of all human acts.

As the epicurean moralist Thomas Rutherforth wrote in *An Essay on the Nature and Obligations of Virtue* (1744), 'The love of God cannot be supposed to oblige us to do any thing in opposition to our true and real interest.'[71] This statement

---

[70] See Tillotson, 'Of Confession, or Sorrow for Sin', in *Works*, iii. 18–19.

[71] Rutherforth, *Nature and Obligations of Virtue*, p. 265.

contradicted the doctrine of contrition, which had clear affinities with Rutherforth's specific target, the benevolism of Shaftesbury, Hutcheson, and others of that group. Not unlike Protestants who denied the validity of attrition, the benevolists claimed that the expectation of reward or punishment ruined the character of a virtuous act. For that reason, John Clarke's refutation of Hutcheson is closely comparable to Johnson's discussion of repentance in Sermon 2:

I desire [Hutcheson] to reconcile this Doctrine to the Scriptures (for he has too much good Sense to be an Infidel, I dare say.) In them the greatest Reward is promised to Virtue, and Vice is threatened with the greatest Punishments, on purpose sure to excite Mankind to the Practice of Virtue; for if they were not designed for that purpose, I should be glad to be informed what they were designed for.[72]

Johnson's acceptance of both contrition and attrition, therefore, is consistent with his support of the Christian epicureans. Moreover, the epicurean movement flourished as it did because of the new pragmatism that infiltrated many areas of eighteenth-century thought. A new acceptance of self-interest, and an impatience with doctrinal quibbles that did little to promote the achievement of virtue, led even leading nonconformists, such as Samuel Chandler, to advocate the supposedly Catholic doctrine of attrition.[73]

We have seen that many leading Anglicans, such as Daniel Waterland, attempted to push the Church away from the legalism which prevailed early in the century, and towards a revived conviction in the importance of love as the foundation of Christian virtue. But here we must readjust our understanding of the traditional divisions within English Protestantism. Although Waterland was advocating something closer to the traditional Protestant doctrine of contrition, he was himself a High-Churchman who also championed the 'Real Presence' in the Lord's supper, a doctrine only narrowly different from the Catholic doctrine of transubstantiation. Waterland's dislike for the legalistic tendencies of latitudinarian divinity was shared by theologians who, like John Wesley, disagreed with his opinion on most other doctrines. On the issue of repentance, as on

---

[72] John Clarke, *Foundation of Morality*, p. 48.
[73] See Samuel Chandler, 'The Scripture Doctrine of Repentance', in *Sermons*, ii. 415.

many others, any neat division between 'Catholic' and 'Protestant' doctrines was breaking down. It is difficult to examine Johnson's thought according to this traditional division because his beliefs addressed modern issues and problems quite different from those which faced theologians of the sixteenth and seventeenth centuries. His views reflect the preoccupations of eighteenth-century Anglicanism—which does not mean that these views were universally favoured. Especially as his doctrinal positions embodied an overriding legalism, he was taking a controversial stand in a divided Church of England.

3. *The Christian Ordinances: The Form and the Power of Godliness*

It was conventional in Restoration divinity to attack those who confined their religion to the observance of the external forms of Christianity while neglecting to maintain a uniform habit of virtue and piety in all parts of their life, a concern shared by Law in *Serious Call*. This lesson had, of course, a strong foundation in the New Testament. St Paul condemned the fault of 'Having the form of godliness, but denying the power thereof' (2 Timothy 3: 5), the text for sermons on the Christian ordinances by Tillotson, Johnson, and many others. And before St Paul, Christ's debates with the Pharisees were traditionally interpreted as a sign of God's new plan for mankind, a plan that replaced the plethora of rituals in the Jewish Church with a simple code of virtue and only a few indispensable ordinances. This, for many theologians, reflected God's recognition that mankind had come of age and could no longer be treated as children. As Samuel Clarke argued, God had given the Jews 'such positive precepts, as had not in themselves any real and intrinsic worth', a practice explicable only by His desire 'to prove the obedience of his peculiar people the Jews'.[74] Now that this obedience had been proved, most of the rituals could be abandoned.

According to Clarke, however, God had always placed a secondary value on ritual. Even under the Jewish dispensation, observance of the moral law was of much greater importance than the various ceremonies enjoined by positive command (a

---

[74] Samuel Clarke, 'The Nature, End, and Design of the Holy Communion', in *Sermons*, iv. 104.

duty directly imposed by Divine will and not entailed by natural religion):

tho' these things *were not to be left undone*, yet the *weightier matters of the Law*, were always *judgment, mercy*, and *truth*. To *these*, God continually exhorted his people by the Prophets; and declared upon all occasions, that their ritual observances, *in comparison of* these more important Duties, were of no value, and *without* them, were even abominations in his Sight. Thinkest thou that I will eat bulls flesh, or drink the blood of Goats? No; But offer unto God thanksgiving, and pay their vows unto the most High.[75]

This passage indicates Clarke's scepticism with the belief that ritual really ever had an important place in a true revelation from God. In Sermon 13 Johnson's scepticism with ritual was perhaps even greater: unlike Clarke, he did not attempt to offer an explanation for what he considered the baffling case of the Jewish ceremonies. 'The religion of the Jews,' he argued, 'from the time of Moses, comprized a great number of burdensome ceremonies, required by God for reasons which perhaps human wisdom has never fully discovered' (xiv. 139). The Jewish dispensation was explicable to Johnson only so far as it subordinated ritual to morality, for in the time before Christ 'even these sacred rites might be punctually performed, without making the performer acceptable to God; the blood of bulls and of goats might be poured out in vain, if the desires were not regulated, or the passions subdued' (xiv. 140). Just as Clarke had asserted that 'ritual observances, *in comparison of* these more important Duties, were of no value', so Johnson left no doubt that 'the moral law [is] exalted over all ceremonial institutions' (xiv. 140). This was especially true of Christianity, which kept only those rituals that served an easily discernible purpose to promote virtue.

But this understanding of the Christian ordinances became the subject of an important controversy between latitudinarian and High-Church divines. When in *An Exposition of the Church Catechism* (1729) Clarke reiterated his stand that there was 'no comparison' between moral duties and the Christian ordinances, Daniel Waterland responded with *The Nature, Obligation, and Efficacy of the Christian Sacraments* (1730). According to

---

[75] Ibid. 105. See Psalm 50: 13.

Waterland, the rituals of Christianity were perhaps the most unique and important contribution of revealed religion. Since we go to church or receive the sacraments from the same love of God that, as Waterland insisted, should motivate all our virtuous acts, 'it is wrong to say that these Institutions are not commanded in that strict and absolute Manner as moral Virtues are'.[76] 'Any Pretense', he wrote elsewhere, 'of setting up *Moral Virtues* in opposition to *Religious Duties*, is undermining Morality instead of serving it.'[77]

Clarke died in 1729 and his case was taken up by his admirer, Arthur Ashley Sykes. Sykes repeated Clarke's position that 'notwithstanding positive institutions were prescribed by God; yet when they and moral duties are compared together, moral duties are always preferred'.[78] According to Sykes, the real point was that the Christian ordinances were merely a *means* to the end of moral virtue. 'To say that a positive duty is of *equal* excellence, or value with a moral one, is just the same absurdity as to say that the means are as valuable as the end.'[79] By calling the sacraments simply 'means', Sykes was recalling the position of Clarke, Tillotson, and other latitudinarian divines that all ritual practices, including the sacraments, served primarily as 'instruments' to strengthen the will and to remind us periodically of our duty.[80] This was the basis for a latitudinarian understanding of Christianity that reduced all ritual and both Anglican sacraments to minor and merely functional additions to the religious life. And it was a view of the Christian ordinances generally shared by Johnson.

Johnson did sometimes refer to the Church ceremonies as 'duties'.[81] Nevertheless, while Waterland suggested that neglecting the sacraments or public worship was as much an offence against God as moral iniquity, Johnson felt few scruples concerning his poor church attendance.[82] His discussions

---

[76] Waterland, *Christian Sacraments*, p. 73.

[77] Ibid. 26–7.

[78] Arthur Ashley Sykes, *A Defence of the Answer to the Remarks upon Dr. Clarke's Exposition of the Church Catechism*, (London, 1730) 39.

[79] Ibid. 14. Other replies to Waterland, such as John Chilton's *Positive Institutions not to be Compar'd with, or Preferr'd before Moral Duties and Virtues* (London, 1730), generally reiterated the case advanced by Sykes.

[80] See, e.g., Tillotson, 'Of the Form and the Power of Godliness', in *Works*, iii. 328.

[81] See, e.g., Sermon 13, xiv. 144.

[82] As discussed by Quinlan, *Layman's Religion*, pp. x–xv.

of religious rites and ceremonies almost always focus on their functional value as instruments to promote virtue. Sermon 13 concludes with a strong statement that 'The form of godliness, as it consists in the rites of religion, is the instrument given us by God for the acquisition of the power' (xiv. 148). Johnson's view of the sacraments is closely associated with his controversial understanding of the will as a 'balance' which could be controlled through the strengthening or weakening of opposing desires.[83] For this reason, his major essay on the will, *Rambler*, No. 7, contains a strong affirmation of the latitudinarian position that religious ritual is a means to facilitate the practice of virtue. 'The great art of piety,' he wrote, '. . . and the end for which all the rites of religion seem to be instituted, is the perpetual renovation of the motives to virtue' (iii. 40). This statement, like much of *Rambler*, No. 7, was highly controversial: an increasing number of Anglicans shared Waterland's concern that the latitudinarians had drained all the spiritual value from Christianity.

Sympathy for Waterland's case had been augmented during the controversy raised by Benjamin Hoadly's *A Plain Account of the Nature and End of the Sacrament of the Lord's Supper* (1735), a work that embodied the boldest and, for many, the most offensive extremes of latitudinarian doctrine. This pamphlet was probably written more for political than religious reasons. In the 1730s the nonconformists were campaigning for the repeal of the Test Act—the act which required members of state institutions to take the Anglican communion. Walpole's government was theoretically sympathetic to the cause of increased toleration, but Walpole was too prudent to commit himself to such a controversial measure as the repeal of this cornerstone of established Church predominance.[84] Hoadly, a powerful Whig bishop made famous by the 1717 Bangorian controversy, was called on to reduce tensions over the Test Act. His anonymously published *Plain Account* portrayed the Lord's supper as merely a commemorative act with no intrinsic power or significance: by implication, nonconformists should not hesitate to take the Anglican sacrament in order to gain

---

[83] See ch. 3, sec. 2, above.

[84] For an account of Walpole's position, and his use of Hoadly, see R. B. Barlow, *Citizenship and Conscience* (Philadelphia, 1962), 88–96.

political employment, nor should Anglicans see this as a profanation of the eucharist. This doctrine was immediately condemned in a small flood of pamphlets by High-Churchmen, including Waterland.

Hoadly's treatment of the Lord's supper was very similar to Samuel Clarke's in both *An Exposition of the Church Catechism* and four well-known sermons 'Of the Nature, End, and Design of the Holy Communion'. As Maurice Quinlan has pointed out, Johnson made extensive notes on these sermons and, in my view, Johnson's Sermons 9 and 22 on the Lord's supper enunciate a doctrine very close to that of Clarke and Hoadly. This, however, was not Quinlan's opinion. Clarke (like Hoadly later on) contended that there is 'no grace annexed to˙ the mere material action' of receiving the Lord's supper, and this, Quinlan argued, 'is in complete contradiction to what Johnson says in Sermon IX'.[85] In Sermon 9 Johnson seemed to acknowledge the supernatural benefits of communion denied by Clarke. The communicant, Johnson wrote, will receive 'the supernatural and extraordinary influences of grace, and those blessings which God has annexed to the due use of the means appointed by himself' (xiv. 99). Johnson's use of the expression 'means', however, suggests that he did not consider the Lord's supper itself to be a supernatural act. Indeed, the connection that Johnson draws between communion and grace is almost identical to that drawn by Clarke in *An Exposition of the Church Catechism*.

As in his sermons on the communion, Clarke argued in the *Exposition* that 'There is no Superstition whatsoever, more mischievous and destructive of True Religion; than men's imagining, that, in a *Sacrament*, the inward and spiritual Benefit is *necessarily* and *in course* connected with the Outward Performance.'[86] Nevertheless, he also made clear that 'The *spiritual Benefit* is, by the Appointment of God, so annexed to the Use of the *Means*; as that every one, not who *partakes*, but who *worthily partakes* of the *outward Sign*, shall be also made Partaker of the *inward Blessing*.'[87] Like Johnson, Clarke's phrase was 'Use of the *Means*'. His point was that the reception of grace depended

[85] Quinlan, *Layman's Religion*, p. 96.
[86] Samuel Clarke, *An Exposition of the Church Catechism* (London, 1729), 288–9.
[87] Ibid. 289.

primarily on the worthiness of the communicant, the reverence and virtue of his disposition upon taking the sacrament, rather than on the act of communion itself. Communion, a mere material act, was simply an instrument by which the worthy communicant received special grace directly from God.

It was Hoadly's similar denial that the *material action* of communion possessed any spiritual benefit which prompted the anger of High-Churchmen. Like Clarke, Hoadly did not dispute that the Lord's supper was indirectly a 'means' to obtain grace, but he went one step further than Clarke by insisting that those spiritual benefits were derived from the prayers associated with the sacrament, not from the worthiness of the communicant:

We are taught, in the *Prayer* annexed to this *Thanksgiving*, to ask God's assistance towards our performance of what is still on our part necessary, in the conduct of our Lives, *after* our having *duly partaken* of the Holy *Communion*. Neither here is the *Grace* of GOD supposed to be a certain and immediate effect of our receiving his *Sacrament* WORTHILY, but is purely left (as it ought to be) as the *Subject* of a *Christian's Prayers*, wholly distinct from the Duty of communicating.[88]

Neither Johnson nor Clarke went so far as entirely to separate grace from the act of communion. Nevertheless, Johnson's sermons on the Lord's supper verge far closer to Hoadly's doctrine than to that of his High-Church opponents. Sermon 9 elaborates at some length on Johnson's point that the Lord's supper has a natural effect to increase virtuous habits 'by the new strength which every idea acquires by a new impression' (xiv. 99). The act of commemorating the death of Christ strengthens the motives to virtue, the purely physical effect of religious rites also described in *Rambler*, No. 7. But Johnson's discussion of the supernatural effects of communion is limited to a paragraph which, as in Hoadly's pamphlet, links the benefits of grace to the prayers accompanying the sacrament, rather than to the sacrament itself:

When we thus enter upon a new life by a solemn, deliberate, and serious dedication of ourselves to a more exact and vigilant service of God, and oblige ourselves to the duties of piety by this sacrament, we

---

[88] Benjamin Hoadly, *A Plain Account of the Nature and End of the Sacrament of the Lord's Supper* (London, 1735), 131–2.

may hope to obtain, by fervent and humble prayer, such assistances from God as may enable us to perform those engagements, which we have entered into by command, and in the manner appointed by him (xiv. 101).

Sermons 9 and 22 do warn against the extreme laxity of doctrines, such as Hoadly's, which portray the Lord's supper as an essentially unimportant ceremony that can be entered into or neglected with indifference. Yet Johnson's doctrine of the Lord's supper has many affinities with Hoadly's. Like Hoadly, Johnson depicts the Lord's supper as primarily a commemorative act;[89] both warn against the dangers of too rigorous a standard for worthy communion;[90] both habitually use the term 'table' instead of 'altar' to describe the place where the Lord's supper is administered.[91]

These affinities are significant because they place Johnson on the side of the latitudinarians and the Whigs in a major controversy with the High-Church. Since Johnson was supposedly a Tory, it seems especially peculiar to find that he has doctrinal affinities with Benjamin Hoadly, the very embodiment of the Whiggism that Johnson is reputed to have despised, a man who made his name by, in Johnson's view, fomenting discord against the dominance of the established Church. But this is less of a paradox than might be imagined. As we will see in the next chapter, Johnson's hostility to religious toleration was unbending and severe. Nevertheless, this hostility resulted not from any strong concern that the dissenters were preaching an erroneous form of Christianity, but from his conviction, based on a sophisticated assessment of human nature, that religious liberty was not compatible with an ordered society. That he himself possessed real doctrinal links with the Low-Church and dissenters made no difference to his political principle that

[89] As the Yale editors note, Johnson's 'firmest verbal association with *communion* is *commemoration*' (xiv. 98 n. 4). This in itself does not establish any connection with Hoadly, for his High-Church opponents did not deny that the Lord's supper was, in part, commemorative. For them, however, it was much more, due to the 'Real Presence' of Christ in the bread and wine.

[90] Cf. Sermon 22, xiv. 230, and Hoadly, *Plain Account*, 81–2.

[91] As Hoadly contended, 'there is no need for an *Altar*, for this sort of *Commemorative* Eating and Drinking' (p. 53). For Johnson's use of 'table', as opposed to 'altar', see xiv. 105 and 236. He also wrote a prayer in preparation for communion, significantly entitled 'At the Table' (i. 358).

there must be one Church allied with the state. As a religious thinker he was broad-minded, and willing to accept a fair amount of latitude in the interpretation of traditional doctrines. Whatever the vagaries and inconsistencies of the various Christian sects, the goal of the individual was always the same—a virtuous life.

8

The Case against Religious Liberty

1. *The Utility of an Established Church*

'The vulgar are the children of the State, and must be taught like children.'[1] Johnson issued this judgement in 1766 during a discussion with Boswell on one of their most frequent topics of conversation—the question of religious liberty for nonconformists. Its harshness surprised Boswell and, along with Johnson's other condemnations of the campaign for full toleration, has perplexed his admirers ever since. How are we to make sense of such an abrupt dismissal of religious freedom by a man who, on other issues such as provision for the poor, the debtors' laws, and capital punishment for theft, seemed so broad-minded and progressive?

A detailed contextual study of this question suggests that we must agree with both Chester F. Chapin and Donald J. Greene that Johnson's opposition to increased toleration did not result from mere 'prejudice'.[2] His various comments and writings on the dissenters reveal that he possessed a sound understanding of the intense and complex debate which surrounded the question of religious freedom. Although his views on toleration were harsh even for his own day, they form a reasonably consistent line of argument. They are founded largely on his belief that liberty for nonconformists would inevitably disrupt social order. We have seen that a concern to preserve order was the underlying basis for a wide range of orthodox beliefs. The Anglican defence of the established Church, which Johnson followed quite closely, makes the rationale of this pragmatism much clearer, and shows why orthodox writers were determined to maintain their doctrines even at some potential cost to 'truth'.

[1] *Life*, ii. 14.

[2] The only full study of Johnson's attitudes on toleration and dissent is the chapter 'Church and State' in Chapin, *Religious Thought*, pp. 118–40. D. J. Greene, who set out to discredit the Victorian assumption that Johnson was a prejudiced Tory, touches on the issue of toleration in *The Politics of Samuel Johnson* (New Haven, 1960), 232–3 and 236.

As in other areas of moral and religious thought, the eighteenth century's debates on toleration were marked by an increasing scepticism with speculative claims of 'right' and 'truth' which lacked a foundation in the real nature and interests of mankind. Early in the century, High-Churchmen such as Henry Sacheverell justified the repression of nonconformists on the grounds that they were wicked apostates from the absolute truths preached by the Church of England. But the violent persecution of dissenters fomented by such dogmatism, most notably following Sacheverell's famous sermon, *The Perils of False Brethren* (1710), offended moderate Anglicans as well as nonconformists.[3] Under Walpole's administration, there were efforts to justify the privileges enjoyed by Anglicans—their legal monopoly over government posts and membership in the universities—as a political necessity rather than the state's endorsement of Anglican doctrines. These efforts were crowned by Warburton's *The Alliance of the Church and State* (1736). Although Chester F. Chapin has already noted some of the similarities between the *Alliance* and Johnson's views on toleration,[4] it is necessary to say something more about Warburton's enormously important and influential book.

There was little original about Warburton's thesis that an established Church was essential to maintain social order. The same thesis had been set forth by, for instance, Machiavelli in his *Discourse on Livy*, quoted during the 1720s in replies to Mandeville.[5] The value of Warburton's treatise lay in its synthesis of a number of familiar philosophical and theological positions into a single cohesive theory of why the Church was essential to a well-organized society. Like John Locke in *An Essay Concerning Human Understanding* (1690), Warburton argued that the values of society were controlled by more than one standard of conduct. The civil law was the primary means to maintain order, but its influence on the citizen was

[3] See Henry Sacheverell, *The Perils of False Brethren, a Sermon Preached before the Lord Mayor, 5 November, 1709* (London, 1710). Sacheverell accused the dissenters of 'Heterodoxy' and 'High-Treason', and was subsequently impeached for 'malicious, scandalous, and seditious libels'.

[4] See Chapin, *Religious Thought*, pp. 122–5.

[5] See Niccolò Machiavelli, *The Discourses*, trans. R. Crick (Harmondsworth, 1970), 142–3. Cited by Dennis, *Public Mischiefs*, pp. 78–81.

necessarily and dangerously limited. It properly concerned itself only with what Warburton called 'perfect' obligations, which imposed an absolute duty to perform or to avoid some action. The law could not control 'imperfect' obligations such as charity and gratitude which left the citizen with a fair amount of personal discretion.[6] Moreover, the civil law had authority only over public transgressions, but none over moral crimes committed in private. The laws 'can have no further Efficacy, than to restrain Men from an *open* Violation of Right, while what is done amiss in private, tho' equally tending to the public Prejudice, escapes their Animadversion'.[7] Hence, the civil law was incapable of exerting full control over society; social order could be preserved only through the additional sanctions imposed by 'the Power of Religion'.

In a 1773 debate with the dissenter Henry Mayo, recorded in Boswell's *Life*, Johnson also distinguished between 'perfect' and 'imperfect' duties.[8] And in Sermon 24 he neatly summarized Warburton's argument on the limitations of legal authority:

Human laws, however honestly instituted, or however vigorously enforced, must be limited in their effect, partly by our ignorance, partly by our weakness. Daily experience may convince us, that all the avenues by which injury and oppression may break in upon life, cannot be guarded by positive prohibitions. Every man sees, and may feel, evils, which no law can punish. . . . These deficiencies in civil life can be supplied only by religion (xiv. 256).

The practical importance of religion was that it guarded against socially disruptive acts which the civil law could not punish. Unlike civil law, its power lay in the conscience of the individual, and the transgression of its laws could not be hidden from the eyes of God.

Theoretically, the nature of the religion which supplemented civil law did not matter, so long as its ethical code conduced to social order. All that was necessary was an established Church, protected by the state, in order to ensure that the influence of religion was as visible and regular as the civil law. The choice of the religion to be established could be made largely on the

6 See William Warburton, *The Alliance of Church and State* (London, 1736), 11–132.

7 Ibid. 10.

8 See *Life*, ii. 250.

basis of what religion generally prevailed in the society. This was the heart of a more conciliatory defence of Anglican privileges because it seemed to imply that any nonconformist sect would be eligible to become the established Church if it were the religion of the majority. Indeed, Anglicans expressed no qualms that the prevailing religion in Scotland, Presbyterianism, enjoyed the same protection as Anglicanism in England. Anglicans even seemed willing to concede that the establishment of Islam or paganism benefited other societies, despite, as the dissenters objected, the sacrifice of religious truth which this admission entailed. It is worth noting the contradictions inherent in the position of orthodox writers who made this admission. Against the deists, orthodox writers claimed that only Christianity provided an adequate code of moral conduct; alternative systems, such as natural law, could result only in chaos. In their debates on religious rights, however, they were faced with the allegation that, as Benjamin Hoadly observed of their arguments, 'A *Mahometan,* A *Pagan,* A *Jew,* a *Papist*, are, Every one of them, under the same Obligation to promote the Profession of their own Religion.'[9] In response to this charge, Anglicans now claimed to be unperturbed. In a 1766 conversation, Johnson seemed indignant when Boswell asked whether 'a poor Turk must be Mahometan, just as a poor Englishman must be a Christian'. 'Why, yes, Sir,' he answered, 'and what then? This now is such stuff as I used to talk to my mother, when I first began to think myself a clever fellow; and she ought to have whipped me for it.'[10]

But Boswell's objection was more pertinent than Johnson was willing to admit, at least in this discussion.[11] In addition, the more subtle implication of Warburton's *Alliance* was that the Church of England was really far more suited for establishment than any other religion. Warburton argued that the influence of religion could only be propagated through an elaborate system of rituals and ordinances. This was because 'a

[9] Benjamin Hoadly, *An Answer to the Representation Drawn-up by the Committee of the Lower-house of Convocation* (London, 1718), 168.

[10] *Life*, ii. 14.

[11] See ibid. iv. 12, where Johnson raised a similar objection against a clergyman who, perhaps, too easily acquiesced that 'the State has a right to regulate the religion of the people'.

mere mental Intercourse with God which makes Religion only a divine Philosophy of the Mind is altogether unfit for such a Creature as Man in his present Station here'.[12] Visible rites were needed to keep religious ideas strong and constant in the mind. This was the basis of the latitudinarian doctrine that the Christian rites were useful primarily as they strengthened the motives of virtue and piety. Since Johnson agreed that this was the major benefit of religious rites, it is not surprising that his understanding of an effective established Church was similarly connected to the belief that only a formally ritualized Church could ensure the influence of religion. As he went on to argue in Sermon 24, 'That religion may be invigorated and diffused, it is necessary that the external order of religion be diligently maintained, that the solemnities of worship be duly observed' (xiv. 257). Consistent with the usual case against increased toleration, Johnson's sermons avoid any explicit claim that the Church of England deserved legal establishment for religious reasons, yet his contention that the established Church must have an 'external order' effectively eliminated Quakerism as a viable candidate for alliance with the state, and greatly weakened the case for most dissenting Churches, with their reduced emphasis on ritual solemnities. Roman Catholicism, the only other alternative, embodied the fault at the opposite extreme, because its rituals were seen to excuse moral laxity rather than propagate virtue.

These affinities between Johnson and Warburton do not necessarily indicate any special interest on Johnson's part with the *Alliance*. Rather they align Johnson with the defence of the established Church which was used by most of his Anglican contemporaries in the 1760s and 1770s. As Joseph Priestley observed in 1769, 'the *Alliance* [is] generally considered the best defence of the present system of church authority, and . . . most other writers [take] their arguments from it'.[13] The *Alliance* was favoured because it provided a means to defend the privileges of the Anglican Church without recourse to the dogmatic assertions of 'truth' associated with outright persecution. As the dissenters quickly realized, however, the liberal

---

[12] Warburton, *Alliance*, p. 37.
[13] Joseph Priestley, *Considerations on Church Authority, Occasioned by Dr. Balguy's Sermon on that Subject* (London, 1769), p. vii.

sounding rhetoric of the *Alliance* brought them no closer to their
objective of religious freedom. It even made persecution more,
rather than less, defensible, because it made the repression of
minorities necessary to maintain social order. While this
allegation was denied by most opponents to full religious
liberty, Johnson adopted quite a different approach. As we will
see, he bluntly acknowledged the potential for persecution, and
then refused to back down.

2. *Public Order and the Spirit of Enquiry*

The controversy over religious rights concerned not only the
specific issue of whether there should be full or increased
toleration for dissenters, but moreover the advantages or
dangers of a free society in which men were at liberty to think
and act as they pleased. According to John Locke in his first
Letter Concerning Toleration (1689), such a free society could only
benefit mankind, for 'Truth certainly would do well enough, if
she were once left to shift for herself.'[14] With the important
exception of atheists (whose disbelief in God made them
incapable of respecting the oaths upon which civil order relied),
individuals should be allowed to espouse and debate any
doctrine or belief they considered important: truth was the
child of vigorous dialectic, and once found it would gain the
immediate assent of all those sincerely concerned to know it.

A great deal occurred in the campaign for religious rights
between Locke's three *Letters Concerning Toleration* (1689–92)
and the debate which constituted the immediate context for
Johnson's remarks on toleration in the 1760s and 1770s. Most
important, there were the Occasional Conformity Bill of 1711
and Schism Act of 1714 (both repealed in 1718), the Bangorian
controversy of 1717, the campaign for the repeal of the Test
and Corporations Act during the 1730s and 1740s, and then,
following Archdeacon Francis Blackburne's *The Confessional*
(1766), the petition for ending subscription to the Thirty-nine
Articles by Anglican clergymen and university students. This
was the petition (rejected by parliament in 1772) which
prompted some of Johnson's most hostile remarks on toleration
in Boswell's *Life*. And this hostility cannot be easily disentangled

---

[14] John Locke, *A Letter Concerning Toleration* (London, 1689), 40.

from a more fundamental opposition to the ideal of free speech: for, after almost a century of campaigning, Locke's principle that truth could be attained only in a society that permitted free enquiry and debate remained the cornerstone of the case for religious liberty. As John Disney wrote in 1775:

> when the establishment shall confine itself to its original platform, and mutual toleration shall be allowed by the municipal law, we shall mutually feel the full force of the gospel, in all our debates on questions which concern religion. Controversy will be the infallible means of discovering truth, and each disputant will candidly argue with that freedom and temper, which will bring the debate to a speedy issue, and crown the laudable endeavour of both with success.[15]

The dissenters' ideal of unrestrained enquiry raised a dilemma similar to that faced by orthodox writers in their debates with the free-thinkers. Anglicans could hardly deny the virtues of free enquiry and debate when they had so often maintained that the truths of religion were reasonable, and could withstand the attacks of any opponent. Thus, proponents of the established Church generally acknowledged that a free enquiry into truth was exceedingly beneficial—if carried out with the proper candour and open-mindedness. As John Rotheram wrote in a 1767 rebuttal of Blackburne's *Confessional*, 'Could we indeed hope to see a free but fair enquiry, under the conduct of men, who with a real zeal for truth unite a temper and patience which alone can bring us to it . . . every friend to our constitution would wish that [truth] might be submitted to such a trial, because from every such trial, it must come out the purer.'[16] On the other hand, Rotheram and others insisted that this theoretical ideal of a candid and disinterested debate could seldom be achieved in practice: 'There be cause to fear that, instead of a concern for the real interests of religion, men would bring only a passionate zeal for the advancement of some particular system.'[17]

This fear that a free debate would almost inevitably disintegrate into violent competition and feuding was more fully expressed by Nathaniel Forster, whose *The Establishment of*

---

[15] John Disney, *Remarks on Dr. Balguy's Sermon* (London, 1775), 31.

[16] John Rotheram, *An Essay on Establishments in Religion* (Newcastle upon Tyne, 1767), 138.

[17] Ibid. 158.

the Church of England (1770) reflects a tendency in these later debates to explore the psychology of holding and espousing strong beliefs:

The passions of men are always very strongly engaged on the side of their opinions. And nothing less than the strong and steady hand of law and government will be able to keep them within due bounds, and prevent their running into the most violent and dangerous excesses. . . . Each man, entirely convinced that his opinion is the right, is naturally led to wish, that it *were* the opinion of all; very soon persuades himself that it *ought* to be so; nay thinks too, that it certainly *would* be so, did the rest of mankind, like himself, divest their mind of prejudice, and discard every authority but that of reason. These obstacles in the way of truth he therefore thinks it incumbent upon him, if possible, to remove. And finding that his work cannot be so easily accomplished by reason, and argument, he feels no scruple to make use of any other means.[18]

As the result of such reasoning, Forster and others claimed that the right of the state to supervise and, if necessary, suppress controversial opinions was, so far from being a hindrance to true liberty, in fact the only way that freedom of enquiry could be *preserved*. They continued to declare their support for free enquiry, with the stipulation that true freedom was safeguarded by the prerogative of the state to check opinions which threatened to disrupt this process. Especially by the 1760s, pamphlets opposing increased toleration were full of liberal sentiments: the established Church was all for religious liberty. The goal of its supporters was only, as Forster asserted, to 'establish by law a national religion, and at the same time to admit and tolerate in the largest sense every conscientious dissent from it'.[19]

As Chapin has noted, Johnson seemed to have little faith in the dictum that 'in the conflict of opinions truth will vanquish error'.[20] Yet, like Forster, he acknowledged that the desire to propagate one's beliefs was natural, and conceivably motivated by the most benevolent intentions: 'A man convinced of the truth of his own tenets, wishing the happiness of others, and

[18] Nathaniel Forster, *The Establishment of the Church of England, Defended upon the Principles of Religious Liberty: A Sermon* (London, 1770), 7.
[19] Ibid. 11.
[20] Chapin, *Religious Thought*, p. 132.

considering happiness as the certain consequence of truth, is necessarily prompted to extend his opinions, and to fill the world with proselytes' (Sermon 23, xiv. 240). But he then went on to argue that the innocent objective of persuading others to adopt one's opinions often gave way to the less justifiable desire for power and dominance: 'We find the teacher, jealous of the honour of his sect, and apparently more sollicitous to see his opinions *established* than *approved*' (xiv. 241). In Sermon 7 he described how open debate almost inevitably disintegrated into a violent struggle for ascendance:

how few there are capable of managing debates without unbecoming heat, or dishonest artifices, how soon is zeal kindled into fury, and how soon a concern for reputation mingles with a concern for truth, how readily the antagonists deviate into personal invectives, and, instead of confuting the arguments, defame the lives of those, whose doctrine they disapprove, and how often disputes terminate in uproar, riot, and persecution, every one is convinced, and too many have experienced (xiv. 78).

Johnson's examination of the psychology of religious controversy is similar to that of contemporary pamphleteers such as Forster, yet Johnson gave this examination an unusual sophistication. He suggested how readily an honest 'concern for truth' becomes mixed with more pernicious motives—pride, envy, a desire for power. This process of corruption, he realized, was largely unwitting, an involuntary and relentless tendency of the human mind rather than a deliberate opportunism. Especially earlier in the century, writers such as John Perceval, the first Earl of Egmont, had alleged against the dissenters that 'there's no-body but sees, 'tis Interest you have at Heart'.[21] But Johnson rejected 'the present mode of speculation to charge these men with total hypocrisy, as wretches who have no other design but that of temporal advancement, and consider religion only as one of the means by which power is gained, or wealth accumulated' (xiv. 241). His dismissal of such a crude conception of the dissenters' campaign did not, however, lead to a more broad-minded liberalism. Precisely the opposite: his conviction that the process which corrupted the

---

[21] John Perceval, 1st Earl of Egmont, *The Controversy in Relation to the Test and Corporation Acts* (London, 1733), 23. Perceval's position was very common: see also John Brown, *An Estimate of the Manners and Principles of the Times* (London, 1757), 122.

sincere desire for truth was natural and usually unnoticed, even by the individual who was espousing his beliefs, made the dangers of a free debate on religious issues all the more insidious and difficult to prevent. It increased, rather than diminished his resolve to keep the spirit of enquiry under the constant and stringent control of the state.

It is the peculiar mark of Johnson's observations on the dissenters that they are free from the liberal rhetoric which characterized the defence of the established Church at that time. While his blunt hostility to religious liberty may discomfort liberal sentiments in our own age, it freed his arguments from the confusions and hypocrisies which the dissenters easily exposed in the conventional defence of the established Church. The more conciliatory and broad-minded tone of Anglican tracts in the 1760s and 1770s did little to silence the allegation that the arguments used by English opponents against full religious liberty could justify any amount of persecution—even the Spanish Inquisition. As Benjamin Hoadly told parliament in 1718, 'by admitting the principle of self-defence and self-preservation in matters of religion, all the persecution of the Heathens against the Christians, and even the Popish Inquisition may be justified'.[22] This contention was repeated and amplified in Blackburne's 1766 *The Confessional*.[23] In 1769 Joseph Priestley challenged his opponents to admit that, for all their noble sounding praises of 'freedom' and 'toleration', they were 'only afraid of the term *persecution*, which, happily for the friends of liberty, lies under an *odium* at present'. If the established Church admitted that 'a certain degree of persecution was just, though certain degrees of it were unjust', their arguments would be 'much clearer . . . and their ideas more free from confusion'.[24]

Johnson, for one, cannot be charged with unclarity and duplicity on this point. In 1763 he defended the Spanish Inquisition in a well-known conversation with Boswell and some unidentified passengers in a stage-coach:

In the afternoon the gentlewoman talked violently against the Roman Catholics, and of the horrours of the Inquisition. To the utter

---

[22] See Benjamin Hoadly, *Works* (3 vols.; London, 1773), Appendix, i, p. lxvi.

[23] See Francis Blackburne, *The Confessional* (London, 1766), 72.

[24] Priestley, *Considerations on Church Authority*, p. 14.

astonishment of all the passengers but myself, who knew he could talk upon any side of the question, he defended the Inquisition, and maintained, that 'false doctrine should be checked at its first appearance; that the civil power should unite with the church in punishing those who dared attack the established religion, and that such only were punished by the Inquisition.'[25]

Boswell was probably right to assume that Johnson was exercising his 'spirit of contradiction', his tendency to 'talk for victory': Johnson's humanitarianism would undoubtedly recoil from the violence of the Inquisition. None the less, the background of eighteenth-century debates on toleration suggests that he meant something more. He admitted what the dissenters had dared proponents of the established Church to admit for almost a century: that their arguments could be used to justify any persecution, any oppression. In an enlightened English society this persecution did not actually take place, but Johnson made clear that he would not back down from his principles in alarm at their *theoretical* potential to justify an Inquisition. As we will see more clearly, it was this habit of openly acknowledging the potential for abuse—rather than retreating into encomiums on 'freedom'—that made him invulnerable to the charge that Anglicans were hypocrites and simply putting a more respectable face on oppressive and potentially violent laws.

A major area of debate centred on the nature of the sects and doctrines which the magistrate could justifiably suppress. Consistent with Locke's position in his *Letters Concerning Toleration*, most writers for the established Church agreed with John Rotheram that the magistrate 'must not carry [his powers] into the regions of pure and unmixed religion'.[26] The state had a right to interfere with private religious beliefs only so far as they promoted the transgression of civil laws, or otherwise threatened to disrupt social order. But surely, the dissenters complained, this left the magistrate with considerable powers of discretion concerning which doctrines posed this potential threat. When Nathaniel Forster attempted to placate such concerns by arguing that the state 'means only to preserve the establishment itself from violence, and from every probable

---

[25] *Life*, i. 465.
[26] Rotheram, *Essay on Establishments*, p. 43.

inlet of violence',[27] the dissenters immediately asked how such a 'probable inlet of violence' would be determined. In a 1771 answer to Forster, Benjamin Dawson argued that this vague criterion left the dissenter entirely at the mercy of the magistrate's fallible private judgement:

> But as for preserving the Establishment from every *probable inlet* of violence, this is a very uncertain ground for the *Legislature* to proceed upon in *framing* the Law, and for the *Magistrate*, in applying the sanctions thereof. For by what rule may probabilities of this kind be *calculated?*—By no certain rule. Or with whom, shall the determination of what is a probable inlet of violence, rest?—With no *fallible* being, without a *more* than *probable* inlet of violence to Religious freedom.[28]

In order to protect themselves from the abuse of the magistrate's considerable powers of discretion, the dissenters contended that his interference should be limited to actual and overt transgressions of civil law, instead of 'probable' misdemeanours. 'The authority of the civil magistrate is bounded by the civil demeanour of the subject,' John Disney wrote in 1774; 'the thoughts of the heart being known only to God, the magistrate has no concern with the consciences of his people—'Till these break out into overt acts . . . they affect not his province.'[29] Moreover, the magistrate possessed no physical power to influence the convictions of a nonconformist, even if he considered those convictions dangerous: this was a major basis for the idea that religious liberty was a 'natural right'. By their very nature, religious opinions were beyond the power of coercion through legal penalties.[30]

Johnson expressed his opinions on this issue in a debate at the house of Edward and Charles Dilly on 7 May 1773. It is worth noting that certain persons in attendance that evening had played a significant role in the controversy aroused by

---

[27] Forster, *Establishment of Church of England*, p. 43.

[28] Benjamin Dawson, *A Free and Candid Disquisition on Religious Establishments* (London, 1771), 29.

[29] John Disney, *A Letter to the Most Reverend Lord Archbishop of Canterbury* (London, 1774), 7.

[30] John Locke elaborated on the inability of judicial penalties to affect the understanding in *Letter Concerning Toleration*, pp. 7–8. For the use of this reasoning to demonstrate the 'natural right' of religious liberty, see, e.g., Peter Peckard, *The Nature and Extent of Civil and Religious Liberty* (Cambridge, 1783), 18.

Blackburne's *Confessional* and the subsequent petition to end subscription to the Thirty-nine Articles. As Richard Burgess Barlow noted in *Citizenship and Conscience*, Dr Henry Mayo had been censured by the General Body of London Dissenting Ministers for carrying his 'disruptive doctrines' before the Bishop of London.[31] Also present was Augustus Toplady, whose attack on the dissenters, *Free Thoughts on the Projected Application to Parliament in the Year 1771 for the Abolition of Ecclesiastical Subscriptions* (1771), had attracted considerable attention. In this company, Boswell glibly 'introduced the subject of toleration', giving no indication that this topic would inevitably spark the heated exchange which followed. It would appear, in fact, to have been a cue for Johnson, who responded energetically:

Every society has a right to preserve peace and order, and therefore has a good right to prohibit the propagation of opinions which have a dangerous tendency. To say the *magistrate* has this right, is using an inadequate word: It is the *society* for which the magistrate is agent. He may be morally or theologically wrong in restricting the propagation of opinions which he thinks dangerous, but he is politically right.[32]

By indicating his preference for the term 'society' rather than 'magistrate', Johnson raised the possibility that the question of 'rights' could be considered from more than one perspective. The dissenters insistently proclaimed the individual's 'right' of private judgement, even if his judgement was dismissed as wrong-headed by the majority of society; Johnson answered that 'society' had the same 'right' of private judgement in deciding which doctrines were dangerous, even if its agents were sometimes 'morally and theologically wrong'. By admitting that the magistrate was fallible, yet refusing to retreat from his position as the result of this acknowledgement, Johnson disarmed one of the dissenters' major arguments in the contemporary debate.

The reader will notice that Johnson, no less than the dissenters, was afraid of 'probable' inlets of violence, but it is characteristic of his political thought that he was far more conscious of probable violence by the people against the state,

[31] See Barlow, *Citizenship and Conscience*, p. 82.
[32] *Life*, ii. 249.

than by the state against the people. While he expressed little fear that the magistrate would seriously abuse his powers of discretion, he often suggested that every doctrine which contradicted the state religion was a potential source of political disruption. Later in the same debate with Mayo, Johnson made clear that he supported the magistrate's right to suppress not only overtly criminal acts, but every doctrine which might promote civil disobedience. In response to Mayo's defence of a father's right to teach his children any doctrine he held to be true, Johnson explained,

> take it thus:—that you teach them the community of goods; for which there are as many plausible arguments as for most erroneous doctrines. You teach them that all things at first were in common, and that no man had a right to any thing but as he laid his hands upon it; and that this still is, or ought to be, the rule amongst mankind. Here, Sir, you sap a great principle in society,—property. And don't you think the magistrate would have a right to prevent you?[33]

Mayo's answer, 'I think this magistrate has no right to interfere till there is some overt act,'[34] echoed the dissenters' standard rebuttal. It may seem curious that Mayo did not challenge Johnson's particular illustration of a dissenting doctrine: even proponents of full religious liberty, such as John Locke, had granted the magistrate the power to suppress doctrines such as the community of goods which so clearly encouraged illegal acts.[35] By the 1770s, however, the very principle of 'probable' illegality was at issue, since this principle, once conceded in an obvious case, could be extended to more vague and uncertain 'probabilities' of civil disruption.

Bennet Langton, however, finally challenged Johnson's illustration, asking 'if there was not a material difference as to toleration of opinions which led to action, and opinions merely speculative'.[36] Johnson answered that even the diffusion of nonconformist doctrines on speculative issues, such as the Trinity, would 'lessen the influence of religion', and for that reason, '*I* think it *not* politick to tolerate in such a case'.[37] This

---

[33] Ibid. 251. Article XXXVIII condemns the doctrine of the community of goods, which was usually attributed to the Anabaptists.
[34] *Life*, ii. 251.
[35] See Locke, *Letter Concerning Toleration*, pp. 46–7.
[36] *Life*, ii. 254.
[37] Ibid.

response returned to Warburton's dictum that the full influence of religion could be achieved only if all doctrines were consistent and uniform. As Thomas Balguy wrote in 1769, 'without *uniformity*, public institutions can never obtain their full effect'.[38] It is easy to see how greatly this position broadened the legitimate powers of the magistrate. There was, according to this, no such thing as 'pure and unmixed religion'; all dissenting doctrines were pernicious because they lessened the influence of religion upon which the order of society relied.

Thus, the hard line taken by Johnson really gave no assurance of toleration of any sort. Early in the debate with Mayo, he seemed to make a considerable concession. 'Every man has a right to liberty of conscience,' he admitted, 'and with that the magistrate cannot interfere.'[39] This will be recognized as the basis for the 'natural right' of religious liberty mentioned above: the magistrate has no physical power to influence the judgement, which is therefore necessarily free. But Johnson went on to turn this argument *against* the dissenters: 'People confound liberty of thinking with liberty of preaching. Every man has a physical right to think as he pleases; for it cannot be discovered how he thinks. . . . But, Sir, no member of a society has a right to *teach* any doctrine contrary to what that society holds to be true.'[40] In other words, the dissenter had the right to contrive what doctrines he pleased—so long as he kept his opinions to himself. It is perhaps a little difficult for the modern reader to take this argument seriously. Surely the case for liberty of conscience always took for granted the right of the individual to harmonize his speech with his convictions. Nevertheless, Johnson was not alone in his use of this rebuttal, for all its apparent irony. For example, in 1772 Bishop Thomas Newton of Bristol used the same reasoning in a speech to the House of Lords. 'Faith cannot be controlled by human laws,' Newton admitted, 'thought and conscience will still be free.'[41] But this admission was used to

38 Thomas Balguy, *A Sermon Preached at Lambeth Chapel, on the Consecration of the Right Reverend Jonathan Shipley* (London, 1769), 13.

39 *Life*, ii. 249.

40 Ibid.

41 Thomas Newton, 'A Speech Designed for the House of Lords, on the Second Reading of the Dissenters Bill, May 19, 1772,' in *Works* (3 vols.; London, 1782), Appendix, i. 143.

support the same argument advanced a year later by Johnson: 'liberty of thinking and judging is one thing, and liberty of public preaching is another. . . . Thought is free, but public preaching should be laid under some restraint.'[42]

The restriction on public preaching supported by Johnson and Newton was not favoured by the majority of Anglicans, and represents the most conservative extreme of the established Church's position. It recalls the restraints imposed by the short-lived Schism Act (1714–18), designed by the Tory administration to stamp out nonconformist preaching.[43] Attitudes had been greatly liberalized since those bitter years of Tory rule and High-Church fervour. On the other hand, we have seen that the new liberalism of the 1760s and 1770s was extremely flimsy and quite lacking in sympathy for real reforms on religious rights. Johnson's hard position was, at the very least, candid and logically coherent, leaving even such an experienced campaigner as Henry Mayo with no recourse save groundless assertions of 'right'. We might also note, in the citations we have examined, that Johnson was generally sceptical of the notion of 'truth'. He rarely alluded to 'truth' as an absolute value recognized by some and missed by others; Johnson almost always referred to what a society 'holds to be true'. In the next section we will explore further into this question of 'truth', and whether this absolute value could ever be found by the serious enquirer.

3. *'Hoadly's Paradox' and Sincerity of Private Judgement*

Both Anglicans and dissenters were deeply suspicious of the conviction that the peace and order of society could be justly sacrificed in the name of 'truth'. This was a lesson of the Civil Wars. For Anglican writers, an established Church would prevent the recurrence of the Civil Wars by checking fanatical dogmatism at its first appearance. For the dissenters, on the other hand, the alliance of Church and state gave Anglicans the power to impose their own doctrines by force.

---

[42] Ibid. 138–9.

[43] The Schism Act required schoolmasters, among whom would be included the nonconformist clergy (known as 'teachers'), to carry a certificate proving that they had taken the Anglican sacrament within the past year.

The Civil Wars, they contended, had been caused not by too much, but by too little toleration.[44] Like the advocates of the established Church, the dissenters idealized a peaceable, well-ordered society, but such a society, they argued, could be attained only through the acknowledgement that a diversity of sects and doctrines was inevitable and that all had an equal right to exist. Most dissenters, and eventually also the advocates of the established Church, saw that it was in the best interest of their cause and of society in general to cast doubt on the belief that any individual had personal access to ultimate religious truths, approved by God to the exclusion of all other sects and doctrines.

For this reason, Benjamin Hoadly's 1717 critique of the belief in ultimate and universal truths was celebrated by the dissenters as 'unanswerable'.[45] And, while his challenge initially outraged High-Churchmen, Sir John Hawkins later ranked the Bishop of Bangor among the 'illustrious divines' of the age, an evaluation which reflects Hoadly's impact on eighteenth-century thought as a whole.[46] Hoadly permanently changed the language of the subsequent debate; thereafter, controversists on both sides spoke less of 'truth', and more of 'persuasion' and 'sincerity'.

The Bangorian controversy was sparked by Hoadly's sermon *The Nature of Christ's Kingdom*, preached before George I on 31 March 1717. Central to this famous attack on Church authority was the argument that while the Church governors and the individual Christian might disagree on the interpretation

---

[44] Locke argued that repressive laws inspired civil disobedience far more than freedom did: see *Letter Concerning Toleration*, pp. 19–21. Although many dissenters diplomatically avoided mentioning the Civil Wars, others blamed them on the 'tyranny' of Archbishop Laud. See, e.g., anon., *The Devout Laugh, or Half a Hour's Amusement to a Citizen of London, from Dr. Pickering's Sermon* (London, 1750); Thomas Gordon and John Trenchard, *The Character of an Independent Whig* (1728), in Thomas Gordon and John Trenchard, *A Collection of Tracts* (London, 1751), 313. But in 'The Vanity of Human Wishes' (ll. 165–74), Johnson blamed Laud's execution by the Puritans on his 'fatal Learning': 'hear his death, ye blockheads, hear and sleep.' This is not just a lesson on the human condition; it is also political rhetoric.

[45] See, e.g., Philip Furneaux, *Letters to the Honourable Mr. Justice Blackstone* (London, 1770), 161.

[46] See Hawkins, *Life*, p. 80. Hoadly has not enjoyed such respect among more recent historians, who have treated him with some derision. See, e.g., Stephen, *English Thought*, ii. 129; Norman Sykes, *Church and State in the XVIIIth Century* (Cambridge, 1934), 294.

of Scripture, the Reformation had discredited the belief that any worldly body had the right to claim infallible judgement on the correct interpretation. Hoadly's case was grounded in a philosophical paradox concerning the nature of belief and the limits of human certainty. No individual could 'know' the 'truth'; he could only be 'sincerely convinced' he knew the truth. Since the individual possessed no objective standard by which to evaluate the truth of his convictions, his endeavour to comply with what he sincerely believed were Christ's commandments could be the only condition of salvation, even if his judgement was in some ultimate sense erroneous.[47] This argument took advantage of the vagueness of the Thirty-nine Articles on the nature of Church authority. Articles XIX, XX, and XXI uphold the authority of the Church to appoint doctrines and ceremonies, yet also concede that the fallible nature of Church authority renders its appointments unnecessary for salvation.

Hoadly's position was rehearsed by dissenters right into the 1770s. As Philip Furneaux argued in his 1770 critique of Blackstone's *Commentaries on the Laws of England* (1765–9):

As every man is accountable only for the use of his own understanding, not for that of other men's; consequently, his safety consists, not in giving up his own to the direction and controul of others, but in using it himself to the best advantage. And should he, in the careful and conscientious use of it, err; that error will never be imputed to him as a crime.[48]

Johnson could rightly observe in Sermon 7 that 'there is no topick more the favourite of the present age, than the innocence of errour accompanied with sincerity' (xiv. 79). Nor did he himself dismiss this opinion as entirely absurd. 'The Judge of all the earth', he went on, '. . . will require in proportion to what he has given, and punish men for the misapplication, or neglect of talents, not for the want of them' (xiv. 79). Thus,

---

[47] See Hoadly, *The Nature of Christ's Kingdom, A Sermon Preach'd before the King 31 March, 1717* (London, 1717), *passim.*; *Answer to the Lower-house of Convocation*, p. 95. Hoadly was, of course, not the first to argue that sincerity rendered doctrinal errors innocent in the eyes of God. In *A Discourse of Free-thinking*, p. 34, Anthony Collins attributed this doctrine to Chillingworth.

[48] Furneaux, *Letters to Blackstone*, p. 35. In 'Of Offenses against God and Religion', *Commentaries on the Laws of England* (4 vols.; Oxford, 1765–9), IV. iv, Blackstone had supported strong laws to protect the established Church.

God would certainly not condemn men who erred in their convictions as the result of limited intellectual capacities. But Johnson refused to make this admission a reason for diminishing the importance of Church authority or leaving the individual at complete liberty to fashion his own beliefs. While he did not claim that any person or institution was in exclusive possession of 'truth', he did insist on the great difficulty of achieving that 'sincerity' which justified error:

That errour . . . may be innocent will not be denied, because it undoubtedly may be sincere, but this concession will give very little countenance to the security and supineness, the coldness and indifference of the present generation, if we consider deliberately, how much is required to constitute that sincerity, which shall avert the wrath of God, and reconcile him to errour (xiv. 79–80).

In Sermon 7 Johnson attempts to show that true 'sincerity' is 'not barely a full persuasion of the truth of our assertions', nor 'a heat of the heart kept up by eager contentions or warm professions, nor a tranquillity produced by confidence, and continued by indolence' (xiv. 80). This effort to expose the instability and carelessness of the sincerity apparently endorsed by Hoadly recalls some of the best defences of Church authority in the Bangorian controversy.

Perhaps Hoadly's most effective opponent was William Law, who made his début as a controversist in *Three Letters to the Bishop of Bangor* (1717–18).[49] Law, like Johnson later in the century, argued that Hoadly's definition of 'sincerity' made the most careless and whimsical belief sufficient for salvation:

according to a maxim of your own, you are obliged to acknowledge that Man to be *sincere*, who *thinks* himself to be *sincere*. . . . So that it is not *Sincerity*, as it contains all that is *rational* and *excellent* which alone justifies, but as it may be an *idle, vain, whimsical* Persuasion, in which People think themselves in the right. This Persuasion, though founded in the Follies, Passions, and Prejudices of human Nature, consecrates every Way of Worship, and makes the Man thus persuaded as

[49] Law's *Three Letters* have been rated as a clear victory over Hoadly by Norman Sykes, *Church and State*, p. 297. But the victory was really less than decisive: Law must practically repeat Hoadly's arguments to vindicate his own position as a nonjuror. Compare Law, *Three Letters to the Bishop of Bangor* (1717–18), in *Works*, i. 181, and Benjamin Hoadly, *An Answer to the Reverend Dr. Snape's Letter* (London, 1717), 24.

acceptable to God, as he who through a right use of his Reason, serves God in that Method which he has instituted.[50]

Hence, while Hoadly questioned the possibility of determining whether one's beliefs were 'true', Law and Johnson pointed to the difficulty of determining whether one's beliefs were really 'sincere'. For Law, however, there was apparently a clear distinction between 'an *Idle, vain, whimsical* Persuasion', and 'a right use of . . . Reason'. As a nonjuror, after all, Law was engaged in his own conscientious resistance to authority. Johnson, on the other hand, suggested that pride, envy, and self-interest were so subtly insinuated into the thoughts, and the process of cleansing the mind of such corrupting drives was so arduous, that wise men were forced to embark on a monastic programme of self-purification in order to achieve real 'sincerity'. Only in retirement could 'the chain of reasoning be preserved unbroken, and the mind perform its operations, without any hindrance from foreign objects' (Sermon 7, xiv. 81).

Unlike even Law, Johnson cast doubt on the assumption that men in the hurry and business of daily life could *ever* justly claim to be sincere. Even a sincere belief in Christianity, as we have previously discussed, was impossible without the special support of grace.[51] This scepticism resulted not only from his belief that the mind inclined naturally towards delusion, but also from his conviction that the complexity of the issues which divided Christian Churches was far beyond the understanding of ordinary people. In April 1778, for example, the Quaker Mrs Knowles informed Johnson that a young woman of their acquaintance had left the Church of England to join the Society of Friends. Johnson remarked angrily that 'she knew no more of the Church which she left, and that which she embraced, than she did of the difference between the Copernican and Ptolemaic systems'.[52] Mrs Knowles answered that 'she had the New Testament before her',[53] reflecting the traditional non-conformist reliance on the individual's personal encounter with Scripture. This was a principle which orthodox Anglicans

[50] Law, *Works*, i. 194.
[51] See ch. 1, sec. 2, above.
[52] *Life*, iii. 298.
[53] Ibid.

could deny only at some risk of self-contradiction. Article VI maintains that the New Testament is an adequate rule of faith, and apologists contended against the deists that the revelation was useful primarily as a means to enlighten the common man, who would otherwise be abandoned to a morass of complex philosophical debates. Against the dissenters, conservative Anglicans now portrayed the Scriptures themselves as beyond the capacities of the common man.

As John Bellward declared in 1774, the Scriptures contained many truths 'hard to be understood, and such as the *unlearned and unstable may wrest to their own destruction*'.[54] This was the position adopted by Johnson against Mrs Knowles:

JOHNSON. 'Madam, she could not understand the New Testament, the most difficult book in the world, for which the study of a life is required.' MRS. KNOWLES. 'It is clear as to essentials.' JOHNSON. 'But not as to controversial points . . . we ought not, without very strong conviction indeed, to desert the religion in which we have been educated. That is the religion given you, the religion in which it may be said Providence has placed you. If you live conscientiously in that religion, you may be safe. But errour is dangerous indeed, if you err when you choose a religion for yourself.'[55]

Both Johnson and Bellward remarked on the 'destruction' and 'danger' that could result from a mistaken choice of religion. This would seem to be an allusion to the sin of schism. Especially in the Restoration and early eighteenth century, High-Churchmen condemned the dissenters as schismatics, despite their own vulnerability to this charge from the Roman Catholics. John Scott's analysis of schism in his popular treatise, *The Christian Life* (1681), stipulated like Johnson that the only safety lay in submitting one's judgement to the authority of the Church on difficult or controversial points of doctrine:

He . . . that *separates* from the Communion of the Church for Causes that he cannot *judg of*, must necessarily separate without Cause or Reason; he cannot have neither *true*, nor *false* Pretence for his *Separation*; because the Arguments *pro* and *con* are beyond the Sphere of his *Cognizance*; and consequently if he there upon *withdraw* from the

54 John Bellward, *A Sermon Preached at the Archdeacon's Visitation, Monday, April 18, 1774* (Norwich, 1774), 11.
55 *Life*, iii. 298–9.

Churches Communion, 'tis not because he *cannot* comply with her *sinful* Impositions, but because he *will not* submit to her just Authority. Whereas by modestly submitting our Judgment to the *Churches*, in Cases where we can not judg for *our selves*, we take an effective Course to secure our Innocence. For though that which the Church injoins should be *materially* sinful, yet to *us* who neither *do*, nor *can* understand it to be so, it will be *imputed* only as an *innocent* Error.[56]

This explanation brings the attitudes of conservative Anglicans into sharp contrast with those of Hoadly and his admirers. Hoadly contended that the individual's faithful adherence to the judgements of his own mind would ensure his salvation, regardless of the possibility that his beliefs were in an ultimate sense erroneous. Scott and Johnson, on the other hand, declared that the individual's safety lay in obeying the authority of the Church, despite the possibility that the authorized doctrines were 'materially sinful'. This was their version of 'innocent error'.

When Mrs Knowles accused Johnson of dictating the need for 'implicit faith', he acknowledged that 'the greatest part of our knowledge is implicit faith'.[57] This statement was not entirely disingenuous, for he greatly doubted the ability of most men to know whether their beliefs were true, or even sincere. Moreover, Johnson tended to trust the knowledge passed down through tradition more than the insights of the individual. This was one reason why he was not greatly shaken by the scepticism of infidels such as Hume. Nevertheless, Johnson did not ordinarily indicate that our submission to traditional wisdom must take the form of 'implicit faith'. Although he considered an irreverence for tradition to be the ruling disease of his age, he did distinguish between a reasonable and mindless veneration for the great writers of the past. A broad consideration of his writings suggests that this balanced view characterized his advice on how the Christian could most responsibly shape his religious convictions. And in this respect, he exemplified a general liberalization of attitudes within the Anglican Church.

[56] John Scott, *The Christian Life* (London, 1681), 443–4.

[57] *Life*, iii. 299. High-Churchmen and Tories were frequently accused of promoting 'implicit faith'. See, e.g., Gordon and Trenchard, *The Independent Whig*, p. 311. Gordon and Trenchard also attacked the 'canting Absurdity' that one must remain in the religion of one's birth, an opinion expressed by Johnson in his discussion with Mrs Knowles.

The Anglican Church carried on a long tradition of Scriptural commentary stretching back to the writings of the Church Fathers. Like the dissenters, Anglicans placed decreasingly less confidence in the ability of the individual to discover ultimate and universal truths, yet the Fathers did provide some access to the one authority that could be relied on with absolute conviction—the direct revelation of God. Having lived close to the time of the Christian revelation, the earliest Fathers could be expected to have a more accurate knowledge of its truths, unadulterated by the corruptions caused by the repeated transcriptions and translations of the New Testament. But Anglican views on the use of the Fathers changed during the course of the century. A controversy early in the century, once again involving the prolific Samuel Clarke, gives some indication of the conflicting views on this subject.

In the preface to *The Scripture-doctrine of the Trinity* (1712) Clarke strongly questioned the authority of the Fathers, arguing that the Church must rely primarily on reason and Scripture. As the remainder of his treatise made evident, Clarke was especially concerned to discredit the authority of the Athanasian Creed.[58] This was the fourth-century document opposed by the followers of Arius, whose teachings on the Trinity seem to have been favoured by Clarke. In response to Clarke's position, Edward Wells wrote a vindication of the Fathers, in which he argued that they 'can't be Reasonably suppos'd but to have *infallibly* Known the True sense of Scripture'.[59] On issues such as the Trinity, we should first 'let the *Testimony* of the Primitive Church *Over-rule our Understanding*'.[60] In his subsequent reply to Wells, Clarke denied that the Fathers were infallible or that they should be followed with 'implicit faith'. He did, however, acknowledge that their teachings should be taken into account and allowed to exercise a limited influence on private judgement:

There is indeed a Sense of the word, *Authority*, in which it may rightly be said the *Primitive Writers* are of *Great Authority*. The opinion or Judgment of every *Learned* Man, carries with it *an Authority*. . . . Now in

---

[58] See Samuel Clarke, *The Scripture-doctrine of the Trinity* (London, 1712), 446–54.
[59] Edward Wells, *Remarks on Dr. Clarke's Introduction to his Scripture Doctrin [sic] of the Trinity* (London, 1713), 21.
[60] Ibid. 23–4.

the like manner as Great *Learning*, so Great *Antiquity* carries with it in This Sense a sort of Authority: Not a Power of obliging any Man to give his Assent implicitly; but only a Power of *so far* influencing a Man's Opinion, as the Author's skill in his own and the Scripture-language, and his better knowledge of the Facts which happened nearer his own Time, compared with what had at the same time been said by Other Writers . . . ought to have.[61]

The 'Other Writers' mentioned by Clarke would apparently include even a heretic like Arius. In keeping with his latitudinarian principles, Clarke wished to loosen the shackles of traditional orthodoxy. Nevertheless, Clarke's understanding of the Fathers' authority gained wide support later in the century, even among conservative writers who might have been expected to side with the more orthodox Wells. The lives and teachings of the Fathers were the subject of repeated attacks throughout the century, most notably by Conyers Middleton in 1749. Not only did these attacks provide ammunition for Blackburne's 1766 attack on Anglican authority,[62] but they undoubtedly took their toll on the prestige of the Fathers among the Anglicans themselves. Wells's dictum of entire reliance on the Fathers lost favour, and Clarke's view that their influence should be maintained, but carefully limited, became the more common line of argument. For example, in a 1772 reply to Blackburne, George Harvest declared that 'the Authority which Dr. Clarke here allows to the ancient Writers' was 'that very Authority which is meant by all reasonable Persons, when they speak of the Authority of Antiquity'.[63]

As usual, Clarke's alleged heresy on the Trinity did not diminish his durable popularity and influence. In Sermon 7 Johnson advised that Christians should follow the 'old paths' as a more secure alternative to private judgement, but his treatment of the Fathers was most akin to the position outlined by Clarke, rather than the 'implicit faith' urged by Wells:

Part of the disesteem into which [the Fathers'] writings are now fallen may indeed be ascribed to that exorbitant degree of veneration in

---

[61] Samuel Clarke, *A Letter to Dr. Wells, in Answer to his Remarks* (London, 1714), 23–4.

[62] See Blackburne, *Confessional*, p. 328. Conyers Middleton attacked the authority of the Fathers in *A Free Inquiry into Miraculous Powers in the Christian Church* (1749). The Fathers were defended by Warburton in his introduction to *Julian* (1751).

[63] George Harvest, *The Reasonableness and Necessity of Subscription to Explanatory Articles of Faith Demonstrated: in Two Letters* (London, 1772), 21.

which they were once held by blindness and superstition. But there is a mean betwixt idolatry and insult, between weak credulity and total disbelief. The ancients are not infallible, nor are their decisions to be received without examination, but they are at least the determinations of men equally desirous with ourselves of discovering truth, and who had, in some cases, better opportunities than we have now. (xiv. 82).

This cautious and measured defence of the Fathers is very similar to the balanced view of tradition and private judgement expressed in the preface to his edition of Shakespeare and elsewhere in his moral essays. It reflects Johnson's desire to promote an intelligent respect for both the Church and its traditions, rather than a passive submission to authority. Once again, we see that his opposition to religious liberty was not founded on a rigid dogmatism, or an uncritical faith in 'truth', or an intolerance of all disagreement and change. More than anything it embodied a desire for caution, and a justifiable sense that society's links with the past were being weakened.

4. *The Conservative Idea of Political Change*

The objective of the dissenters was in important respects to diminish the influence of the past on contemporary thought. Not only did they have to persuade Anglicans that new forms of doctrine could be accommodated within orthodox Christianity, but they had to prove that they were not the bellicose Puritans of old. With regard to this second objective, they enjoyed moderate success. Unlike many Anglicans of the Restoration and early eighteenth century, later Anglicans rarely linked contemporary nonconformists with those who had fomented the Civil Wars. The sermons preached every 30 January to commemorate the death of Charles I increasingly used this occasion not to condemn dissent, but to plead for peace and restraint. Johnson's Sermon 23, which was among the many sermons preached on this day, makes only a brief allusion to the Civil Wars, and focuses more generally on the dangers of religious fanaticism to promote 'strife' and 'confusion'. It seems to have been modelled on a sermon by John Tillotson, 'The Danger of Zeal without Knowledge'.[64] Since Tillotson

---

[64] Sermon 23 and Tillotson's 'The Danger of Zeal without Knowledge' enumerate the same 'marks', or what Johnson calls 'tokens', which indicate a fanatical zeal for

had enjoyed the favour of that great advocate of toleration, William III, this is a good indication of how much even Johnson had moderated the rhetoric surrounding the question of religious dissent.

Moreover, Johnson did indicate that there were times when the violent upheaval of social order was necessary and even inevitable. As he told Sir Adam Fergusson in 1772, '. . . in no government power can be abused long. Mankind will not bear it. If a sovereign oppresses his people to a great degree, they will rise and cut off his head. There is a remedy in human nature against tyranny, that will keep us safe under every form of government.'[65] This may strike us as a justification of revolution that could be used to defend the Civil Wars. It even seems to anticipate the slogans of the French Revolution. In eighteenth-century England, however, Johnson's reasoning was used by the most conservative writers to justify not the reformation of society, but the maintenance of the present system. In his 1767 defence of the established Church, for example, John Rotheram also acknowledged that the overthrow of governments was sometimes necessary: 'There are times when corruption prevails so far, that the distemper is visible to every eye; when every good principle is in danger of being lost, and when the cause of religion calls loudly upon every one to whom its interests are dear to rise up for its preservation.'[66] As Rotheram explained, however, the time for such upheaval had certainly not arrived. Real tyranny could not be mistaken, and when the corruption of religious truth was 'visible to every eye' revolution would take place with the full consensus of society. It was fomented not by factions, but by an entire mass of people urged forward by concerns intrinsic to human nature. Such an argument blocked the route to the more modest reformation desired by the nonconformists because it suggested that change would ultimately take care of itself. Change was an historical inevitability that occurred only occasionally. Most

---

reform prompted by pride and envy rather than a genuine love of truth. These marks included the use of violence disproportionate to the importance of the end, the use of illegal methods, and a hostility to all types of authority. Even Johnson's phrasing is like Tillotson's, strong evidence that the Archbishop's sermon was indeed his source. Compare Sermon 23, xiv. 242–3, and Tillotson, *Works*, ii. 178.

[65] *Life*, ii. 170.
[66] Rotheram, *Essay on Establishments*, p. 141.

Anglicans agreed that this had been the case at the Reformation and at the Glorious Revolution of 1688.

Until these historical moments occurred, change in religious and political institutions should be resisted: it was destabilizing and ordinarily moved society further away from rather than closer to truth. 'Innovations of a public nature are ever dangerous', wrote John Bellward in 1774, 'and generally productive of greater evils, than those which they are meant to remedy. They ought therefore never to be attempted, but upon great and urgent occasions.'[67] It was this principle which also seemed to govern Johnson's understanding of change in governments and religious establishments. As Johnson admitted in Sermon 7, the need for social reformation was sometimes necessary, but always threatened to be more destructive than beneficial. The human mind was always vulnerable to the corrupting drives of pride and envy which promoted unnecessary violence and overwhelmed the zeal for truth:

changes of conduct or opinion may be considered as the revolutions of human nature, often necessary, but always dangerous. Necessary, when some favourite vice has generally infected the world, or some errour, long established, begins to tyrannize, to demand implicit faith, and refuse examination. But dangerous, lest the mind, incensed by oppression, heated by contest, and elated by victory, should be too far transported to attend to truth, and out of zeal to secure her conquest, set up one errour to depress another (xiv. 75-6).

Until such revolutions of conduct or opinion became necessary, men must be patient with the inevitable imperfection of all human institutions. 'All institutions are defective by their nature,' he wrote in Sermon 24, 'all rulers have their imperfections, like other men' (xiv. 259). This conviction in the faults of all the political and religious systems of mankind formed the basis of the strong conservatism of writers who opposed the broadening of civil rights for dissenters. If political and religious change occurred through the continual improvisation of existing systems—the understanding of change which seemed to underlie the campaign for religious freedom—then society would be in a perpetual state of instability and

[67] Bellward, *Sermon at Archdeacon's Visitation*, pp. 19-20.

uncertainty. As Thomas Balguy complained in a 1769 pamphlet against the dissenters, 'No human institution is free from faults: none therefore is free from the attacks of a willing adversary.'[68] Similarly, Johnson's hostility to insurgency in political pamphlets such as *The False Alarm* (1770) or *Taxation no Tyranny* (1775) was not grounded on any belief that the existing systems were ideal or without the potential for abuse. His consistent argument was that the innovations advocated by his opponents were unnecessary; the historical moment for change had clearly not arrived. Everywhere he tries to put modern controversies into their true perspective; he accuses his opponents of vastly overrating their grievances, of raising a spectre of political abuse absurdly disproportionate to the modest reality of present events, of generally threatening the peace of society by a 'false alarm'.

It would seem appropriate to conclude this study on a note which stresses Johnson's fundamental conservatism. This is not to question that a slightly different selection of citations, organized in a different manner, might bring other aspects of his thought and character to the foreground in our final impression. While we reflect on Johnson's conservatism, for example, we must try to keep in mind his extraordinary willingness to promote humanitarian reform in the laws governing provision for the poor, the debtors, and capital punishment. Nevertheless, it was Johnson's desire for stability and order which forms the most consistent link between the various areas of his thought. He was a thinker of enormous complexity, yet everywhere he takes those positions which, in his view, best served the welfare of man and society. At different times we are best served by positions which are theoretically inconsistent and even contradictory, a phenomenon which helps to account for the ambiguities in Johnson's thought as we move from one work or statement to the next. What we almost never lack in Johnson, however, is a thinker who has in mind the wider repercussions of his views on his immediate audience and on society at large.

Johnson's conservatism does not ordinarily reflect dogmatism or bigotry. His thought is filled with doubt concerning the

---

[68] Balguy, *Sermon at Lambeth Chapel*, p. 21.

ability of men to achieve a knowledge of truth or even a real 'sincerity' in their convictions. It is important to consider, however, that doubt of this sort does not necessarily cause anxiety and desperation. Having resolved that it is impossible to achieve absolute confidence, the next step may be to accept a limited confidence as the best that any man can hope for. It was this stabilizing resignation, rather than a desperate clinging to the need for truth, which most fully characterized Johnson's religious and moral beliefs. This disposition was shared by many orthodox writers of his century. There is perhaps no label that would adequately summarize the complexities of Johnson's thought or, even more obviously, the wider context of eighteenth-century England. Yet the most compelling lessons of its moralists and divines concern the need for moderation, pragmatism, and care.

BIBLIOGRAPHY

Anon., *Animadversions on a Late Book, Entituled the Reasonableness of Christianity* (Oxford, 1697).

Anon., *The Case of Insolvent Debtors Considered* (London, 1724).

Anon., *The Devout Laugh, or Half a Hour's Amusement to a Citizen of London, from Dr. Pickering's Sermon* (London, 1750).

Anon., *An Essay on the Freedom of Will in God and in Creatures* (London, 1732).

Anon., *Hanging not Punishment Enough for Murtherers, High-way Men, and House-breakers* (London, 1701).

Anon., *The Religious, Rational and Moral Conduct of Matthew Tindal, LLD., Late Fellow of All Souls College in Oxford: In a Letter to a Friend* (London, 1735).

Anon. (ed.), *Twenty-five Sermons Preached at the Anniversary Meetings of the Children Educated in Charity-schools in and about the Cities of London and Westminster* (London, 1729).

ABBEY, CHARLES, and OVERTON, J. H., *The English Church in the Eighteenth Century* (2 vols.; London, 1878).

ABBOT, J. L., *John Hawkesworth: Eighteenth-century Man of Letters* (Madison, Wis., 1982).

ADAMS, WILLIAM, *An Answer to Mr. Hume's Essay on Miracles* (1752) (3rd edn; London, 1767).

ADDISON, JOSEPH, *The Spectator*, ed. D. F. Bond (6 vols.; London, 1965).

ALCOCK, THOMAS, *Observations on the Defects of the Poor Laws* (London, 1752).

—— *A Sermon on the Late Earthquakes* (Oxford, 1756).

ALKON, P. K., *Samuel Johnson and Moral Discipline* (Evanston, Ill., 1967).

—— 'William Law, Robert South and Samuel Johnson', *SEL* 6 (1966), 499–528.

ALTHAUS, P., *The Theology of Martin Luther*, trans. R. C. Schultz (Philadelphia, 1966).

ATTERBURY, FRANCIS, *Sermons and Discourses on Several Subjects and Occasions* (2 vols.; London, 1726).

AUGUSTINE, St, *The Confessions*, trans. E. Pusey (London and New York, 1909).

AYSCOUGH, FRANCIS, *A Sermon Preach'd before the Honourable the House of Commons, January the 30th, 1735/6* (London, 1736).

BACON, FRANCIS, *Works*, ed. J. Spedding, R. Ellis, and D. Heath (14 vols.; Boston, 1861).

BAILEY, NATHANIEL, *Dictionarium Britannicum* (London, 1721).

BALDERSTON, K. C., 'Dr. Johnson and William Law', *PMLA* 75 (1960), 382–94.

BALGUY, JOHN, *The Foundation of Moral Goodness, or a Further Inquiry into the Original of Our Idea of Virtue* (London, 1728).

—— *Divine Rectitude, or a Brief Inquiry Concerning the Moral Perfections of the Deity* (London, 1730).

BALGUY, THOMAS, *A Sermon Preached at Lambeth Chapel, on the Consecration of the Right Reverend Jonathan Shipley* (London, 1769).

BANGS, CARL, *Arminius: A Study in the Dutch Reformation* (Nashville and New York, 1971).

BARLOW, R. B., *Citizenship and Conscience* (Philadelphia, 1962).

BARROW, ISAAC, *Works* (4 vols.; London, 1686).

BATE, W. J., *The Achievement of Samuel Johnson* (New York, 1955).

BAYLE, PIERRE, *Miscellaneous Reflexions, Occasion'd by the Comet which appear'd in December 1680* (1683) (trans., 2 vols., London, 1708).

BECCARIA, CESARE, *On Crimes and Punishments* (1764), trans. Henry Poalucci (Indianapolis and New York, 1963).

BELLWARD, JOHN, *A Sermon Preached at the Archdeacon's Visitation, April 18, 1774* (Norwich, 1774).

BENSON, GEORGE, *The Reasonablenesse of the Christian Religion* (1741) (2nd edn.; London, 1746).

BENTHAM, JEREMY, *An Introduction to the Principles of Morals and Legislation* (London, 1789).

BENTLEY, RICHARD, *Remarks upon a Late Discourse of Free-thinking, in a Letter to F.H.D.D. by Phileleutherus Lipsiensis* (London, 1713).

BERKELEY, GEORGE, *Alciphron, or the Minute Philosopher* (2 vols.; London, 1732).

BICKNELL, E. J., *A Theological Introduction to the Thirty-nine Articles* (London, New York, and Toronto, 1919).

BIRD, EDWARD, *Fate and Destiny Inconsistent with Christianity* (London, 1726).

BLACKBURNE, FRANCIS, *The Confessional* (London, 1766).

BLACKBURNE, T. C., 'Friday's Religion: Its Nature and Importance in *Robinson Crusoe*', *Eighteenth-century Studies*, 18 (1985), 360–82.

BLACKSTONE, WILLIAM, *Commentaries on the Laws of England* (4 vols.; Oxford, 1765–9).

BLEWITT, GEORGE, *An Enquiry whether a General Practice of Virtue tends to the Wealth or Poverty, Benefit or Disadvantage of a People* (London, 1725).

BLOUNT, CHARLES, *The Oracles of Reason* (London, 1693).

BOLINGBROKE, HENRY ST JOHN, 1st Viscount, *Philosophical Works* (5 vols.; London, 1754).

BOSWELL, JAMES, *Life of Johnson* (1791), ed. G. B. Hill, rev. L. F. Powell (6 vols.; Oxford, 1934–50).

BRAMHALL, JOHN, *A Defence of True Liberty from Antecedent and Extrinsecall Necessity* (London, 1655).

BROAD, C. D., *Leibniz: An Introduction*, ed. C. Levy (Cambridge, 1975).

BROUGHTON, THOMAS, *Christianity Distinct from the Religion of Nature* (3 pts.; London, 1732).

BROWN, JOHN, *Essays on the Characteristics* (London, 1751).
—— *An Estimate of the Manners and Principles of the Times* (London, 1757).

BROWN, S. G., 'Dr. Johnson and the Religious Problem', *English Studies*, 20 (1938), 1–17.

BROWNE, PETER, *A Letter in Answer to a Book, Entituled, Christianity not Mysterious* (London, 1697).

BULKLEY, CHARLES, *A Vindication of My Lord Shaftesbury, on the Subject of Ridicule* (London, 1751).

CAMPBELL, ARCHIBALD, *An Enquiry into the Original of Moral Virtue* (Edinburgh, 1733).

CAMPBELL, GEORGE, *A Dissertation on Miracles* (Edinburgh, 1761).

CHANDLER, SAMUEL, *Sermons* (4 vols.; London, 1759).
—— *A Vindication of the Christian Religion* (London, 1725).

CHAPIN, C. F., *The Religious Thought of Samuel Johnson* (Ann Arbor, 1968).
—— 'Samuel Johnson and the Scottish Common-sense School', *Eighteenth Century: Theory and Interpretation*, 20 (1979), 50–64.

CHESTERFIELD, PHILIP DORMER STANHOPE, 4th Earl of, *Letters to His Son*, ed. E. Strachey (2 vols.; London, 1901).

CHILTON, JOHN, *Positive Institutions not to be Compar'd with, or Preferr'd before Moral Duties and Virtues* (London, 1730).

CHUBB, THOMAS, *The True Gospel of Jesus Christ Asserted, to which is added, A Short Dissertation on Providence* (London, 1738).

CHURCH, THOMAS, *An Analysis of the Philosophical Works of Lord Bolingbroke* (London, 1755).

CICERO, DE OFFICIIS, trans. W. Miller (London and Cambridge, Mass., 1913).

CLARKE, JOHN (1682–1757), *An Enquiry into the Cause and Origin of Evil* (London, 1720).

CLARKE, JOHN (1687–1734), *An Examination of what has been Advanced Relating to Moral Obligation, in a late Pamphlet, Entitled, A Defence of the Answer, &c.* (London, 1730).

—— *The Foundation of Morality in Theory and Practice Considered* (London, 1726).

CLARKE, SAMUEL, *A Discourse Concerning the Being and Attributes of God* (1705) (4th edn.; London, 1716).

—— *A Discourse Concerning the Unchangeable Obligations of Natural Religion and the Truth and Certainty of the Christian Revelation* (London, 1706).

—— *An Exposition of the Church Catechism* (London, 1729).

—— *A Letter to Dr. Wells, in Answer to his Remarks* (London, 1714).

—— *Remarks upon a Late Book, Entituled, A Philosophical Enquiry Concerning Human Liberty* (London, 1717).

—— *The Scripture-doctrine of the Trinity* (London, 1712).

—— *Sermons* (1730) (10 vols.; 2nd. edn.; London, 1731).

—— and Leibniz, Gottfried von, *A Collection of Letters Relating to the Principles of Natural Philosophy and Religion* (London, 1717).

COLE, WILLIAM *Legal and Other Reasons . . . Why the Subjects of England should not be Imprisoned for Debt or Damages* (London, 1675).

COLLIER, JEREMY, *Essays upon Several Moral Subjects* (1697–1709) (4 pts.; 6th edn.; London, 1722).

COLLINS, ANTHONY, *A Discourse Concerning Ridicule and Irony in Writing* (London, 1729).

—— *A Discourse of Free-thinking* (London, 1713).

—— *A Philosophical Inquiry Concerning Human Liberty* (London, 1717).

—— *The Scheme of Literal Prophecy Considered* (London, 1727).

CONYBEARE, JOHN, *A Defence of Reveal'd Religion* (London, 1732).

—— *A Sermon Preach'd in the Parish-church of Christ-Church, London* (London, 1738).

COX, L. G., *John Wesley's Concept of Perfection* (Kansas City, Mo., 1964).

CROUSAZ, JEAN-PIERRE, *A Commentary on Mr. Pope's Essay on Man* (1737), trans. Samuel Johnson (London, 1739).

CUDWORTH, RALPH, *The True Intellectual System of the Universe* (London, 1678).

CUMBERLAND, RICHARD, *A Philosophical Enquiry into the Laws of Nature* (Dublin, 1750).

DAWSON, BENJAMIN, *A Free and Candid Disquisition on Religious Establishments* (London, 1771).

DENNIS, JOHN, *Vice and Luxury Public Mischiefs* (London, 1724).

DISNEY, JOHN, *A Letter to the Most Reverend Lord Archbishop of Canterbury* (London, 1774).

—— *Remarks on Dr. Balguy's Sermon* (London, 1775).

DODDRIDGE, PHILIP, *The Perspicuity and Solidity of Those Evidences of Christianity to which the Generality of its Professors among us may Attain, Illustrated and Vindicated* (London, 1742).

DODSLEY, ROBERT, *The Preceptor* (2 vols.; London, 1748).

DODWELL, HENRY, *Christianity not Founded in Argument* (London, 1741).

EDWARDS, JOHN, *Socinianism Unmask'd: A Discourse Shewing the Unreasonableness of a Late Writers Opinion Concerning the Necessity of Only One Article of Faith* (London, 1696).

ELMYN, SOLLOM, Preface to *A Complete Collection of State Trials* (2nd edn.; London, 1730).

EPICURUS, *Morals*, trans. Walter Charleton (London, 1655; repr. London, 1926).

ERASMUS, DESIDERIUS, *Enchiridion militis christiani* (1503), trans. Raymond Himelick (Bloomington, 1963).

ESPRIT, JACQUES, *Discourses on the Deceitfulness of Humane Virtues* (1691), trans. William Beauvoir (London, 1706).

FANCOURT, SAMUEL, *An Essay Concerning Liberty, Grace, and Prescience* (London, 1729).

FIDDES, RICHARD, *The Body of Divinity* (2 pts.; Dublin, 1718).

—— *A General Treatise of Morality form'd upon the Principles of Natural Reason Only* (London, 1724).

FIELDING, HENRY, *Amelia* (1751), ed. M. C. Battestin (Oxford, 1983).

—— *Complete Works*, ed. W. E. Henley (16 vols.; London, 1903).

—— *Joseph Andrews* (1742), ed. D. Brooks (London, 1970).

—— *The History of Tom Jones, a Foundling* (1749), ed. M. C. Battestin and F. Bowers (2 vols.; Oxford, 1974).

FLEETWOOD, WILLIAM, *The Perfectionists Examin'd* (London, 1741).

FLEMING, CALEB, *Necessity not the Origin of Evil, Religious or Moral* (London, 1757).

FLEW, R. NEWTON, *The Idea of Perfection in Christian Theology* (London, 1934).

FORDYCE, DAVID, *The Elements of Moral Philosophy* (London, 1754).

FORBES, DUNCAN, *Some Thoughts Concerning Religion, Natural and Revealed* (Edinburgh, 1750).

FORSTER, NATHANIEL, *The Establishment of the Church of England, Defended upon the Principles of Religious Liberty: A Sermon* (London, 1770).

FOSTER, JAMES, *Sermons* (4 vols.; London, 1733).

—— *The Usefulness, Truth, and Excellency of the Christian Revelation Defended* (London, 1731).

FRANKS, R. S., *The Doctrine of the Trinity* (London, 1952).

FURNEAUX, PHILIP, *Letters to the Honourable Mr. Justice Blackstone* (London, 1770).

GAY, JOHN, *A Dissertation Concerning the Principles and Criterion of Virtue and the Origin of the Passions* (1731) (2nd edn.; London, 1732).

GIBSON, EDMUND, *The Bishop of London's Pastoral Letter to the People of His Diocese, by Way of Caution against Lukewarmness on One Hand, and Enthusiasm on the Other* (London, 1739).

—— *The Great Work of Our Redemption by Christ* (London, 1735).

GORDON, THOMAS, and TRENCHARD, JOHN, *A Collection of Tracts* (London, 1751).

GRAY, J., *Johnson's Sermons: A Study* (Oxford, 1972).

GREENE, D. J., *The Politics of Samuel Johnson* (New Haven, 1960).

—— 'Samuel Johnson and "Natural Law"'. *Journal of British Studies*, 2 (1963), 59–75 and 84–7.

GROTIUS, HUGO, *The Rights of War and Peace* (1625), trans. William Evats (London, 1682).

GROVE, HENRY, *A System of Moral Philosophy* (2 vols.; London, 1749).

GRUNDY, I., *Samuel Johnson and the Scale of Greatness* (Leicester, 1986).

HAGSTRUM, J. H., 'The Nature of Dr. Johnson's Rationalism', *ELH* 17 (1950), 191–205.

HALE, MATTHEW, *The Works, Moral and Religious* (2 vols.; London, 1805).

HARVEST, GEORGE, *The Reasonableness and Necessity of Subscription to Explanatory Articles of Faith Demonstrated: in Two Letters* (London, 1772).

HAWKINS, SIR JOHN, *The Life of Samuel Johnson* (2nd edn.; London, 1787).

HILL, G. B. (ed.), *Johnsonian Miscellanies* (2 vols.; Oxford, 1897).

HOADLY, BENJAMIN, *An Answer to the Representation Drawn-up by the Committee of the Lower-house of Convocation* (London, 1718).

—— *An Answer to the Reverend Dr. Snape's Letter* (London, 1717).

—— *The Nature of Christ's Kingdom, A Sermon Preach'd before the King, 31 March, 1717* (London, 1717).

—— *A Plain Account of the Nature and End of the Sacrament of the Lord's Supper* (London, 1735).

—— *Works* (3 vols.; London, 1773).

HOBBES, THOMAS, *English Works*, ed. Sir William Molesworth (11 vols.; London, 1839; repr. Scientia Verlaag Aalen, 1962).

HOOKER, SIR RICHARD, *Works*, ed. John Keble (7th edn.; Oxford, 1888).

HUDSON, N. J., 'Johnson, Socinianism and the Meaning of Christ's Sacrifice', *Notes and Queries*, NS 32 (1985), 238–40.

HUME, DAVID, *Philosophical Works*, ed. J. H. Greene and J. H. Grose (4 vols.; London, 1882; repr. Scientia Verlaag Aalen, 1964).

HUTCHESON, FRANCIS, *An Inquiry into the Original of Our Ideas of Beauty and Virtue* (1725) (3rd edn.; London, 1729).

JENYNS, SOAME, *A Free Inquiry into the Nature and Origin of Evil* (London, 1757).

JOHNSON, C. L., 'Samuel Johnson's Moral Psychology and Locke's "Of Power"', *SEL* 24 (1984), 563–82.

JOHNSON, SAMUEL, 'Considerations on the Case of Dr. T's Sermons, Abridged by Mr. Cave, 1739', *The Gentleman's Magazine*, 62 (1789), 555–7.

—— *Diaries, Prayers and Annals*, ed. E. L. McAdam, Jun., with D. and M. Hyde (New Haven, 1958), *The Yale Edition of the Works of Samuel Johnson*, i.

—— *A Dictionary of the English Language* (1755) (2 vols.; 4th edn.; London, 1773).

—— *The Idler and the Adventurer* (1753–60), ed. W. J. Bate, J. M. Bullit, and L. F. Powell (New Haven and London, 1963), *Yale Edition*, ii.

—— *Johnson on Shakespeare*, ed. A. Sherbo (New Haven and London, 1968), *Yale Edition*, vii and viii.

—— 'The Life of Dr. Boerhaave', *The Gentleman's Magazine*, 9 (1739), 37–8, 72–3, 114–16, 172–6.

—— *Lives of the English Poets* (1781), ed. G. B. Hill (3 vols.; Oxford, 1905).

—— *Poems*, ed. E. L. McAdam, with G. Milne (New Haven and London, 1964), *Yale Edition*, vi.

—— *The Rambler* (1750–2), ed. W. J. Bate and A. B. Strauss (New Haven and London, 1969), *Yale Edition*, iii–v.

—— *Sermons*, ed. J. Gray and J. H. Hagstrum (New Haven and London, 1978), *Yale Edition*, xiv.

JONES, CHARLES, *Some Methods Proposed towards Putting a Stop to the Flagrant Crimes of Murder, Robbery, and Perjury* (London, 1752).

JONES, M. G., *The Charity-school Movement: A Study of Eighteenth-century Puritanism in Action* (Cambridge, 1938).

JORTIN, JOHN, *Sermons on Different Subjects* (7 vols.; London, 1771).

KAMES, HENRY HOME, LORD, *Essays on the Principles of Morality and Natural Religion* (Edinburgh, 1751).

KING, WILLIAM, *An Essay on the Origin of Evil* (1702), trans. Edmund Law (1731-2 vols.; 2nd edn.; London, 1732).

LA BRUYÈRE, JEAN DE, *Works* (2 vols.; London, 1713).

LA ROCHEFOUCAULT, FRANÇOIS, duc de, *Moral Reflections and Maxims* (London, 1706).

LAW, WILLIAM, *A Serious Call to a Devout and Holy Life* (1729), ed. P. G. Stanwood (London, 1978).

—— *Works* (9 vols.; London, 1762; repr. Setley, Hants., 1892-3).

LELAND, JOHN, *An Answer to a Late Book, Intituled Christianity as Old as the Creation* (2 vols.; Dublin, 1733).

—— *Remarks on a Late Pamphlet, Entitled Christianity not Founded on Argument* (London, 1744).

LOBB, SAMUEL, *The Benevolence Incumbent on us, as Men and Christians, Considered* (London, 1746).

LOCKE, JOHN, *The Correspondence of John Locke*, ed. E. S. de Beer (8 vols.; Oxford, 1979).

—— *An Essay Concerning Human Understanding* (1690), ed. P. H. Nidditch (Oxford, 1979).

—— *A Letter Concerning Toleration* (London, 1689).

—— *A Letter to the Right Reverend Edward [Stillingfleet] Ld. Bishop of Worcester, Concerning Some Passages Relating to Mr. Locke's Essay of Human Understanding* (London, 1697).

—— *The Reasonableness of Christianity* (London, 1695).

—— *The Reasonableness of Christianity*, ed. I. T. Ramsay (London, 1958).

LOVEJOY, A. O., *The Great Chain of Being* (Cambridge, Mass., 1936).

—— *Reflections on Human Nature* (Baltimore, 1961).

MACHIAVELLI, NICCOLO, *The Discourses*, trans. R. Crick (Harmondsworth, 1970).

MANDEVILLE, BERNARD, *The Fable of the Bees* (1724), ed. F. B. Kaye (2 vols.; Oxford, 1924).

MASON, JOHN, *Self-knowledge* (London, 1745).

McINTOSH, C., 'Johnson's Debate with Stoicism', *ELH* 33 (1966), 327-36.

MIDDLETON, CONYERS, *A Free Inquiry into Miraculous Powers in the Christian Church* (London, 1749).

MILL, JOHN STUART, *Utilitarianism* (London, 1863).

MILLINGEN, J. G., *The History of Duelling* (2 vols.; London, 1841).

MONTESQUIEU, C. DE SECONDAT, BARON DE, *The Spirit of the Laws* (1748), trans. Thomas Nugent (2 vols.; London, 1823).

MORE, SIR THOMAS, *Utopia* (1516), ed. E. Surtz and J. H. Hexter (New Haven and London, 1965).

NELSON, ROBERT, *A Companion for the Festivals and Fasts of the Church of England* (London, 1705).

NEWTON, THOMAS, *Works* (3 vols.; London, 1782).

NYE, STEPHEN, *A Discourse Concerning Natural and Revealed Religion* (London, 1698).

OLLYFFE, GEORGE, *An Essay Humbly Offer'd for an Act of Parliament to prevent Capital Crimes, and the Loss of Many Lives* (London, 1731).

OVERTON, J. H., *William Law: Non-juror and Mystic* (London, 1881).

PASCAL, BLAISE, *Pensées* (1669), trans. A. J. Krailsheimer (Harmondsworth, 1962).

PECKARD, PETER, *The Nature and Extent of Civil and Religious Liberty* (Cambridge, 1783).

PERCEVAL, JOHN, 1st Earl of Egmont, *The Controversy in Relation to the Test and Corporation Acts* (London, 1733).

PIERCE, C. E., jun., *The Religious Life of Samuel Johnson* (London, 1983).

PITT, MOSES, *The Cry of the Oppressed* (London, 1691).

POPE, ALEXANDER, *An Essay on Man* (1734), ed. M. Mack (New Haven and London, 1950), *The Twickenham Edition of the Poems of Alexander Pope*, vol. iii, pt. 1.

PRIESTLEY, JOSEPH, *Considerations on Church Authority, Occasioned by Dr. Balguy's Sermon on that Subject* (London, 1769).

PUFENDORF, SAMUEL, *The Law of Nature and Nations* (1672), trans. Basil Kennet (London, 1749).

QUINLAN, M., 'The Rumour of Dr. Johnson's Conversion', *Review of Religion*, 12 (1948), 243–61.

—— *Samuel Johnson: A Layman's Religion* (Madison, Wis., 1964).

RANDOLPH, THOMAS, *The Christian's Faith a Rational Assent* (London, 1744).

RICHARDSON, SAMUEL, *Sir Charles Grandison* (1754), ed. J. Harris (3 vols.; London, 1972).

RADZINOWICZ, L., *A History of English Criminal Law* (3 vols.; London, 1948).

ROGERS, JOHN, *The Necessity of Divine Revelation, and the Truth of the Christian Revelation Asserted* (London, 1727).

ROTHERAM, JOHN, *An Essay on Establishments in Religion* (Newcastle upon Tyne, 1767).

RUTHERFORTH, THOMAS, *The Credibility of Miracles defended against the Author of Philosophical Essays* (Cambridge, 1751).

―― *An Essay on the Nature and Obligations of Virtue* (Cambridge, 1744).

SACHEVERELL, HENRY, *The Perils of False Brethren, a Sermon Preached before the Lord Mayor, 5 November, 1709* (London, 1710).

SCHWARTZ, R. B., *Samuel Johnson and the Problem of Evil* (Madison, Wis., 1975).

SCOTT, JOHN, *The Christian Life* (London, 1681).

SECKER, THOMAS, *Fourteen Sermons on Several Occasions* (London, 1766).

SEWARD, THOMAS, *The Late Dreadful Earthquake no Proof of God's Particular Wrath against the Portuguese: A Sermon Preached at Lichfield, Sunday, December 7, 1755* (London, 1756).

SHAFTESBURY, ANTHONY ASHLEY COOPER, 3rd Earl of, *Characteristics of Men, Manners, Opinions, Times etc.* (1711), ed. J. M. Robertson (2 vols.; London, 1900).

SHERLOCK, THOMAS, *The Tryal of the Witnesses* (London, 1729).

SHERLOCK, WILLIAM, *A Discourse Concerning the Divine Providence* (London, 1694).

―― *A Practical Discourse Concerning Death* (London, 1689).

―― *Sermons Preach'd upon Several Occasions* (2nd. edn.; London, 1702).

―― *A Vindication of the Doctrine of the Holy and Ever Blessed Trinity* (London, 1690).

SKELTON, PHILIP, *Ophiomaches, or Deism Reveal'd* (1748) (2 vols.; 2nd edn.; London, 1749).

SKINNER, Q., 'Meaning and Understanding in the History of Ideas', *History and Theory*, 8 (1969), 3–53.

SMALRIDGE, GEORGE, *Sixty Sermons Preached on Several Occasions* (Oxford, 1724).

SMITH, ADAM, *The Theory of Moral Sentiments* (London, 1759).

SNAPE, ANDREW, *A Sermon Preach'd before the Right Honourable the Lord Mayor* (London, 1731).

SOUTH, ROBERT, *Sermons Preached upon Several Occasions* (11 vols.; London, 1734–44).

STEBBING, HENRY, *A Discourse Concerning the Use and Advantages of the Gospel Revelation* (London, 1730).

—— *Discourses upon Several Subjects* (London, 1722).

—— *A Treatise Concerning the Operations of the Holy Spirit* (London, 1719).

STEELE, RICHARD, *The Christian Hero: An Argument Proving that No Principles but those of Religion are Sufficient to make a Great Man* (London, 1701).

STEPHEN, L., *History of English Thought in the Eighteenth Century* (2 vols.; London, 1962).

STILLINGFLEET, EDWARD, *A Discourse in Vindication of the Doctrine of the Trinity* (London, 1697).

—— *Works* (6 vols.; London, 1710).

STROMBERG, R. N., *Religious Liberalism in Eighteenth-century England* (Oxford, 1954).

STRUTT, SAMUEL, *A Defence of the Late Learned Dr. Clarke's Notion of Natural Liberty* (London, 1730).

SWIFT, JONATHAN, *Irish Tracts 1720-23 and Sermons*, ed. H. Davis and L. Landau (Oxford, 1963).

SYKES, ARTHUR ASHLEY, *A Defence of the Answer to the Remarks upon Dr. Clarke's Exposition of the Church Catechism* (London, 1730).

—— *The Principles and Connexion of Natural and Revealed Religion Distinctly Considered* (London, 1740).

SYKES, NORMAN, *Church and State in the XVIIIth Century* (Cambridge, 1934).

TAYLOR, JEREMY, *The Whole Works*, ed. Charles Eden (10 vols.; London, 1848).

TAYLOR, JOHN, *The Scripture Doctrine of Original Sin* (London, 1741).

TILLOTSON, JOHN, *Works* (1696) (3 vols.; 4th edn.; London, 1728).

TINDAL, MATTHEW, *Christianity as Old as the Creation* (London, 1730).

TOLAND, JOHN, *Christianity not Mysterious* (London, 1696).

TOPLADY, AUGUSTUS, *Works* (London, 1853).

TOTTIE, JOHN, *A Charge Relative to the Articles of the Church of England* (Oxford, 1772).

TRAPP, JOSEPH, *The Nature, Folly, Sin and Danger of Being Righteous Over-much* (London, 1739).

—— *A Reply to Mr. Law's Earnest and Serious Answer (as it is called) to Dr. Trapp's Discourse* (London, 1741).

TRUMAN, BEN C., *The Field of Honor* (New York, 1884).

VOITLE, R., *Samuel Johnson the Moralist* (Cambridge, Mass., 1961).

WAHBA, M. (ed.), *Johnsonian Studies* (Cairo, 1962).

WALLACE, D. D., *Puritans and Predestination* (Chapel Hill, 1982).

WARBURTON, WILLIAM, *The Alliance of Church and State* (London, 1736).

—— *A View of Lord Bolingbroke's Philosophy* (1754) (3rd edn., London, 1756).

—— *Julian; or a Discourse Concerning the Earthquake and Fiery Eruption which defeated that Emperor's Attempt to rebuild the Temple at Jerusalem* (London, 1751).

—— *Works* (12 vols.; London, 1811).

WATERLAND, DANIEL, *Sermons on Several Important Subjects of Religion and Morality* (2 vols.; London, 1742).

—— *The Nature, Obligation, and Efficacy of the Christian Sacraments* (London, 1730).

—— *Scripture Vindicated in Answer to a Book intituled, Christianity as Old as the Creation* (3 pts.; London, 1733–4).

—— *A Supplement to the Treatise, Entituled, The Nature, Obligation, and Efficacy of the Christian Sacraments* (London, 1730).

WATTS, ISAAC, *An Essay towards the Improvement of Charity Schools* (London, 1728).

—— *The Improvement of the Mind, or a Supplement to the Art of Logic* (1741) (London, 1784).

—— *Works* (6 vols.; London, 1753).

WEARMOUTH, R. F., *Methodism and the Common People of the Eighteenth Century* (London, 1945).

WELLS, EDWARD, *Remarks on Dr. Clarke's Introduction to his Scripture Doctrin [sic] of the Trinity* (London, 1713).

WESLEY, JOHN, *An Earnest Appeal to Men of Reason and Religion* (1743), ed. G. R. Cragg (1975), *The Works of John Wesley*, gen. ed. F. Baker (Oxford and Nashville (1975–), xi.

—— *Works* (14 vols.; London, 1830).

WHITEFIELD, GEORGE, *An Answer to the Bishop of London's Last Pastoral Letter* (London, 1739).

WILBUR, E. M., *A History of Unitarianism* (2 vols.; Cambridge, Mass., 1952).

WILLEY, B., *The English Moralists* (London, 1964).

WILSON, THOMAS, *Works* (2 vols.; London, 1781).

WOLLASTON, WILLIAM, *The Religion of Nature Delineated* (1722) (5th. edn; London, 1726).

WOOLSTON, THOMAS, *A Sixth Discourse on the Miracles of Our Saviour* (London, 1729).

YOUNG, EDWARD, *The Complaint, or Night Thoughts on Life, Death and Immortality* (London, 1750).

ZIRKER, M. R., *Fielding's Social Pamphlets* (Berkeley and Los Angeles, 1966).

INDEX